High-Leverage Leadership

D0070929

Globalisation of world trade, international media, technological innovation and social change are creating opportunities and challenges that today's pupils will inherit and build on. A pupil's academic, technical and social capacity will define their success or failure. Therefore, educational outcomes and wellbeing for young people across emerging and developed economies, and the crucial role of education and leaders of education, have never been more important.

Schools are under pressure to think more clearly about their place in children's lives beyond the passage of learning in classrooms. The processes inside schools, the organisation of school systems and the relationship between communities and educators are critical elements in a complex mix that must balance correctly if it is to benefit school children properly.

Using the term 'high-leverage leadership' to describe leadership that is associated with higher outcomes than would normally be found in similar contexts, this timely book:

- demonstrates how successful educational leaders apply contextual, social and professional expertise to the three distinctive leadership tasks of navigation, management and partnership;
- offers an insight into the complexity of the educational leadership and practices of school leaders who, against the odds, produce high outcomes for young people;
- provides an overview of the development of educational leadership research;
- validates the idea that a renovation of educational leadership is necessary to maximise educational outcomes.

High-Leverage Leadership will be an indispensible text for school leaders, public sector officers, postgraduate students and researchers in leadership, policy, school improvement and educational change.

Denis Mongon is a Visiting Professorial Fellow at the Institute of Education, University of London, UK and a Senior Research Fellow at the University of Manchester, UK.

Christopher Chapman is Professor of Education at the University of Manchester.

High-Leverage Leadership

Improving outcomes in educational settings

Denis Mongon and Christopher Chapman

Routledge
Taylor & Francis Group

LONDON AND NEW YORK

First published 2012
by Routledge
2 Park Square, Milton Park, Abingdon, Oxon OX14 4RN

Simultaneously published in the USA and Canada
by Routledge
711 Third Avenue, New York, NY 10017

*Routledge is an imprint of the Taylor & Francis Group, an informa
business*

British Library Cataloguing in Publication Data
A catalogue record for this book is available from the British Library

Library of Congress Cataloging-in-Publication Data
Mongon, Denis.
High-level leadership : improving outcomes in educational settings /
Denis Mongon, Christopher Chapman.
p. cm.
Includes bibliographical references and index.
1. School management and organization--Great Britain. 2.
Educational leadership--Great Britain. 3. School improvement
programs--Great Britain. I. Chapman, Christopher. II. Title.
LB2900.5.M64 2012
371.2'07--dc23
2011028904

ISBN: 978-0-415-68952-6 (hbk)
ISBN: 978-0-415-68953-3 (pbk)
ISBN: 978-0-203-15691-9 (ebk)

Typeset in Galliard
by Fakenham Prepress Solutions, Fakenham, Norfolk NR21 8NN

MIX
Paper from
responsible sources
FSC® C004839
www.fsc.org

Printed and bound in Great Britain by
TJ International Ltd, Padstow, Cornwall

Contents

List of illustrations   vi
Preface   vii

1   Educational leadership: Professional imperative or misguided optimism?   1

2   High-leverage leadership   14

3   Navigation   35

4   Management   61

5   Partnership   84

6   Organisational pathology and high-leverage leadership   111

7   Governance, accountability and impact   127

8   Reflections on high-leverage leadership in education   150

References   162
Index   178

Illustrations

Figures

1.1   A framework for exploring emerging forms of school leadership   10
2.1   A model for high-leverage leadership   23
6.1   Performance map of Family 6 Greater Manchester schools   115
6.2   Leadership and improvement in challenging circumstances   120
6.3   School capacity and leadership focus   121
7.1   Framework for discussing impact   145
7.2   Sources of evidence   146

Tables

2.1   The distinction between *asymmetric partnerships* and *associate partnerships*   33
3.1   Learning or performance orientation   55
4.1   School stages of inquiry   67

Preface

We have had the privilege of working with many talented people in a diverse range of educational settings. For the most part this has involved working with schools in challenging and urban settings. This book draws together our practical experience and research findings to explore the nature of educational leadership that gives 'the most bang for its bucks' in terms of student outcomes. Put simply, we set out to describe the practices and processes associated with high-leverage leadership.

We are all too aware of the energy and tenacity required to achieve outstanding outcomes, particularly in difficult contexts, and we have attempted to provide practical accounts that are relevant to school leaders and combine them with deeper theoretical insights. We hope this combination will challenge thinking, raise questions and stimulate discussion in both practitioner and academic communities. This book does not offer simple solutions or recipes; rather, it attempts to capture the complexity of context and the nuanced practices that underpin successful leadership.

Inevitably a book of this type is only possible with the support of colleagues working in education. Without support from the sponsors of our research, including the Department for Education, the National College for School Leadership and the National Union of Teachers, our projects never would have got off the ground.[1] We are particularly grateful to John Bangs, Maggie Farrar, Toby Greany and Jill Ireson for their support over the years and to Barbara Spender for her keen eye. We are also indebted to our academic colleagues' challenge and insight. In particular, a special thanks must go to our colleagues at the Universities of Manchester and London and beyond. You know who you all are! Finally, perhaps the most important thanks goes to the school leaders and their staff who, despite the challenges they face, have been so open with their thoughts and generous with their time. You made this book possible and we hope we have captured the essence of the remarkable work you do with adults and young people.

Denis Mongon and Christopher Chapman
Universities of London and Manchester

1 Over the course of our work, the central government department responsible for education in England has changed its name several times, variously being The Department for Education, for Education and Employment, for Education and Skills, for Children, Schools and Families and most recently again for Education. In the text and references we have used the corresponding acronyms. England's National College for School Leadership was for a time known as the National College for Leadership of Schools and Children's Services. In the text and references we have describes it simply as the National College.

1 Educational leadership
Professional imperative or misguided optimism?

Introduction

It is hard to imagine a world without leaders or leadership. In one form or another there are those who are seen to be leading others by directing, influencing and organising collective effort. In most societies we look to our 'leaders' (whether they be religious, political, military, industrial or public servants) for guidance and inspiration. For centuries these leaders have been a cornerstone of society. The best of them are trusted, perceived to hold a strong set of values and beliefs and, perhaps most importantly, to possess unwavering integrity and humility.

During the past two to three decades the context for leadership appears to have changed at a rapid pace. With the accelerating expansion of e-technology and the emergence of 24-hour 'real time' media, leadership has become ubiquitously visible. This has presented a new set of challenges for our leaders. Some have gained prominence, even celebrity status. However, this swift rise can be fragile and temporary, ending in mockery and disgrace. For example, Lord Sugar, the former Chairman of both Amstrad and Tottenham Hotspur Football Club, is an international industrial leader, but is now better known as a television star. His television programme follows potential apprentices competing for a business partnership or a £100,000-salary job in one of his companies, achievable only if they can avoid being told 'You're Fired' by a growling Sugar. Steve Jobs, the CEO of the computer giant Apple, was also an internationally recognised leader. He built the Apple brand and range of i-products, and his personal image was and remains deeply and inextricably linked to the brand and its success. Until his recent death, no Apple product launch would be complete without images of Jobs flooding the e-networks. On the other hand we see leaders whose celebrity status is derived from major mistakes – such as Gerald Ratner, whose careless remark about the quality of his goods was so disastrous for the business, or Sir Fred Goodwin, who seems, in the public mind, to carry so much personal blame for the international banking crisis. Increased visibility and the potential rewards, not least in the international finance sector, have brought leadership into global focus. This phenomenon is not the preserve of industry leaders. While political and religious leaders have always had a relatively high profile, recent decades have also seen military leaders move further into the public spotlight. It has become common to witness military commanders on television explaining the rationale for and outcomes of a military strike, and their memoirs and accounts of conflict fill the shelves of airport bookshops.

Leadership has come into sharp focus in the public sector, especially within education. In England, state-school headteachers are now under a public spotlight previously reserved for a few high-profile headmasters of independent schools. One example is Sir William Atkinson, Headteacher of the Phoenix School in London. In the late 1990s and 2000s he was recognised as the catalyst for 'turning around' the fortunes of a very difficult school in a tough area of the city. He was recognised for his efforts, gaining a knighthood and becoming an adviser to the then Prime Minister, Tony Blair. He could also be heard sharing his views about leadership and change on TV and radio phone-in and panel discussions. He sat on the Question Time panel, the BBC's leading current affairs and political debate show. Initially the BBC1 soap opera Waterloo Road, charting the development of a school 'rising from the ashes', was based on his story, with the first head having similar character traits and bearing a notable physical resemblance. The media reporting of his work, along with that of a number of other high-profile headships in England, has reinforced the attention given to school leadership as the key element in making a difference to the outcomes and ultimately the life chances of young people. Some of these heads rose to prominence only to be 'dethroned' from their newly-found status. One of the most high-profile falls from grace was that of Dame Jean Else, who has recently had her title revoked. In England the rewards for this generation of leaders have been substantial, but the stakes were high and the pressure colossal.

This book aims to unpack the work of principals and headteachers like Sir William Atkinson, who are successful against the odds, to expose the complexity of their educational leadership and offer accessible insights into their key practices. We use the term 'high-leverage leadership' to describe leadership that is associated with higher outcomes than would normally be found in similar contexts. Put simply, the outcomes achieved are disproportionately higher than one might expect. High-leverage leadership reaches out to the holy grail of 'excellence and equity', not only achieving outstanding outcomes but promoting fairness (recognition and redistribution) for young people and also, as we explain in Chapter 5, for the adults who work with them. Importantly, high-leverage leadership ensures that the system gets the most 'bangs for its bucks'. Our argument is that high-leverage leaders engage in three forms of related activity, Navigation, Management and Partnership, to produce high outcomes for the young people.

The purpose of this chapter is to set the context for that argument. First, we provide an overview of the development of educational leadership research. Second, we discuss a number of theories and practices associated with educational leadership, and third, we reflect on the emerging challenges that lead us to conclude that a reconceptualisation of educational leadership is necessary if we are to maximise educational outcomes for all.

Why educational leadership: why the attention?

In the introduction to this chapter we focused on the rise in visibility of leadership in general, and specifically of educational leadership, over the past few decades. In this section we move on to consider whether it is just the visibility that has increased or whether and how other aspects of leadership have developed in their importance, and if there is any evidence to underpin this rise in profile. We are guided by two questions. Are we dealing with a veneer, a fad of our time? And, is there any substance backing up the investment made by governments in developing educational leadership and leaders in the hope of generating improved outcomes?

If there is a leadership fad, it is significant. The sheer volume of academic literature generated over the past two decades demonstrates this. In May 2011 a search on Google Scholar offered over 1,410,000 hits for the term 'educational leadership'. Leadership development programmes, Master's degrees and other accredited schemes have swollen in numbers.

It is not only academics who have become preoccupied with educational leadership. Related publications and articles can be found in the popular press; news stories about schools often focus on 'leadership issues', and there are unprecedented numbers of consultants offering coaching, mentoring and critical friendship to school leaders. Governments and policymakers have also shown their commitment, investing millions of dollars in educational leadership. In England the National College for School Leadership was established in 2000, other national governments and states around the world have followed suit, developing various types of school leadership academies. In schools, principals have higher status than ever before; in England, secondary headteachers can earn more than hospital consultants, lawyers and arguably the Prime Minister. The importance and profile of leadership seems to permeate education systems. We are told that success needs – even demands – 'strong leadership'. But where is the evidence? How did we ever get by without our obsession with leadership?

Some of us almost did in the 1970s and 1980s. In England, an interest in alternative schooling ran parallel to a *laissez faire* approach to headship that contributed to the events at Risinghill and William Tyndale Schools, to which we refer in Chapter 3. Gronn (2003) has reflected on the near death of educational leadership as an academic interest in the USA during the 1970s and 1980s. He argues that this can be accounted for by the lack of legitimacy of leadership, rooted in the culture and ideas of the time. This arose from a situation whereby those in the system became reluctant followers and leadership as a concept did not fit the way either academia or society saw themselves. At the same time:

> ... the wider field of leadership spawned its own peculiar brand of melancholia – a rash of anti-leadership thinking. From the mid 1970s a number of scholars began voicing their disquiet.
>
> (Gronn, 2003, p. 61)

Some American scholars (e.g. Miner, Argyris, Calder, Pfeffer) argued that leadership had become outmoded, had outlived its usefulness and that the field of organisational behaviour and management provided a more optimistic way forward in developing understanding about how and why organisations worked and performed. In contrast to the 1970s, the mid-to-late 1980s saw the emergence of ideas relating to 'transactional' and 'transformational' leadership. These developments brought new energy to the field, and by the early 1990s they were quickly adapted to form the bedrock of contemporary educational research (e.g. Gronn, 1996).

These advances coincided with, and were at times related to, the emergence of international research on effective schools, confirming the relationship between leadership and effective schooling. The seminal paper by Ronald Edmonds (1979) in the United States reported findings linking effective schools for the urban poor to institutional leadership, expectations and atmosphere. In the same year, Rutter and colleagues (1979) also highlighted the relationship between school leadership and effective schooling. Since these early studies, this relationship has been confirmed by numerous studies and reviews (Leithwood, 2002; Hallinger and Heck, 1996; Sammons *et al.*, 1995; Leithwood *et al.*, 1999; Hallinger and Heck, 2010). As the knowledge base has expanded, the detail and complexity of the relationships have became the focus of interest (see Davies and West-Burnham, 2003). This has included the nature of leadership in schools at different phases of development (Chapman, 2004), in different socio-economic contexts (Chapman and Harris, 2005) and at different levels within the organisation, focusing on departmental (Harris *et al.*, 1995; Sammons *et al.*, 1997) and teacher leadership (Leiberman and Miller, 2004; Harris and Muijs, 2004).

Day and colleagues (2010, pp. 3–17) have undertaken some of the most recent work exploring the relationship between leadership and student outcomes. Their three-year study identifying 10 strong claims for the importance of educational leadership draws together a range of evidence to offer a contemporary summary of the field. The claims are:

1 *Headteachers are the main source of leadership.* Staff perceive heads as the main source of leadership in schools. Headteachers' values, reflective strategies, and leadership practices are key to improving student outcomes.
2 *There are eight key dimensions of successful leadership.* Successful leaders define their values and vision to raise expectations; set direction and build trust; reshape the conditions for teaching and learning; restructure parts of the organisation and redesign leadership roles and responsibilities; enrich the curriculum, enhance teacher quality; enhance the quality of teaching and learning; build collaboration internally and build strong relationships outside the school community.
3 *Headteachers' values are key components in their success.* Successful leaders hold a set of common characteristics and core values. These include a strong sense of moral responsibility and a belief in equal opportunities, respect for

others and a commitment to and passion for learning, achievement and the school community.

4 *Successful heads use the same basic leadership practices, but there is no single model for achieving success.* Successful heads draw on elements of transformational and instructional leadership, working intuitively from experience to mix and match approaches and strategies to their specific context.

5 *Differences in context affect the nature, direction and pace of leadership actions.* Schools at different phases of development require different forms of leadership.

6 *Heads contribute to student learning and achievement through a combination and accumulation of strategies and actions.* Successful heads focus on narrowing within-school variations by looking for strategies to develop approaches to foster collaborative teacher cultures, assessment for learning, monitoring pupil and school performance, the coherence of teaching programmes and the provision of extracurricular activities.

7 *There are three broad phases of leadership success.* Heads identified three phases of leadership. In the first, the foundation phase, heads tended to prioritise issues including improving the physical environment and setting directions and communicating expectations. For the middle, developmental phase, heads prioritised distributing leadership roles and promoting the use of data to inform decision-making; and in the third, enrichment phase, heads focused on personalising and enriching the curriculum as well as the further distribution of leadership.

8 *Heads grow and secure success by layering leadership strategies and actions.* Heads build on an initial leadership framework to develop multiple layers of leadership strategy, making decisions about what is continued and what has become less relevant to priorities for development.

9 *Successful heads distribute leadership progressively.* There is a connection between a distributed approach to leadership and the improvement of student outcomes. Distribution of leadership is common, but Day and colleagues (2010) note that patterns vary and the distribution of leadership responsibility and power varies depending on local context.

10 *The successful distribution of leadership depends on the establishment of trust.* Trust underpins successful leadership. It supports the distribution of leadership and the development and maintenance of a positive ethos.

These 'strong claims' highlight a number of key messages relating to successful leadership. Perhaps most potent is the importance of context. As we have argued previously (Chapman, 2004), differing approaches are needed for different school contexts. A key question we seek to address in this book is what does high-leverage leadership look like in these different contexts? What works, and why? And what form of leadership has the highest leverage in a given context? Here we look to our framework of Navigation, Management and Partnership to offer a way forward.

Despite the volume of quantitative and qualitative evidence suggesting the importance of school leadership, there remains a number of doubts about the substance of the relationship. These doubts are often underestimated and sometimes ignored, and they raise some important issues.

The first issue is that the relationship between leadership and school improvement is not as well established as one might think, given the current policy discourse. In England this is highlighted by the government's own inspection evidence. Over the past decade we have seen an upward trend in inspection judgements regarding the quality of leadership, the quality of teaching and student progress. The paradox is that the first has increased at a greater rate than the last two. This challenges the arguments claiming a strong relationship between leadership and improved student outcomes

The second issue relates to research funding. Much of the leadership research over past decades has been undertaken on behalf of government and its agencies. The nature of this type of funding raises the possibility of interference by sponsors, and therefore, potentially, issues of objectivity. For some researchers in the field of leadership and policy studies, it is seen as a 'badge of honour' not to have undertaken this type of work. This raises questions about the objectivity of the alternative, so-called 'independent' research, which itself may be biased by an anti-government political position. Both the nature of funding bodies and the values and beliefs of researchers can muddy the waters.

The third issue relates to stability and sustainability of effects over time. There is a growing body of work exploring how leadership practice can vary over time. Some of the most recent work in this area conducted by Day and colleagues (2011) offers useful insights into how leaders' actions, approaches and the strategies they employ change as their school becomes more effective. However, understanding about the complexity of the relationship between leadership and school effects over time remains elusive.

The fourth issue relates to managerialism and performativity (Gleeson and Husbands, 2001). Some would argue that 'leadership' has developed a dominant discourse located with the official policy doctrines of central governments. And furthermore, this has generated an orthodoxy of the 'right kind' of leadership. One only has to look around any centrally administered, accredited leadership course. The candidates speak in the same language, think in similar ways, they often dress and look similar. We have a conveyor belt of cloned leaders. This is a form of the Panopticon (Foucault, 1977) at work, whereby leaders are trained in an orthodoxy and placed under surveillance through mechanisms such as inspection regimes. Foucault (p. 201) argues that the major effect of the Panopticon is to:

> ... induce in the inmate a state of conscious and permanent visibility that assures the automatic functioning of power. So to arrange things that the surveillance is permanent in its effects, even if it is discontinuous in its action; that the perfection of power should tend to render its actual exercise unnecessary ... Bentham laid down the principle that power should be visible and

unverifiable. Visible: the inmate will constantly have before his eyes the tall outline of the central tower from which he is spied upon. Unverifiable: the inmate must never know whether he is being looked at in any one moment; but must be sure he may always be so.

Internationally, school leaders are being corralled into a form of 'panoptic leadership' which promotes behaviours and practices prescribed by the state, to conform to an orthodoxy of standards-based reform, effectiveness and improvement.

Fifth, it is dangerous that educational leadership has come to be viewed by some as a panacea. In many systems, principals are identified as both the key change agents and the primary unit of analysis for accountability purposes. Therefore, the stakes are high. As we commented earlier, heads tend to be paid handsomely for their work. However, they are often removed from office when student outcomes decline.

Notwithstanding these issues, and reflecting upon the weight of evidence offered by leadership, effectiveness and improvement research, we consider that the attention given to educational leadership is worthwhile. Therefore, we are of the opinion that leadership research is a valid strand of inquiry within the field of educational effectiveness and improvement (see Chapter 5). However, we do urge a sense of caution. Educational leadership might be a key ingredient but it is not unproblematic and, as we have highlighted, should not be viewed as a panacea. Furthermore, the exact nature of leadership required in different settings as times change and policy evolves would seem to be far less clear. This uncertainty leads us to outline some of the theories of educational leadership that have informed our understanding.

Understanding theory and practice

There is a massive collection of writing about the theory and practice of educational leadership. One might think that all that can be written about leadership has been written and that the field of educational leadership research is staggering to a satiated halt. If we lived in static environment, this might well be the case, but, as Leithwood and his colleagues (1999) remind us, times change. Effective leadership is closely related to the context in which it is exercised. Therefore, as the social and organisational context changes – to which we would add the legal and constitutional – so does the nature of leadership required to effect change. What works in leadership, and why it works, changes as the context evolves.

A question of leadership and management?

Leadership is closely related to the concepts of 'management' and 'administration'. Dimmock (1999) helpfully sets out the differences between them, claiming leadership to be concerned with higher-order tasks designed to improve staff, student and school performance, while management is concerned with maintenance activity and administration associated with lower-order activities. For others, leadership is concerned with doing the right things and management with doing things right. Differentiate leadership from management by linking management to systems and leadership to people. Put simply, in education, management has a history of being associated with the maintenance of systems and structures and leadership with values, vision and direction setting. Brighouse and Woods (2006) argue that most schools are over-managed and under-led, but there is nothing worse than an over-led and under-managed school. Leadership and management go hand in hand but a headteacher with great ideas and the ability to influence and bring people together for collective effort will soon lose followership if plans cannot be operationalised and the mechanisms are not in place to support the work of the community. We take the stance that management is a key aspect (along with navigation and partnership) of leadership, rather than vice versa. This argument is developed further in Chapter 2 and in more detail in Chapter 4 of this book.

From models of leadership to 'new' models of leadership

Building on the work of Bush and Glover (2002), Bush (2007) outlines six models of educational management and nine associated models of educational leadership:

Formal management models assume schools are hierarchical and leaders use their authority and power, gained from their formal position within the hierarchy, to achieve their goals. The type of leadership that tends to be associated with these models is 'managerial'. This is leadership that takes a technical, rational perspective focusing on the completion of tasks to achieve desired outcomes.

Collegial management models such as the interpersonal model use discussion to determine policy and make decisions. Some power is shared across the school and there is a shared sense of purpose across the organisation. There is a plethora of literature pertaining to the type of leadership closely associated with collegial models. Transformational leadership became a buzzword of the 1990s and 2000s, and its characteristics and variants are well documented. Examples can be found within both private- and public-sector organisations, and in education it has been associated with improved student outcomes (Day *et al.*, 2011). Participative leadership is associated with the collegial model. Leithwood and colleagues (1999) argue that democratic principles and group decision-making form the kernel of this type of leadership.

Political management models assume organisations function through the process of negotiation and bargaining, with micro-politics creating factions and interest groups which interact to serve their own agendas. Within this model Bush (2003) argues that 'conflict is viewed as a natural phenomenon and power accrues to dominant coalitions rather than being the preserve of formal leaders' (p. 89). Transactional leadership is associated with political models. Here, action occurs through a set of 'exchanges' of a valued resource. These 'transactions' or 'deals' are linked to resource dependency theory and tend to lead to maintenance of operations rather than developmental activity.

Subjective management models are underpinned by individuals' own constructions of reality. Therefore, participants experience the organisation in different ways, often rooted in their own values and beliefs. Therefore, organisations have 'different meanings for each of their members and exist only in the experience of those members' (Bush, 2003, p. 113). Most forms of leadership rest uneasily with the subjective model. One notable exception is the recently coined post-modern leadership. In this form of leadership there are, as yet, no clearly agreed definitions although, as one might expect, individuals' constructions of reality underpin understanding of the organisation and its development and there are links with the collegial model (Bush, 2003).

The ideas surrounding the final two models of leadership are even more underdeveloped. Bush (2003) suggests ambiguity management models assume organisations are opaque in nature and shrouded in uncertainty and turbulence. They are dominated by a lack of clarity as individuals opt in and out of the decision-making process and relate to notions of 'contingent leadership'. Finally, Bush asserts that cultural management models are driven by the beliefs, values and ideas held within the organisation and the norms that develop within the organisation can be identified by the traditions, rituals and symbols exhibited by it. This is related to forms of moral and instructional models of leadership.

Bush's thoughtful work in this area provides us with a starting point and helps us begin to understand leadership and management through a lens of 'models'. There have been other attempts to build 'models' of leadership. Unfortunately, some of these are less than helpful, reducing the ideas to a model that serves only to describe organisational governance and structures. If we are to develop our understanding about the nature of leadership and how it interacts with organisational development, we need to cast the net back and develop the ideas of Bush, or move beyond the current position where 'academy leadership' and 'federation leadership' are thought of in terms of 'models' (PWC, 2007) to where we articulate 'new models' as 'emerging patterns of practice' (Chapman *et al.*, 2008 and 2009).

A further observation worthy of mention concerns the relationship between leadership and pedagogy. As some models and approaches to educational leadership have moved closer to pedagogical leadership (e.g. instructional leadership) it is interesting to note the increased interest in system leadership. This form of leadership depends on the basic idea that school leaders have a role to play in shaping the education of young people beyond the limits of their own schools and can make a contribution to the knowledge and capacity that resides within and across the system. In practice this has involved headteachers running groups, chains or federations of schools to improve student outcomes (Chapman *et al.*, 2011), working in coaching and mentoring roles with other leaders, as in the case of National Leaders of Education in England (Higham *et al.*, 2007) or working for the strategic management executive of a chain of schools to provide quality assurance or to spread good practice across schools, as in the case of charter schools in the US or academies in England. Whether this form of leadership offers the possibility for 'real' systemic reform is an issue we pick up in more detail in Chapter 8.

Confronting the challenge: developing leadership practice that is fit for purpose – Navigation, Management and Partnership

Research suggests that leaders are increasingly recognising the limitations of existing arrangements. Consequently they are exploring how new arrangements, both structural and through redefining relationships within the system, provide opportunities to develop more appropriate leadership, management and governance practices. Thus, there is a high level of naturally occurring experimentation within many mature education systems. This tends to be shaped by the context from which it emerges. Much of this experimentation involves collaboration at unprecedented levels between schools and with a range of other stakeholders.

In some systems there is also evidence signalling a move towards a more coordinated and systematic approach to educational provision. Schools are collaborating with a range of partners to a greater degree than we have seen over the past two decades. This move towards increased collaboration can be seen as a positive shift which, under the right conditions, will play a major role in strengthening the capacity of the education system and enhancing equity. Increased collaboration, new structural arrangements and the emerging patterns of practice have had a significant impact on the work of school leaders. Figure 1.1, reported in our work on New Models of Leadership (Chapman *et al.*, 2008), provides a framework for exploring the impact of these changes on school leadership, management and governance.

Figure 1.1 highlights what seems to be a significant change in headteacher roles and responsibilities. It illustrates how headteachers have been drawn into important cross-boundary leadership activity, connecting at a strategic level with governors, other services, the wider community and local and national agencies (represented by arrow 1). Unlike in the past – when the majority of

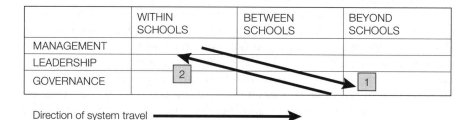

Direction of system travel ⟶

Figure 1.1   A framework for exploring emerging forms of school leadership

the headteacher's life was spent 'in school', leading and managing within clearly defined structures and relationships – these emerging activities operate outside of traditional line management hierarchies. They involve relationships that are quite different and require a complex set of skills, where those involved need to be expert in analysing the wider contexts in which their schools operate. They also have to develop skills as negotiators, facilitators and brokers within often diffuse relationships with minimal history and competing agendas.

These trends have major implications for other senior staff within schools (represented by arrow 2). Increasingly, they are taking on tasks previously carried out by headteachers. This provides new opportunities for such colleagues to take on responsibility and, in so doing, to have greater possibilities to develop their leadership and management skills, particularly within their own schools. All of this can be seen as an overall change in the ways in which schools position themselves in their local communities, represented by the 'direction of system travel' arrow. Such a re-positioning is demanded by policy agendas focusing on closing the gap in the achievements of different groups of learners. It also makes sense in terms of international research, which indicates that school improvement, particularly in socio-economically disadvantaged contexts, will only be sustainable if it is connected to effective programmes of community regeneration (Payne, 2008).

In terms of developing capacity for innovation within the system, such arrangements can be seen as a means of resolving what some writers have described as the maintenance–development dilemma (Hargreaves and Hopkins, 1996). This arises from the tensions that occur when established organisations are faced with the need to change. Put simply, they have to continue carrying out existing requirements (maintenance) whilst, at the same time, inventing responses to new requirements (development). This is experienced as a dilemma in that, however an organisation responds, there are associated risks: too much emphasis on maintenance means that the organisation gets left behind, whilst an over emphasis on development may damage the quality of what is already in place.

Separation of roles, of the sort seen in some schools, seems on the surface at least to offer a promising way of dealing with all of this. For example, the head of a successful hard federation concentrates mostly on further innovations, leaving each of his two deputies to manage one of the two sites. Governors continue to take responsibility for all day-to-day policy issues, leaving the trustees to focus on next steps. In this case the head is the only person attending meetings of both groups, thereby confirming his overall strategic role.

Interesting as such arrangements are, they are not without tensions. So, for example, in another group of schools that has developed a remarkable capacity for development, some members of staff complain that the headteacher has taken his eye off routine matters. As a result, they argue, some aspects of the school's work have deteriorated.

Looking to the future, it will be important for the next generation of school leaders to learn about what is involved in this wider role, not least because this may not have been part of their previous work experience. Clearly, there are implications here for programmes of continuing professional development and how current heads relate to their senior leaders and to their induction into their extended professional networks. This signals the rise and potential future dominance of partnership working as the key role for tomorrow's leaders (see Chapters 2 and 5 for further details).

In conclusion, our analysis leads us to identify the following issues that will shape the nature of navigation, management and partnership as key dimensions of tomorrow's educational leadership. These are important if we are to develop further our understanding of emerging forms of leadership, management and governance and of how they impact on schools and their communities:

1   In many systems across the world there is a range of interesting develop-ments taking place regarding the conceptualisation and implementation of leadership practices. Many of these seem to have the potential to increase the capacity of schools to innovate. Such developments are vital if the system is to find ways of continuing to improve overall standards while, at the same time, reducing the gap between high- and low-achieving groups of learners. But it is also clear that these examples are closely tied to the local contexts in which they have developed. Consequently, it is unlikely that there are 'solutions' here that will transfer easily across boundaries. Rather, we need to generate understandings about particular approaches that can enable a more informed development of ways forward in other contexts, as starting points for the design of specific structures that will meet specific, local needs, rather than as models to be replicated. It is clear that traditional understandings of leadership and management are outmoded and will not serve schools and their communities in this context. Here we believe that conceptualising educational leadership on the dimensions of navigation, management and partnership offers a productive way forward.

2   Though all of these developments have been driven by the desire to improve educational outcomes and, in some, there are early indications of progress, the production of knowledge related to the impact of such developments on student outcomes is very limited at this stage. Therefore, further research investigating the impact of new models of leadership on student outcomes (cognitive and non-cognitive) will be needed. Furthermore, we need to generate deeper understandings about the relationship between leadership and school development phase and context. In Chapter 6 we focus on the relationship between organisational pathology and navigation, management and partnership.

3   Our experience of working and researching with school leaders and other professionals suggests a number of emerging patterns of practice. We see evidence that many headteachers are rethinking their priorities, looking much more outside the school, leaving their senior colleagues to manage day-to-day arrangements. We also see that collaboration between schools and between schools and other agencies is increasingly a process that directly involves staff from a variety of levels in the school in discussions and decision-making.

Such practices have major implications for how navigation, management and leadership play out at all levels within the organisation and the shaping of professional development programmes to support those enacting leadership.

In summary, in this chapter we have outlined the current context and summarised some of the literature relating to the theory and practice of educational leadership to argue that current conceptions of leadership are not fit for purpose. If leadership is to continue to play a major role in the development of schools throughout the 21st century, we need to develop high-leverage approaches. It is our belief that such approaches must be underpinned by navigation, management and partnership. We now move on to outline the key characteristics of each of these elements and how they can serve to offer high-leverage leadership.

2   High-leverage leadership

Introduction

There are some schools which simply appear to buck the trends; schools where pupils' academic attainment and other outcomes are so much better than national averages for similar pupils and similar neighbourhoods. High-leverage is the phrase we are using to describe leaders who work in those schools and contribute to an impressive effect on a range of outcomes for children and young people. From somewhere in the recesses of our school-level science we recall that a lever is a bar resting on a fulcrum which multiplies the effect of a force. We remember being told about Archimedes' claim that, with a long enough lever and a place to stand, he could move the earth – apparently using the moon as a fulcrum. In a different context, organisational theory, Peter Senge (1990) used 'leverage' to describe small, well-focused actions that produce significant and enduring improvements. More recently, leverage became temporarily tainted by its association with the first great financial crisis of the 21st century and the misuse of financial leverage that appeared, misleadingly, to multiply financial gains. Our interest is in school leaders whose leverage, their application of effort to critical factors, has both substantial and sustainable consequences: high-leverage leaders.

We use the concept of 'leverage' and its associated multiplier effect because the relationships we have observed between high-leverage leaders and the people with whom they are working have a strength which seem at times analogous to a physical force. Those relationships create a connection through which energy can be generated and transferred. It is a connection which distinguishes high-leverage leaders from other, apparently effective leaders whose approach is aloof, characterised by short-term tactics and transitory. The high-leverage leaders we have worked with and write about do not, as Archimedes hypothetically might, stand at a distance and apply a massive effort against an inert weight – in their case, 'the school'. They position themselves, as we shall show, alongside staff, students and communities so they can nudge and use the momentum of which they believe everyone is already capable. They do not, as some financiers might, use leverage to raise performance in the short term (for share values read exam passes) and so boost their esteem and pay at the expense of the organisation's long-term stability and success. In contrast, they use leverage to secure the short term and simultaneously to invest for the longer term. Hargreaves and Shirley recognise this important leadership approach in their evaluation of the Raising Achievement for Teaching and Learning (RATL) Programme in which leaders managed to balance the tension between achieving short-term gains in attainment with the demands of longer-term capacity building (Hargreaves and Shirley 2009).

We use 'high' alongside 'leverage' simply because the leaders we are describing have a multiplier effect which is uncommonly powerful. In part, that reflects the places where we have usually met them; most often these are areas with a disproportionate number of socio-economically disadvantaged families. It is easier to track the multiplier effect in those areas or with pupils from those backgrounds. Schools with predominantly wealthier students will tend to have continuous and above-average outcomes that are driven by social – in effect, family – factors and are largely immune from school effects. It is where outcomes have historically been poor that the highest leverage is possible. That is a long way from saying that high-leverage leadership is easy. It is not. If it were, then public education systems and social mobility across the world would have been transformed already.

Over the past decade or so our work in a variety of roles and contexts has drawn us into regular contact with leaders who fit our 'high-leverage' description. That work has always embraced a development and research perspective even when, on occasions, it also involved operational and managerial responsibilities. It has included:

- supporting schools to establish new relationships with professional and neighbourhood communities;
- facilitating schools which want to explore new, often combined leadership and governance arrangements;
- working with local authorities, the equivalent in England of school districts, to sponsor new relationships between their schools and between the schools and local authority officers;
- developing new organisational arrangements (called Children's Trusts in England) so that all the services for children in a locality could work collaboratively and more effectively together;
- working with national inspection agencies and with policymakers.

It will become apparent that we have worked with leaders who share a common set of values and aptitudes while pursuing differing emphases in their immediate priorities and managerial tactics. Those values and aptitudes lead them to:

- work in 'challenging circumstances';
- create networks of schools to challenge underachievement;
- exploit legal, organisational and even premises opportunities to design 'new patterns of leadership';
- successfully 'close gaps' in attainment by raising the performance of the lowest achievers;

- contribute to community cohesion and create 'public value', a high degree of local commitment to the school.

We have been fortunate to work with leaders whose approaches and leverage are so remarkably impressive. Certain that we could not do what they do, though equally certain we could learn from them, we wondered whether we could understand what they did well enough to describe its essential features to others, in particular to other leaders and potential leaders. When we set out to do that, we were not helped by the recurring modesty of these leaders, many of whom are unwilling to accept that what they do is exceptional, still less of wider interest. Many also find it difficult or distracting to articulate what they do, and show a strong preference for 'getting on with it'. What follows is our best effort to respect their work and to distil what we have observed and concluded. We are dependent on and deeply grateful to the school leaders who have allowed us to use and sometimes quote their experiences.

We are also grateful to those leaders for confirming that our analysis resonates with their perspective. They have given us confidence in the validity of our thesis, and reassurance that we are close to doing justice to their efforts and to their skills.

In our work on white working-class attainment (Mongon and Chapman, 2008a) we wrote:

> The best of school leadership raises the work of adults and the attainment of young people to levels that exceed expectations and, sometimes, even their own ambitions. It combines relentless focus and management skill with wide professional knowledge and profound empathy, wrapped in a bag of energy and tied with robust optimism. It has its most remarkable expression in circumstances where poverty and culture might otherwise corrode the potential of young people to fulfil their talent.
>
> (Mongon and Chapman, 2008a, p. 1)

That sentiment has not changed, though we feel that our understanding of just what it means is clearer. Our conclusion is that high-leverage leaders have no access to a magic secret or silver bullet which will cure most, still less all, the ills of the education system in England. The way high-leverage leaders spend their time, their day-to-day activity, will be familiar to anyone who has read the major texts on school effectiveness and school improvement. We therefore want to go beyond those analyses of what they do and to describe how they do it. We conclude that they have characteristics that are not individually rare but are uncommon in their combination and application. It is the second part of that equation – the active combination and application of skills – which is the particular focus of this book. We will illustrate how those elements come together for these leaders by using a framework that we will introduce and explain shortly. We need first to summarise how we arrived at this point and to outline the background to the framework.

In our experience, the basic strategies and tactics followed by high-leverage leaders do not diverge noticeably from the approaches that are repeatedly rehearsed in the school effectiveness and school improvement literature. We referred to that literature and its broad conclusions in Chapter 1. For some time we used the quartet of four core practices identified in Chris Day's comprehensive review of that literature (Day *et al.*, 2008) with one addition. Our addition, a fifth core aspect of practice, is founded on the increasing sophistication with which high-leverage school leaders in England analyse and use the recently available and rich sources of numeric data and other information. We proposed that leadership in high-leverage schools was based around five core practices (Mongon and Chapman, 2008a, p. 6):

- *Building vision and setting directions*
  There is a strong, shared sense of purpose; expectations are high for staff and students alike.
- *Understanding and developing people*
  Staff and students are provided with intellectual and emotional stimulation (including purposeful professional development for the adults).
- *Designing the organisation*
  The structure and culture of the organisation is engineered to match its purpose. Lines of authority are clear for adults and students, close attention is paid to the appearance of the environment and there are strong outward connections.
- *Managing and supporting the teaching and learning programme*
  The leaders are relentless in their application to the highest standards of teaching and learning.
- *Collecting, monitoring, analysing and using information*
  Close attention is given to regular performance measurement for students and staff. Analysis and review are used to inform strategic planning and personalised learning.

So far, so simple and straightforward – the work of high-leverage leaders fits neatly into the canon of established literature. Yet, so puzzling: if high-leverage leaders are 'only' following the common repertoire, why is their impact so particularly effective? Can every or even most leaders learn to be so effective? In the many countries where schools are increasingly autonomous, how will high-leverage leadership permeate the national system and percolate to the places where high leverage from within schools is most needed? These key questions have motivated us to dig deeper into the complexities of contemporary high-leverage leadership.

Understanding the work of high-leverage leaders

To understand for ourselves and to help us articulate why high-leverage leaders are so successful, we began to reflect on the kind of people they seemed to be. Was any insight available for us in the stories they told about themselves or in the stories told by governors, staff and students about them? We have concluded that there are elements of character and what we call, for reasons we will explain, 'intelligences' which recur amongst most of these leaders.

Before we begin to describe those common elements, we need to make it clear that we are very far away from and not searching for a formula for school leadership. High-leverage leaders vary too much in the detail of their approaches for us to think formulaic uniformity is desirable or even possible. Although the elements are common, the chemistry in their combination creates a unique blend on each occurrence. We can illustrate that point:

- high-leverage leaders are attentive to the quality of teaching and learning: some through introducing a banding system, others through a deep commitment to mixed ability groups;
- high-leverage leaders are attentive to the non-negotiables of student behaviour: some through quiet affirmation and understated determination, others with public and often vigorous assertion;
- high-leverage leaders are attentive to pupils at the margin: some through having as many as possible designated as having special educational needs, others through avoiding that as an inappropriate stigma;
- high-leverage leaders are attentive to student appearance: some requiring a blazer-and-tie uniform, others having T-shirts and sweatshirts;
- high-leverage leaders are attentive to their relationships with difficult students and families: they are described as being good at that, some because 'they always stay calm', others because 'they're prepared to fight fire with fire'.

In our observations, the common thread across these otherwise varied styles of leadership is the combination of three personality traits with three 'intelligences'. The three personality traits are:

- *Self confidence*: High-leverage leaders tend to believe in their own ability to cope with the job. This is sometimes called self-efficacy (Day *et al.*, 2008). It is what makes high-leverage leaders more likely to tackle a task and to persist even if success is not immediate. Importantly, high-leverage leaders are prepared to reflect and persist if they then think it is right to do so, even in the face of initial failure. Our experience with high-leverage leaders confirms Day's conclusion that effective school leaders have high levels of self-confidence and that their staff appreciate that aspect of them.
- *Personal responsibility*: High-leverage leaders tend to take personal responsibility for their behaviour and its consequences. In one study of schools with 'positive cultures' this has been called an internal locus of control, attributing events in one's life to one's own control and effect (Engels, 2008). The leaders we have met and worked with are not inclined to blame staff, students, parents, community, local authority or national government for problems (though some would say that the last two are not always helpful). They are inclined to see the destiny of the school as being in its own hands.
- *Conscientiousness*: High-leverage leaders pay attention to detail. They tend to be painstaking, verging on the perfectionist, self-disciplined, organised, careful before acting and striving to achieve. One of us has previously written that

they have 'the confidence to be contentious and to deal with conflict, highly pragmatic, resilient and determined' (Harris and Chapman, 2002, p. 3). High-leverage leaders, we will explain in Chapter 5, are as conscientious about the quality of the relationships they create as they are about student outcomes.

High-leverage leaders also have a set of skills that we describe as 'intelligences' and by which we mean simply what Gardner (1983, p. 60) calls human intellectual competence. Gardner describes this as the ability to resolve genuine problems or difficulties and create appropriately effective outcomes. He argues that a prerequisite of intellectual competence is the ability to find or create problems, an ability which, he claims, is 'the groundwork for the acquisition of new knowledge' (1983, pp. 60–1). In our experience, high-leverage leaders resolve existing problems, explore previously unrecognised problems and produce effective solutions by applying three dimensions of 'intelligence': Professional, Social and Contextual (Chapman *et al.*, 2006). If you are uncomfortable with 'intelligence' as a concept in this context, you might prefer to think in terms of disposition, capacity or literacy (Southworth, 2004).

Professional Intelligence

High-leverage leaders employ Professional Intelligence, a kind of practical, problem-solving wisdom which we will describe in Chapter 3 as something akin to 'savvy'. They know their core business well: leadership and management that nurture excellent standards of teaching and learning. They focus intensely on guaranteeing the quality of the interactions between adults and young people and the quality of the pedagogy in their schools. The leaders we have worked with appeared to hold in their heads:

- *A clear, strong view about what constitutes good teaching and learning.*
  They can describe it and model it and they expect it to permeate their school. They believe that everyone can learn and improve. They demonstrate that belief by supporting their staff with high-quality professional development.
- *Good insight into what is happening across their school.*
  If they don't know, and usually they do, then someone in the leadership team will know and can tell them on demand. They arrange for the handling of information across the school to be thorough. Information is harvested and prepared to be organisationally nutritious, to create energy for action.
- *A view of their work with a long field of focus.*
  They scan across the short term and through into the long term. They can apply the quick-fix tactics that create momentum in school improvement, Jim Collins's flywheel effect (Collins, 2001), and still keep an eye on the future. They understand that *what is done* in the short term, and above all how it is done, will carry a long echo.
- *A willingness to take and to encourage disciplined risk.*
  They expect occasional errors and misjudgements to be made. They accept

that, as long as the consequent learning and development are exploited. This applies to everyone, whatever their age or status.

- *An ability to modulate their approach to match the school.*
  They know that the life of a school is cyclical, subject to ebb and flow, sometimes accumulating quality and sometimes haemorrhaging confidence. They constantly move their colleagues towards what we call 'earned autonomy'. In Chapter 5, we claim that this moves beyond 'distributed leadership' into what we call 'Association', relationships based on trust and commitment rather than status and power.

- *Knowledge about how to improve schools and maintain their effectiveness.*
  That knowledge is drawn in part from their own operational experience, not least working with effective leaders. It also draws on their personal inquisitiveness that has attracted them into more or less formal professional enquiry and learning.

- *Sharpness on funding, funding streams and budget deployment.*
  They constantly scan for new funding sources. They deploy the budget to support what the school needs to do next, not what it has always been doing. They fly very close to the wind of financial regulations and grant requirements to ensure that funding streams are aligned with the school's priorities and no-one else's.

- *An ability to turn external pressure into internal impetus.*
  Sometimes momentum can be derived from a sense of conspiracy: 'us round here against the rest ... and we will come out best'. Targets and measured performance are very important to these leaders, but they are a means; the end is to improve the quality of people's lives.

- *The vital priority of staff quality.*
  They are both methodical and imaginative about filling staff vacancies. They believe that their students are entitled to the best teachers and their staff to the best colleagues. Many tell of times when they engaged in personal head-hunting and arm twisting, or called on loyal friends.

Social Intelligence

High-leverage leaders employ Social Intelligence, meaning that they are sensitive to the emotional states of their pupils and colleagues. They know that their effect on student outcomes is mainly indirect and mediated through the activities of teachers and other students, the organisation of the school and relationships with parents and the wider community (Bell *et al.*, 2003). Social Intelligence informs their thoughts and actions even when some members of staff and some students would find that hard to credit. In turn, they are generally well thought of and often admired by their colleagues and pupils. Many of their colleagues, asked what they would do if the headteacher left, have told us they would be torn between their personal admiration and their professional responsibility, wondering whether they would also leave, possibly even follow, or whether they were somehow tied 'to finishing the work we've started'. Many teachers, middle and senior leaders, tell us they are aware that their experience with a high-leverage leader is a great foundation or stepping stone for their own careers. In Chapter 3 we explain just how important this is.

The high-leverage leaders' interpersonal skills are based on their evident respect for the adults and children around them. Their behaviour is rooted in personal value systems that include clear views about how people should behave towards one another. They model that perspective as they move around the school – a word for everyone, however large or small and whatever their status. They drive high expectations without losing their sense of empathy or intending to erode anyone's dignity. As individuals, their behaviour in moments of tension and crisis varies, but their colleagues believe that they are always in control of themselves and the situation, uncompromising in their protection of the school's values and practices. Consequently, they can usually create an atmosphere in which high expectations are seen as evidence of care and concern and not as surveillance or constraint. However, high-leverage leaders know that their work also has its contrary aspects and does not work for every adult or for every child. When we write that high-leverage leaders don't *intend* to erode anyone's dignity and that they *usually* create an atmosphere of care, we know that is not always how their approach is experienced. Sometimes, even with considerable support, some adults or pupils experience high expectations as demanding and unreasonable: they simply cannot respond positively. For a small number this experience feels just as if they are being picked on, in effect bullied. High-leverage leaders are not insensitive but cannot always counter alienation or avoid difficult consequences associated with those feelings. It is a fine line that we observe them treading.

Contextual Intelligence

High-leverage leaders employ Contextual Intelligence, showing a profound respect for the contexts they are working in without ever becoming patronising. We use the plural, 'contexts', because each high-leverage leader is politically tuned to working in several contexts simultaneously. In Chapter 5 we will explore in some detail their sense of responsibility to what we will call five 'authorising environments':

- their own conscience;
- their school community;
- the school governing body;
- local communities (neighbourhood and professional);
- national statutory requirements.

Many, though by no means all, of the high-leverage leaders we worked with referred to their own background and childhood in low-income communities as the basis of their respect for the often economically poor communities in which they work. For that group, this appeared to be an important part of their professional and personal identity. It was even more common for the high-leverage leaders to claim that they had chosen to work in challenging contexts. Although this might be rationalising after the event, it was, so far as we could judge, consistent with their career history.

High-leverage leaders are sensitive to the school's external environment without being condescending to the social or professional communities they work with. 'It is hard,' one said to us. 'It's difficult out there, but that's no excuse for any of us ...' They prefer to talk about the strengths of the local community rather than its shortcomings. For them, the neighbourhood provides more opportunities than problems. They will not tolerate anyone, especially anyone from their school, making comments along the lines of 'What do you expect with kids or parents or places like these?' They combine the personality traits of self-confidence, personal responsibility and conscientiousness we described earlier to create a personal expectation that they can help a community to overcome disadvantage. The same expectation in turn feeds the ethics that informs their work and their relationships around the school. They see the value of what, in Chapter 5, we call Association: close cooperation between service providers to design service delivery around the needs of young people. Their contextual intelligence places their school as a powerful partner, an Associate in our terms, capable of contributing to the full range of outcomes for young people. Their core activity, excellent teaching and learning, is for them both an end in its own right and a contribution to other outcomes. High-leverage leaders know that other services' activities will have their own ends, and believe that these are often capable of enhancing educational outcomes. High-leverage leaders see and understand the pattern of partnerships and associations that produce mutual optimisation of contributions. They have a 360-degree view of their position in local educational networks. They understand the political environments in which they operate, locally and nationally. 'They adopt the education service's initiatives for their school, drain the contribution and divert the constraints' (Mongon and Chapman, 2008a, p. 8).

Having identified the three personality traits, self-confidence, personal responsibility and conscientiousness, and the three intelligences, professional, social and contextual, as key ingredients, we then had to explain, as we do in the following section, how the blend works so effectively in different contexts.

Towards a model of 'high-leverage' leadership

The model on the following page is our analysis of how high-leverage leaders create the positive outcomes associated with their work. The building blocks of the model are located in three key roles: Navigation, Management and Partnership. We opt for Navigation to describe a role that might more often be referred to as 'leadership'. This allows us to avoid the stereotypical juxtaposition in which leadership becomes virtually synonymous with change processes and softer aptitudes while management is associated with system maintenance and tough attitudes. That does not fit the real world in which change often needs careful management and maintenance often needs subtle leadership. In turn, this allows us to propose that leadership is a word best used to describe the combination of the three elements. Navigation, Management and Partnership are indivisible components of leadership and of high-leverage leadership in particular. Our explanatory metaphor is that these three are like three strands of leadership DNA. Like DNA, they need to be taken apart and examined individually in order to understand their composition and relationship to one another. That is what we will do in increasing detail over the next few pages and the following three chapters. Like individual strands of DNA, however, they are virtually lifeless on their own. Their meaning, purpose and effect can only be realised in combination with the other strands. Without that chemistry, each of the strands is inert and dysfunctional.

Role	Function	Activity
Navigation	Securing the vision: setting a direction and nurturing development	**Awareness:** recognising and prioritising issues the organisation will need to address
		Acceptance: understanding that current practice may be a barrier while believing that improvement is possible
		Advocacy: creating a 'living vision' and participating in focused workforce development to introduce sustainable change
Management	Organising: problem-solving, creating order and providing consistency	**Analysis:** using data and other information to create a high-definition picture of how issues manifest themselves locally
		Action: emphasising priorities, and ensuring that change is explicit, funded and managed
		Application: relentless focus, in particular ensuring that the quality of teaching and learning – the basic compact between a school and its community – is first-class
Partnership	Modelling Partnership: treating partners with equal esteem and deep respect	**Association:** being socially aware: nurturing the school as a community in its own right, as a member of its neighbourhood community and as a unit in a wider professional community
		Alignment: improving the alignment of the students' home and school experiences – without bias as to what might change and where
		Area focus: engaging with the wider community in a partnership role because for young people there is no 'one size fits all'

Figure 2.1   A model for high-leverage leadership

The model is designed to share our experience in accessible terms with school leaders and researchers. For each of the three key roles, we describe three key activities, nine in all. In an earlier work we identified five distinct features of the work of leaders who are successful with white working-class students. Those five were Awareness, Acceptance, Area Focus, Alignment and Action (Mongon and Chapman, 2008a, pp. 15–16). The insights gained from those leaders and our further research referenced in this book, especially in schools exploring new forms of local leadership, gradually brought into focus four other features of high-leverage leadership. The four could be squeezed into the same alliteration: Advocacy, Analysis, Application and Association. Time after time we have asked individuals and groups: 'Does this resonate? Have we understood what you are saying and what we have seen? Does this framework make sense to you?' The three-part model (see Figure 2.1) and nine activities consolidate what leaders have told us about their work, what we have observed and what we know from the literature.

Navigation

Navigation, the first of the three roles in our framework, is explained in detail in Chapter 3. We use it to create an analogy between the part played by a navigator on a ship or aircraft and some functions of a school leader. The analogy works like this: a navigator, above all else, has to know the position of her vessel in relation to three critical factors:

- the destination;
- the route; and
- the patterns of weather and currents.

A navigator deploys experience, aptitude and training along with appropriate charts and equipment. If positioning is inaccurate then the direction of travel becomes uncertain, timing unpredictable and fuelling unreliable: an eventful ride is guaranteed and a crash is quite likely.

We think something similar occurs in schools when high-leverage leaders deploy their knowledge and insights.

- They identify the destination – which we have called 'securing the vision'.
- They finalise the route – which we have called 'setting a direction'.
- They anticipate the weather and currents – which we think of as the surrounding political trends, professional standards and community expectations.

To complete the set of functions for a school 'navigator' we have stretched the analogy and added 'nurturing development' because of the overwhelming evidence, some of which we will reference in Chapter 3, that support for professional development is the most powerful tool in the high-leverage leaders' kit.

Awareness and Acceptance – recognising priorities and acknowledging the need for change – are important Activities in Navigation. 'The collective act of reconsidering and transforming the school program means that the school staff becomes a more collegial community which provides ongoing support to its members as they struggle with the ongoing problems of practice' (Knapp, 2001, p. 191). Knapp proposes that there is evidence from the Accelerated School Network in the United States to show that these approaches work because they deal with the pathologies of schools in which students are underachieving rather than assuming that remedial strategies aimed at the students' skill deficits can work in dysfunctional circumstances. Knapp concludes that such approaches 'represent a major shift in theory of actions from a model highlighting learners' deficiencies ... to one emphasising those of the school and its capacity to transform itself'. Not all high-leverage leaders work in schools that require transformation, but most have spoken to us about the balance they try to create between changing the adults' practice and changing the pupils' behaviour.

For that reason, Advocacy, the style in which high-leverage leaders operate their Navigation, demands the greatest part of our attention in Chapter 3. Our experience of working with high-leverage leaders coincides with Ainscow and West's (2006) explanation of how successful leaders operate (p. 9). They draw on the field of social psychology (Johnson and Johnson, 1994) for a tripartite model – competitive, individualistic or cooperative – of the way leaders may structure working relationships. Ainscow and West conclude that studies of schools that have achieved and [importantly] sustained success in urban contexts tend to report leadership that is more cooperative than it is competitive or individualistic. This echoes Bryk and Schneider's (2002) conclusion that one of the most powerful, positive factors in school improvement is the leadership's capacity to nurture the broad base of trust, respect and personal regard which is a critical lubricant in complex circumstances.

In the section on Advocacy in Chapter 3, we will explore how high-leverage leaders use their cooperative disposition – their commitment to equity of voice and social justice and their sense of mutual personal regard – to mould personal relationships and educational practices in their schools. We will borrow the concept of 'living vision' from the work of the Innovation Unit (2009) to show how high-leverage leaders avoid the sterile verbosity into which so many corporate mission statements descend. Instead of the unarguable and ill-defined commitment to parenthood and apple pie which characterises so many vision statements, high-leverage leaders create a powerful connection between the moral grounding and working practices of the school and the goals at which they are aiming. A 'living vision' does not need to be written down, though if it were then it might be a bit longer than the catchy sound bites we are all familiar with. It will not be written to be memorised, it will be written to be acted out. To achieve that, high-leverage leaders use two predominant tactics:

- consistent personal modelling, especially of the learning expected of everyone; and
- consistent use of language to express the values and practices of the school.

High-leverage leaders, in effect, use Advocacy to espouse their values and preferred practices by 'capillary transmission – reaching into the very grain of individuals, touching them and entering into their actions and attitudes, their discourses, learning processes and everyday lives' (Foucault, 1980).

At the core of Advocacy is the high-leverage leaders' commitment to the progress and development of every individual at the school, whatever their age or status. There were many occasions in our conversations with them when we could not immediately tell whether they were talking about children or adults. They are clear that the medium is the message and that their approach to the adults and the adults' approach to their own learning are powerful models for young people. The international research that consistently shows that a commitment to staff development is a key feature of good schools confirms what these leaders already know they need to do.

Management

Management, the second element in our three-part framework, is explained in detail in Chapter 4. Management, through careful attention to detail, guarantees that high-quality Navigation is translated into operational effectiveness. Management means making sure the necessary work gets done, agreed activity happens and that quality is consistent. This second element in our framework is not occupying second place in status or in chronology. *Navigation* and Management are inseparable even when, occasionally, one or the other dominates. High-leverage leaders work to the principle that 'linking management activities and tasks to school or college aims and objectives remains vital' (Bush, 2003, p. 1). Their approach to Management is always rooted in their Advocacy and in the 'living vision' we write about in Chapter 3. High-leverage leaders create overlap between Navigation and Management to ensure that what people are motivated to do and what they actually do are consistent with the purposes of the organisation.

In some circumstances Management activity might take up more of a leader's time than Navigation. Leaders who, for example, inherit a school that is 'failing' may have to manage a lot of detail directly and assertively to create a dependable launch pad. If we can stretch our metaphor of a journey again, high-leverage leaders arriving at a collision site might need to stabilise the injured, stop the leaks or mend the axle before anyone can travel safely onwards. In Chapter 6 we will explore this requirement for leaders to differentiate their approach to match the immediate circumstances facing them. In Chapter 4 we will focus on Management and reflect on how high-leverage leaders organise the work of their institutions, solve problems, create order and provide consistency.

Management is to some degree a technical matter – though not to be confused with administration. High-leverage leaders are not above 'mucking in' when circumstances demand, but are careful to avoid being drawn regularly into tasks which do not demand their skills or experience. High-leverage leaders also avoid managerialism that emphasises procedures over purpose, efficiency over values and external policies over internal commitment. Instead, their management behaviour is suffused with the personality traits and intelligences that also underpin their approach to Navigation. To that extent, Management draws heavily on the Professional Intelligence, but also to some degree on the Social Intelligence, of high-leverage leaders.

Action, emphasising priorities and ensuring that change is explicit, funded and managed, is a vital Management activity, but it is Analysis and Application which, we will show in Chapter 4, do most to distinguish high-leverage leaders from the rest.

The information available for Analysis by school leaders, policymakers and researchers in England has been transformed over the past two decades. The national data on school performance, on individual attainment and on financial deployment is sophisticated and in many ways remarkable. It is not without its shortcomings, not least because the format of its collection and publication reflect national priorities but not necessarily local needs. For that reason, high-leverage leaders are neither mesmerised by data sets nor dependent on them. They also use stories and narratives that are produced in a range extending from everyday conversation through to professional enquiry. In that context, Analysis has become a relatively easy aid to ambition and accountability. It can be used prospectively to inform the next steps in performance development or retrospectively to report how well performance has developed.

Continuous improvement depends on the good use of shared information. 'Good use' means that Analysis permeates the work of high-leverage leaders – it is not a marginal activity. They use enquiry, and therefore Analysis, as a contribution to the trust and to the culture of professional development that we referred to as part of Advocacy. High-leverage leaders also know that one of the richest sources of information about a school resides in the students who have so much contact with and, given the chance, a lot to say about teaching and learning. Analysis in collaboration helps pupils and teachers to understand their different perspectives and to build more collaborative and communicative relationships.

If Analysis is the fuel for high performance, Application is the piston set – the remorseless transfer of force to the moving parts. We describe this in our Framework as 'relentless focus, in particular ensuring that the quality of teaching and learning – the basic compact between a school and its community – is first class'. High-leverage leaders know that, without high-quality teaching, their students will not learn. They also know that, without high-quality teaching and learning behind them, their attempts to build bridges into their surrounding neighbourhood and professional services will fall flat. Their credibility depends on doing the core tasks well. If, for example, external accountability has deemed the quality of teaching and learning to be unsatisfactory, high-leverage leaders might put all their effort into regenerating that core work before thinking about bridges beyond the school. Even good is not – according to high-leverage leaders – good enough. The right to be active beyond the school boundaries has to be earned by demonstrating professional competence within those boundaries.

High-leverage leaders are therefore uncompromising about their recruitment of high-quality staff. Their practices do not always sit comfortably with the expectations of personnel services. They will head hunt and manipulate to recruit the person they want – personal recommendation is often important to them. They are equally uncompromising about staff who will not meet their expectations of professional standards. Everyone is given some opportunity to learn and to develop, but if that is not taken up, their employment will be changed, more or less comfortably. High-leverage leaders do not believe that needy children should have anything but the very best teaching. Inconsistency and variation within the school are particularly monitored and challenged. The performance of everyone in the school is regularly and carefully assessed before it is discussed with them and the next steps of their development agreed. All of this we will explore in more detail in Chapter 4.

Partnership

The final element in our three-part framework, Partnership, is explained in detail in Chapter 5. Partnership (and by implication its converse, isolation) are emerging as dominant issues for leadership and governance in the English public education system during the second decade of the 21st century. Successive governments in England have offered schools increasing autonomy as individual legal entities. The coalition government formed by Conservatives and Liberal Democrats in 2010 announced that it would take the policies of the previous Labour Government to a new level. These include a tranche of deregulation opportunities for every school, encouraging existing schools to become Academies and allowing independent groups to start up new 'Free Schools'. Legally, Academy Schools and Free Schools are independent schools funded by the national government. As independent schools they will be free from many of the national legislative requirements of state schools, not least those prescribing the pay and conditions of their staff.

While schools are becoming more autonomous, many school leaders are aware that families, communities and other services outside the school can make a significant contribution to young people's wellbeing and attainment. Many school leaders also know that the converse is true, that their school's contribution to Partnerships can enhance a range of 'non-educational' outcomes across a community. At its most extreme, this is visible in places such as the one where a leader said to us, 'it's not a matter of how many exam passes they get, sometimes it's a question of whether they will be alive to take the exam'. There is also an increasing awareness that schools linked in networks or chains can work together effectively in the interests of young people. Autonomy is compatible with partnerships, and higher standards of academic attainment are compatible with raising other outcomes. There are many examples in high-leverage schools where the one thrives on the other.

However, these are complex, finely balanced matters and, as schools in England become more autonomous, some leaders will abandon any significant attempt to engage with wider Partnerships and retreat towards the technical management of the classroom experience in their school. In contrast, close and effective Partnerships with students, families, neighbourhood communities and other services have been characteristic of the high-leverage leaders with whom we have been involved. Typically, these Partnerships strive for an egalitarian approach to the rights, privileges and interests of their members. We have been fortunate that our work has allowed us to explore with the leaders where the impetus for those Partnerships comes from and how they are sustained.

The historic ebb and flow of community connection: is the tide moving in or out?

There is a distinguished and long tradition of schools in England working with neighbourhood communities and with other providers of services for children and families. That is not the same as saying it has been a widespread practice, though it was already a well established feature in some areas as long ago as 1870. The Education Act of 1870 effectively founded the state education system in England by bringing a large part of the diverse and complex range of independent, voluntary school provision into public ownership. 'System' would be a hopelessly misleading word to apply indiscriminately to the Ragged Schools, Union Schools, National (Anglican Church) Schools, British (Non-conformist Church) Schools, Industrial Schools or any number of other local variations on provision which operated across England in the 19th century. Given that context, autonomy in the 21st-century English system seems more of a renovation than an innovation. Significantly, as their titles often implied, those schools were not simply places for teaching and learning, they were often an extension of their benefactors' other commitments and aspirations. These other dimensions were variously philanthropic, communitarian, sometimes quite penal and frequently intended to promote industrial efficiency.

Robert Owen's early 19th-century experiments in New Lanark, Scotland, were the iconic model for developments across the United Kingdom. Owen, a Scottish industrialist, pioneered model communities which would be familiar to some of our current innovators, including as they did infant schools, crèches, medical care and education for young and old (Donnachie, 2000). Approaches like Owen's and others, organised for example by churches, trade unions and mutual societies, were maintained largely by philanthropy through the 19th century. Following the 1870 Act, and by the start of the 20th century, state intervention, compulsory school attendance, the mass recruitment of poorly educated and ill-nourished youths to fight imperial wars, and the work of pioneering researchers like Seebohm Rowntree had exposed to public scrutiny the extent of child poverty, abuse and exploitation in England. The response, a pioneering tradition which first sponsored and then demanded legislation for the provision of school meals, school medical examinations, employment rights and curbs on alcohol sales to protect young people, was the predecessor to the communal inclinations of high-leverage leaders.

As the 20th century unfolded, Henry Morris picked up similar themes in the Cambridge Village Colleges which would bring together the 'vital activities of village life' and:

> ... would create out of discrete elements an organic whole; the vitality of the constituent elements would be preserved, and not destroyed, but the unity they would form would be a new thing. For, as in the case of all organic unities, the whole is greater than the mere sum of the parts. It would be a true social synthesis – it would take existing and live elements and bring them into a new and unique relationship.
>
> (Morris, 1925)

This work was continued into the second half of the 20th century, notably by local authorities in the East Midlands of England and particularly in Leicestershire's community colleges. In the 1960s and 1970s, the Plowden Report's emphasis on parent participation, pre-school involvement, education priority areas and positive discrimination (Plowden, 1967) were allied with Eric Midwinter's descriptions of community education in Liverpool (Midwinter, 1972, 1973). These contributors kindled an intellectual spark and then provided solid fuel for the community school movement in inner cities.

The modern high-leverage leaders we have collaborated with are inheritors of this longstanding inclusive seam in English state-sector education. They believe, like their predecessors in this tradition, that a school can only operate with moral authority or provide effective learning if it is attentive to the needs of young people beyond their immediate hunger for learning. But that is a contested view, and during the second half of the 20th century some schools became, for many families, daunting, tightly focused and professionally dominated institutions. Some schools in England would even draw lines on the playground beyond which parents were not allowed without an appointment. During the 1970s in particular, collaboration and community involvement came under increasingly sceptical scrutiny. By 1981 the then Minister of Education, Rhodes Boyson, could inform Parliament that there were no designated Education Priority Areas (Hansard, 1981). The few that had been established had disappeared, first into the cloud of political and operational confusion that surrounded their nature and purpose, and then washed away by the wave of individualism and competition which characterised policy for 20 years or so from the late 1970s.

The consequence is that, for many in the current generation of school leaders in England, the recent emphasis on partnerships involving school-to-school collaboration – and even more so involving schools and other services – has been a radical shift. The strong individual head of a single institution has been their dominant leadership model through a large part of their careers and through most of their leadership experience. Idiosyncratic, heroic leadership was a model pursued in the mid-20th century and based on the enduring 19th-century English independent school tradition in which most English policymakers had been educated. For the two decades from 1980, national policy and academic writing focused school leaders on the internal dynamics of their schools. Assertive local management of teaching and learning was the holy grail of school improvement.

Even as it established its dominance, that approach was increasingly questioned at national and neighbourhood levels and by some academics (Wrigley, 2003, ch. 1). The election of the 'New Labour' government in 1997 '... marked a sharp swing back to neighbourhood projects – 'area-based initiatives' (rapidly shortened to ABIs) now seen as the answer to the geography of disadvantage' (Smith *et al.*, 2007, p. 143). Local leaders in England interested in exploring whether partnerships and networks could raise student outcomes found what we will call 'an authorising environment' (Chapter 7) in policy strands such as Education Action Zones (EAZs), Excellence in Cities (EIC), Beacon schools and Specialists schools, Leadership Incentive Grants, the Leading Edge Partnership Programme, Networked Learning Communities and 14–19 Pathfinders. These were substantially funded national initiatives that purposefully required or encouraged schools to collaborate with other schools and often with other kinds of partners. Educationally focused, many of these initiatives could still be used by school leaders to align their work with initiatives sourced from outside education. This included the Single Regeneration Projects funded by the Department of the Environment, Transport and the Regions to support economic regeneration in 'deprived' areas. Some of the local partnerships managing these projects directed funding into collaborative projects around school management, classroom practices, school–industry links and early years skill development (DfEE, 1999).

Partnerships were further encouraged when the then Labour Government began its promotion of 'extended schools' (Department for Education and Skills, 2005). The intention was that, by 2010, children and families would be able to access a range of core services 'through schools located at the heart of the community'. The core offer did not have to be provided by a school. There was encouragement to create partnership so that the offer could include:

- a varied range of activities including study support, sport and music clubs, combined with childcare in primary schools;
- parenting and family support;
- swift and easy access to targeted and specialist services;
- community access to facilities including adult and family learning, ICT and sports grounds.

Since the change of national government in England in 2010, partnerships have continued to be part of the common currency of educational conversation in England, and generally – though not universally – held to be 'a good thing'. The National College for Leadership of Schools and Children's Services in England (National College) promotes 'the need for new thinking' about leadership models and partnerships and lists examples including federations, legal collaborations, Trusts, co-locations with other services, chains of schools and various combinations of these (National College, 2010a). It has published a 'think piece' by David Hargreaves arguing that a sustainable, self-improving school system requires the development of school clusters, local solutions, co-construction and 'system leaders' (Hargreaves, 2010). The new national government has made partnership a requirement of a kind in its flagship educational reforms in 2010. Schools which want to become Academies – state funded, independent schools – must sign up at least 'in principle' to supporting another school (DfE, 2011a). There is further scope for schools to develop their partnership roles with other schools and communities under the 2010 Coalition Government's 'Big Society' proposal for people and communities to be 'given more power and take more responsibility' (Cabinet Office, 2010, p. 1). Some schools may use their increasing autonomy to retreat from the extended concept into a narrower focus on the management of teaching. This will not be true of all schools, seems unlikely to be true of most and may not be true at all for many.

High-leverage leaders in partnership

If there is a comfort zone for school leaders, it is more likely to be within school, where their formal status should be secure, than beyond school in circumstances where their organisation might even be regarded as 'the problem'. Working beyond that zone requires confidence and courage. If zone is the right word at all, then high-leverage leaders tend to operate in a 'learning zone' both inside and outside their schools. They apply an expectation of learning to everyone including themselves. They are the embodiment of the quip that, if you can choose between work with a leader who knows everything or one who is still learning, you should go for the latter – it will be more fun and more personally useful. In Chapter 3 we will write about high-leverage leaders advocating the core importance of learning and development for everyone in their schools, irrespective of age or status and including themselves. The section on *Association* in Chapter 5 will explain how high-leverage leaders seamlessly translate that core approach – the school being a community where outcomes will improve if relationships allow everyone to learn together – into their encounters with initially unfamiliar groupings outside the school.

High-leverage leaders, we will note in Chapter 3, are less susceptible than many to the swings and roundabouts of national policy. They combine single-mindedness about what needs to be achieved with open-mindedness about how it can be done. They are skilful at adapting and localising national policy so that it enhances and does not inhibit their work. They are also clear that educational attainment is one important outcome for young people. They do not accept that it is the only important outcome and they resist allowing it to overwhelm other outcomes. For these leaders, the main purpose of education is working out how to live together with dignity and in harmony – attainment is one of the steps towards that. They recognise that the cultures in a neighbourhood and the work of other providers can also contribute to that purpose. They therefore work to ensure that the ways in which they and the people around them behave are matched to what they are all trying to achieve.

In Chapter 5, to help us explain more about the kind of Partnership which high-leverage leaders create, we adopt the words Associate and Association. Associate partnerships, we will explain, are bonded cooperations founded on equal respect and mutual esteem. In contrast, asymmetric partnerships are predominantly based on control, the political management of connections and the administration of power between groups. Despite the ubiquitous rhetoric of professional unity in England, associate partnerships are a novel and demanding dimension of leadership for many school leaders. It is that which makes the approach of high-leverage leaders compelling to observe.

Partnerships come in so many shapes and sizes that we need to explain in simple, broad terms a distinction that we want to make between 'asymmetric partnerships' and 'associate partnerships' (see Table 2.1).

Table 2.1 The distinction between 'asymmetric partnerships' and 'associate partnerships'

	Asymmetric partnerships	Associate partnerships
Source	Prefabricated	Cultivated
Framework	Legal	Ethical
Authority	Based on position	Based on trust

- *Asymmetric partnerships* are defined by powerful agencies that might be external or internal to the partnerships: for example, statutory requirements from national government or leverage from local high status institutions. The framework for asymmetric partnerships is predominantly legal: activity is based on technical relationships. Authority is based mainly on position: particular posts or organisations will be associated with power.
- *Associate partnerships* are held together by common interest, defined and cultivated by the partners. Their framework is predominantly ethical: activity is based on expectations of 'the kind of people we are'. Authority is based mainly on trust: hierarchical assumptions are challenged.

We would not pretend that these two are ever simply distinct and separable. In particular they might overlap in improving circumstances when associate partnering is made gradually and purposefully to supersede asymmetric partnering, both in and around the school (see Chapter 6). Our proposal is simply that high-leverage leaders tend to develop and sustain associate partnerships as the core of their leadership inside and outside their school.

The high-leverage leaders we have worked with are intuitive community builders and investors in social capital. Their leadership therefore nurtures associate relationships between people of different ages and status in their schools. Because they then bring the same intuition to bear outside their schools they are comfortable as 'associate partners'. They are comfortable even when their authority cannot rest on the powers of statute and position: they do not rely on that in school and do not expect to rely on it outside. In summary:

because they treat their school as a community of which they are a member, they can see themselves and their school as partners, one of the associates, in wider neighbourhood and professional communities. We will return to this in detail in Chapter 5.

3 Navigation

Role	Function	Activity
Navigation	Securing the vision: setting a direction and nurturing development	Awareness: recognising and prioritising issues the organisation will need to address
		Acceptance: understanding that current practice may be a barrier while believing that improvement is possible
		Advocacy: creating a 'living vision' (see page 52) and participating in focused work force development to introduce sustainable change

Introduction

In the previous chapter we introduced the three key roles in which high-leverage leaders engage: Navigation, Management and Partnership. This chapter focuses on the first of those, Navigation. It explores in more detail how Navigation requires the three activities which we have labelled Awareness, Acceptance and Advocacy:

- *Awareness*: high-leverage leaders are constantly anticipating the priorities their organisations need to address. They hold the moral and professional ground around which the school's work is designed. They scan the political horizons so they are not surprised by initiatives and policy shifts.
- *Acceptance*: they understand that current practice may be a limitation while believing that improvement is possible. They believe that they and their staff are responsible for the outcomes of their work. They never say 'What would

you expect with people like this?' – whether they are talking about pupils, local communities or policymakers!

- *Advocacy*: they build a 'living vision' which is compelling, specific, grounded and can be tested in action (Innovation Unit, 2009). 'Living vision' is the antithesis of platitude. These leaders also promote personal development and learning: for themselves, their colleagues, their students and their communities.

Before looking at those three activities, we need to make a comment about governance. It is a coincidence useful to our Navigation analogy that 'governance' derives from ancient Greek *kubernâo* and Latin *gubernare*, meaning to pilot a ship or chariot. Plato, in the 4th century BC, was one of the first to use *kubernâo* to describe communal oversight. Even though, internationally, modern governance arrangements for schools are enormously varied, there is still an inevitable and therefore universal relationship between those arrangements and Navigation. We will explore that connection in detail when we discuss the accountability of high-leverage school leaders in Chapter 7. Through the present chapter we need to bear in mind that governance – the arrangements for accountability – always contribute to or constrain the leader's capacity to promote a living vision, a sense of direction and an appropriate development programme. In England and some other countries, school governance is a local and predominantly lay matter, conducted by school governors who might share that role with other groups when wider provision, services or partnerships are included. Elsewhere, it remains a predominantly professional and administrative matter in the hands of local or central government officers and, through them, elected local government.

In the present chapter we will briefly expand on what we mean by Awareness and Acceptance, before reflecting in more detail on what we have seen as a power pack in the high-leverage leader's toolkit, Advocacy.

Awareness

Navigation
Securing the vision, setting a direction and nurturing development
Awareness: recognising and prioritising issues the organisation will need to address

Our proposal is that high-leverage school leaders have a highly developed sense of Awareness, constantly anticipating the issues their organisations will need to address.

They do so by:

- helping to define and then holding the moral ground around which the school's work is designed; and

- scanning political horizons so the school is not surprised by initiatives and policy shifts.

'We had been steadily improving attendance and attainment to the level where we were judged to be outstanding. We had celebrated our achievements with parents and the community, a real partnership effort. A local survey then revealed just how limited the ambitions of our successful pupils were – low paid work and teenage pregnancies. It struck us that after all of our work on raising attainment, our children and community had not understood what this could mean for their life chances and future options.'
Sheila Audsley, Headteacher, Clifton Green Primary School

Moral authority and personal morality have been associated with school leadership in England for as long as memory extends – though not in the way that many school leaders now refer to 'moral leadership'. For most of the 20th century, the moral role of many school leaders was associated with personal rather than professional behaviour. Their private behaviour had to be beyond reproach and they had primary responsibility for supervising the personal moral rectitude of staff and students. The moral dimension of professional actions has emerged relatively recently. So has the need for school leaders to scan political horizons.

These changes need to be considered in their historical perspective. They have been quickly taken for granted even though they are quite novel in the great scheme of things. In England, many current headteachers had their first experience of leadership in schools when the leadership model was very different to modern expectations. Understanding the rationale and context for the current practice is an important part of the Awareness that high-leverage school leaders use to improve processes and outcomes.

The person who heads or leads a local school acts as a valve regulating often conflicting pressures between the free expression of professional teachers on one hand and the external expectations of lay or political interests on the other. Recent attempts, internationally as well as in England, to determine and to manage the balance of power between those pressures have highlighted the historically unprecedented importance of the design and quality of that valve. In England, the 1988 Education Reform Act fundamentally changed the legal and constitutional relationship between central government, local government and school governing bodies (what might elsewhere be called School Boards). Inevitably, that also radically altered the relationship between school governing bodies and headteachers. In our discussion of Accountability in Chapter 7 we will write in more detail about how the Act gave both governors and headteachers increased and distinct powers. The governing body was to be responsible for the strategic direction of the school and the appointment of the headteacher. The headteacher was to be responsible for the day-to-day running of the school. These changes gave impetus to the active and wide-ranging phrase 'school leader' which to some extent has challenged the narrower and more passive use of 'headteacher'.

Until 1988, school management in England operated in what appears, retro-spectively, to have been a mess of paradoxes but which, for most of the time, was proudly regarded as a national system locally administered. Six decades after it was written, halfway between the English state system's foundation at the end of the 19th century and the present day, the following assessment of that national compact from the then Ministry of Education manages to appear well inten-tioned and complacent at the same time:

> This is the story of a progressive partnership between the central department, the local education authorities and the teachers. To build a single, but not uniform, system out of many diverse elements; to widen educational oppor-tunity and, at the same time, to raise standards; to knit the educational system more closely into the life of an increasingly democratic and industri-alised community: these are among the main ideas which, despite two major wars, have moved legislators and administrators alike ... the Ministry has traditionally valued the life of institutions more highly than systems and has been jealous for the freedom of schools and teachers.
>
> (Ministry of Education, 1951, p. 1)

This mid-century deference to professional freedom and minimal intervention was shared by local authorities. Typical was the former Chief Education Officer of two English authorities, rural Essex and urban Manchester, writing in 1957:

> No freedom that teachers in this country possess is so important as that of determining the curriculum and methods of teaching. Neither the Minister nor indeed the Local Education Authority exercises authority over the curriculum of any school beyond that of agreeing the general educational character of the school and its place in the local educational system.
>
> (Smith, 1957, p. 161)

Headteachers, not surprisingly, shared the perspective of their local officers and national government. As recently as 1989, one of the authors was working with a local authority team on a school inspection in southern England. The headteacher, advised about a poor science lesson, responded, 'Why are you telling me? I've given [the teacher] the timetable and the head of department has given him the syllabus. What he does in the lab is his business, not mine.'

As a result, in England as in many systems across the world and for most of the last century, the headteacher was in part the on-site public administrator and in part the lead professional in the organisation, though not always the lead for the organisation. It really was not clear what the headteacher was responsible for and how that was separated from the role of teachers, governing bodies and local or central government. That uncertainty was tolerable and perhaps even comfortable as long as no profound or challenging questions were asked about the system and its outcomes. However, in England during the last quarter or so of the 20th century, increasing parental dissatisfaction, government impatience and improved data systems began to expose an education service with significant variations in the quality of its inputs, processes and outcomes. Those variations became associated with a wide range of causes, among them the role of some complacent and underachieving providers – schools and local authorities. The 'jealous protection of freedom for schools and teachers' had sometimes created a space in which great, innovative practice could flourish but which sometimes accommodated a sterile vacuum that nurtured nothing of value and was – because nature abhors a vacuum – eventually filled with second-rate practice and chronically poor attainment. Which of these you encountered seemed to depend very much on which school you attended or which school employed you.

In effect, this was an education service that was struggling to create a compromise between two ideas whose incompatibility still resonates across school leadership. On the one hand there was affection for the idealised model of the independent school headmaster (and, rarely, headmistress). This was the model that the majority of senior politicians and civil servants treasured from their own private schooldays: 'personal, powerful, moralising and patriarchal' (Grace, 1995, p. 11). On the other hand, publicly funded provision for the middle and lower classes needed control:

> ... headteachers were regarded as key subaltern agents in the maintenance of moral and political hegemony and this was regarded by managers and governors [school boards] as their most important responsibility.
>
> (Grace, 1995, p. 10)

The wider social changes of the 1950s and 1960s, alongside changes in the class origins of the teaching force and of governing bodies, were paralleled by changes in the way school leadership worked. In most areas, decisions about admissions, staffing and budgets remained with the local authority, but the day-to-day operation of the school was ceded to headteachers who could intervene, more or less as they chose, in the curriculum and pedagogy. Importantly, 'The extent and nature of this delegation varied by category of school (being more developed in secondary than in primary schools) and also regionally by local authority ...' (Corbett, 1972, p. 12). Consequently, as strategic decisions rested with the local authority and day to day decisions with the headteacher, there was 'a great fog about what school governors are entitled to do' (p. 12).

The profound change in the final two decades of the 1900s – from a system characterised by the rhetoric of professional hegemony in a national compact to a system driven by accountability – can be traced to a point in the mid-1970s when the social, regional and professional tensions in the prevailing system surfaced. They became clear in a speech by the then British Prime Minister, Jim Callaghan, and in a furore at William Tyndale Primary School in Islington, Central London. Callaghan's speech in 1976 at Ruskin College, Oxford, vented the frustration of a Labour Prime Minister and former Chancellor of the Exchequer who could pull few if any levers to improve a vital and expensive public education service which was failing in many ways and not least in its provision for poorer children. The Prime Minister announced, controversially for the time, that local government and schools were to be held responsible by central government for curriculum, standards and the value to the public for the large sums spent on public education. At about the same time, William Tyndale Primary School became the site of a confused though furious argument about who was responsible for the work of its 'progressive' school leadership, whose 'free' methods had alienated most parents and governors alike (Jackson and Gretton, 1976). This led to confrontations between the Department for Education, the national inspectorate, the school's local authority, school governors, parents and staff. Finally, after the suspension of the headteacher and some members of staff, there was a highly critical Committee of Enquiry which recorded widespread confusion about responsibility and authority across the system (Auld, 1976). The combination of these two events produced a political and media impetus at times approaching frenzy.

From 1976 onwards, across governments of different complexions, education policy in England has struggled to square the circle which increases the autonomy of schools on one hand while increasing central control of the curriculum and student outcomes on the other. The shift of the headteacher's role from administrative officer to executive leader has been maintained throughout this period, as it has in other countries.

> In France [for example] schools were redefined as 'school communities' (pupils, teachers, administration, parents) whose actors 'could better serve its users'. The redefinition of the headteacher's role as managerial rather than administrative has resulted in a challenge to the autonomy of teachers in their pedagogic practice.
>
> (Pelage and Evetts, 1998, p. 462)

For most schools in England, autonomy initially led headteachers into a preoccupation with the unfamiliar managerial issues of financial planning, resource management and budget balancing. Before local management could become a systemic vehicle for improvement, it had to move on from that reactive position which, in the main, ensured that the books balanced. This was a shift from knowing which resources were available and how they are accounted for to a wider understanding of how resources might be adapted and deployed to better ends – from maintenance to Navigation. For most school leaders this was a move from resource management to '... leadership and the building of professional capacity to achieve an alignment of curriculum, pedagogy and resources with the mix of learning requirements at the school level' (Caldwell, 2008, pp. 235–49). Our experience is that this is exactly the focus which high-leverage leaders adopt – they don't manage their resources primarily to make sure the bottom line is not in the red, they manage them purposefully to meet the needs of the organisation. Balancing the budget is important, but it is only one of the means to the end.

The modern role of headteacher as Chief Executive Officer with responsibility for every aspect of the organisation has demanded new approaches. School leaders with autonomy are expected to improve their schools more quickly and make them more efficient than had been thought possible when local government officers managed schools at a distance. The headteacher is now held responsible not just for how well the school is organised but above all for its students' academic attainments and other outcomes. *What* a school does might be defined largely by a statutory national curriculum statement of some kind. *Whether* it is successful might be defined largely by external inspection and exam targets driven by strong external pressures. Authoritative autonomy lies with those school leaders capable of seizing on *why* and *how* things will be done.

Purposeful community

We wrote above that high-leverage leaders help to define and then hold the moral ground around which the school's work is designed. We should have added that they are not neutral about what the purpose should be and can articulate it unequivocally.

Over the past few years, school leaders across the English-speaking world have become familiar with the development of 'moral purpose' and 'ethical leadership' as guiding concepts (Oplatka and Addi-Raccah, 2009, p. 399). Michael Fullan defined moral purpose as 'acting with the intention of making positive difference in the lives of employees, customers and society as a whole' (Fullan, 2001, p. 9). He has projected the language of 'moral compass' and 'moral imperative' into the professional conversations of most headteachers (Fullan, 2003a). He has written about the need for leaders to 'pay close attention to whether they are generating passion, purpose and energy – intrinsic motivation' without which, he says, any strategy for fundamental change will fail (Fullan, 2003b, pp. 62–3). Although Fullan recognises that there are pluralistic motives and competing versions of the 'right purpose', he chooses to identify four key ingredients of moral purpose (Fullan, 2004, p. 10):

- commitment to raising the bar and closing the gap in student achievement;
- treating people with respect – which is not the same as having low expectations;
- orientation to improving the environment, including other schools within and beyond the local authority;
- engaging in the big picture of national policy and societal goals.

These four dimensions of moral purpose would be broadly accepted by the high-leverage leaders in our studies. However, they are not universal values for all school leaders: we have heard some argue, for example, that these ideals are not compatible with their school's moral purpose – academic excellence in a single institution.

In a similar vein, Kenneth Strike has written about 'ethical leadership' (Strike, 2007). He claims that '… one very general way to characterise the role of leaders is that they must create healthy, functional, and good educational communities' and that '… this requires a view of educational communities that is informed by a conception of human flourishing and by how moral principles shape the interactions of the members of educational communities to realise their vision' (2007, p. 11). His repetition of 'community' would, we will say in Chapter 5, resonate profoundly with our high-leverage school leaders' own sense of Partnership. The challenge they face, which Strike acknowledges, is in deciding what the key value adjectives in those sentences mean when they have to be translated into professional ethics and personal morality – in effect, when they need to be translated into actions. Strike writes that three ideals are central to ethical decision-making: respect for persons, benefit maximisation and community. 'The first invites us to view others as ends in themselves and entitled to equal respect, the second to maximise good outcomes and the third to create and sustain healthy communities' (2007, p. 14).

Thomas Sergiovanni's work on moral dimensions in leadership is also widely referenced. Sergiovanni frequently refers, in turn, to Robert Greenleaf's concept of the 'servant leaders' whose leadership serves the ends of helping people to become healthier, wiser, freer, more autonomous, capable of service while benefiting, or at least not further depriving, the least privileged in any context (Greenleaf, 2003). 'Remembering the moral aspects of leadership' is one of Sergiovanni's basic principles for school leadership (Sergiovanni, 2001, p. 5). He describes leadership as a responsibility, not a right, its purpose to enhance the enterprise and not the leader. 'Leadership combines management know-how with values and ethics ... doing things right and doing right things' (2001, p. 14).

Sergiovanni describes this process as 'the management of commitment', one of the 'basic competencies of leadership'. The management of commitment involves 'moving leadership away from bureaucratic and personal factors towards cognitive factors – towards ideas'. Then moral authority – 'the sense of common good and the promises and obligations that good requires from everyone' – predominates, and, 'As ideas and commitment are shared, so is leadership' (2001, p. 54).

Fullan, Greenleaf, Sergiovanni, Strike and others with similar perspectives are evidently describing the territory occupied by the high-leverage leaders we know. However, we sense that 'moral purpose' and associated ideas are at risk of losing the impetus which these writers have imparted, and at risk of appearing so commonplace in professional conversations and presentations that they become clichés trotted out to the beat of a hollow drum. We regularly meet school governors who remark that a downside to the national accreditation of prospective headteachers in England is that candidates at interview can reproduce the lexicon without showing insight into the action. Many school leaders we meet appear to think that 'effective moral purpose' simply means 'if my intentions are good, then the consequences will be better'. We have also encountered school leaders who sit, disoriented, between the introduction of morality and ethics into leadership discourse and the moral guardianship of specific cultural values which, we noted above, was an expectation of headteachers for much of the 20th century. That is not what writers such as Fullan, Greenleaf, Sergiovanni and Strike are claiming, nor is it what high-leverage leaders do.

It takes a strong sense of purpose and direction to solve intransigent problems, and the high-leverage school leaders in our studies are capable of infusing and enthusing the adults and children in their school communities with a compelling sense of purpose. They do not do that by dwelling on whether their purpose is based on values, morals or ethics. They believe that their purpose is good and their pursuit of it the right thing to do. The ends are not negotiable although, because they know that the medium is the message, they are prepared to discuss and co-create the means with the people around them. Passion is a word for this:

> Great school leaders have discovered a reason, a consuming, energising, almost obsessive purpose that drives them forwards. It galvanises them to become bigger, bolder people and sustains them through difficult times ... [it is] a passion to make a lasting difference to a school and the people there. They are also passionate about the way in which this will be achieved.
>
> (Ryan, 2008, p. 5)

Our high-leverage leaders' sense of purpose and passion is characterised by its focus on community: a school community. We will return to the detail of that aspect in Chapter 5 when we write about Partnership and their sense of Association.

Equality of opportunity

> When wedded to a relentless commitment to equity, voice and social justice, [school leaders'] efforts in the tasks of sense making, promoting inclusive cultures and practices in schools, and building positive relationships outside of the school may indeed foster a new form of practice.
>
> (Riehl 2000, cited in Ainscow and West, 2006, p. 10)

In our work with high-leverage leaders who have been particularly successful with England's otherwise chronically poor and under-achieving white working-class children, we wrote about the contextual intelligence, social intelligence and rapport which those leaders showed (Mongon and Chapman, 2008a). We described how those high-leverage leaders had been drawn to their work by the challenge of improving the lives of children at the margins of society. Many had come from economically poor backgrounds themselves, and spoke passionately about a duty or an opportunity to offer children life-changing experiences like their own. 'Working-class' origins were not a defining feature of the group, but a similar sense of purpose was: the position that these children find themselves in offends social justice and it needs to be put right. They show a profound respect for the context they are working in without ever patronising it. 'It is hard, difficult out there, but that's no excuse for any of us ...' (Mongon and Chapman, 2008a, p. 8). They tend to talk about the strengths of the local community rather than its weaknesses, they see the locality as an opportunity rather than a problem, they approach the area as a resource rather than an obstacle: no-one in their schools is ever allowed to say 'What do you expect with kids or parents or places like these?' Instead, 'You can actually make a difference here ...' (Mongon and Chapman, 2008a, p. 8). They expect to overcome disadvantage and that expectation feeds into the values which inform their work. They see the value of integrated service delivery to the needs of young people and the contribution that schools can make to the full range of outcomes for them. They have a clear, all-round view of their position in local education and other networks. They understand the political environments in which they operate, locally and nationally. They adapt national initiatives to the needs of their schools, extract the maximum from them and divert the constraints.

Those conclusions are echoed in a series of reports from other research, from England's national inspectorate (Ofsted) and from government reports. In a study of schools in predominantly white working-class areas in former coalfields, Harris and colleagues (2003) found that the more successful schools were those with purposeful and distributed leadership, creating a climate of high expectations and with a strong focus on the quality of personal relationships. Building vision and setting direction, in effect combining morality, values and behaviour, was the first of the four 'basic' leadership practices reported in Day's summary of research into the impact of school leadership on pupil outcomes (Day *et al.*, 2008). Englefield (2002), studying 14 successful primary schools in varied but challenging contexts, described 'can do cultures' and a concern for every pupil. Harris and Chapman (2002) succinctly summarised this phenomenon as 'leadership that is value-driven with a strong moral purpose and deeply concerned about the welfare and education of all pupils in their care' (2002, p. 3). That research has been endorsed by Ofsted reviews of schools that are successful with their Black Caribbean pupils (Ofsted, 2002a and 2002b) and with white boys from low-income backgrounds (Ofsted, 2008a). Those inspectorate summaries drew attention to how the schools valued every student and their backgrounds, treating staff and pupils alike with fairness, trust and respect. Government reports on schools that succeeded against the national trends also continually emphasise the underpinning commitment of their leaders to social justice and equity (Tikly *et al.*, 2006; Walker, 2004; DCSF, 2008a).

High-leverage leaders know that the way adults work with one another in a school will be reflected in the way that adults and students work together. The moral purpose apparently shared by the staff of a school is only as sound as the common ethics and values that underwrite that purpose and the consequential behaviour of the staff. High-leverage leaders understand the negative consequences if purpose becomes disconnected from values and behaviour – especially in fragile environments. They know that inconsistency between purpose, values and behaviour will undermine the social fabric of the organisation. They can therefore spell out for themselves and for their colleagues 'why we do what we do', and then spell out the connection between 'why' and 'how we do what we do'. In the section on Advocacy later in this chapter, we will reflect on how these leaders bring their sense of purpose to life and commit others to share it with them. For now we want to consider how these leaders also scan the political horizon.

Political horizons

Writing about 'authentic leadership', Robert Evans refers to 'integrity' and 'savvy'. Integrity describes the strong moral and ethical features we have just written about. Savvy, to which we turn now, is 'a practical, problem solving wisdom that enables leaders to make things happen'. Being clear about philosophy 'does not automatically make one savvy any more than it makes one charismatic; it does not create the wisdom that comes from experience' (Evans, 2007, p. 141). High-leverage leaders are 'savvy' and the particular aspect of their savvy that we want to note is their scanning of political horizons. They do this in part to influence policy as it is created, in part to anticipate the next set of policy demands on the school, and in part to domesticate those demands, to bring them under the school's control.

Like many other systems, the English publicly-funded education service is a remarkably complex phenomenon to which the word 'systematic' should be applied with some caution. It is the conjunction of different statutory and non-statutory organisations or groupings operating sometimes with apparently incompatible if not contradictory purposes. It accommodates national and local government, the latter in a very wide variety of formats, with more or less clear oversight for the provision of school places. There is a national curriculum with a core that is increasingly reduced by expedient exemptions. The day-to-day running of most schools is largely autonomous and in some cases independent, though state funded. Around 22,000 schools serve thousands of very diverse local communities. Inside those schools, staff will be represented by as many as half a dozen or more trade unions, each with its own interests. For a century these waters were mainly calm and only occasionally agitated. For the past 20 years they have been a series of white-water rides.

Navigation in these circumstances does require high-leverage school leaders to pay attention to both the immediate rapids and the rocks ahead. 'Buffering staff from distractions to their core work' was one of the effective leadership tactics highlighted in the literature review by Day and his colleagues cited above (Day *et al.*, 2008). However, twitching their political antennae does not come easily or intuitively to all school leaders. There is a tendency in the profession to believe that political issues are 'unworthy' of school leaders (Fink, 2005, p. 13), or to 'cast politics as an unprofessional or unsavoury enterprise' (Malen, 2005, p. 208).

High-leverage school leaders who scan the political horizon protect their schools more than most from the day-to-day consequences of the muddle that can be created by the demands of national, local and even neighbourhood politics. They also position their schools to take advantage of whatever opportunities those politics create for them. They are aware of the ebb and flow of political currents (and occasional torrents) from national government as well as, if the metaphor may be stretched, of the sidewash from the tributaries of local government and community politics. They use this knowledge to protect the day-to-day operations of their school and help their staff to understand the context in which they are working. Their staff members, in turn, expect them to mediate the impact of external turbulence and to reduce to a minimum the dissonance between political expectations and their sense of practical reality. This horizon-scanning involves the school leader 'in standing back from the traditional operational and incremental thinking approaches and analysing broad global and national trends which are likely to impact on education over the next ten to fifteen years' (Fink, 2005, p. 12). Those trends do not, in the longer run, play out in the abstract – they eventually become operational in local contexts. Anticipatory school leaders will already have positioned their schools so that they can go with the wave while purposefully selecting the flows whose energy they want to ride on. The high-leverage school leader is astute at filtering out the policies that will not promote substantive improvement at her school and adopting those that will. Muijs and colleagues describe one member of staff in awe of the 'inspirational' headteacher's horizon scanning: 'He always seems three or four years ahead of everyone else, we'll be doing things and then a few years later it will be on the news as something that schools should be doing. It's a lot of new ideas, but always with a bit of enjoyment to them as well' (Muijs *et al.*, 2010, p. 151).

Acceptance

Navigation
Securing the vision, setting a direction and nurturing development
Acceptance: understanding that current practice may be a barrier while believing that improvement is possible

Our proposal is that high-leverage leaders are prepared to Accept that the historic practices of their school may themselves be limiting its capacity for improvement. They accept that those practices should be considered for change at least as much as any external factors or inputs.

A good navigator knows that, however determined she might be to take a particular route, she has to allow for the power of nature: mountains and chasms, rivers and seas, storms and droughts. The route has to reflect the skills of the crew and the durability of the vessel. If the journey does not end with a safe arrival, it has not been a good trip. Something similar can be said about schools, where the destination is to improve outcomes for young people. If the chosen craft is not capable of making the journey, or the crew is not up to the task, or the directions have turned out to be misguided, then irrespective of how personally or institutionally precious those might be, the problem has to be acknowledged and a new way found. External accountability limits the options for changing destination so either the vessel or the crew have to change.

'When I first came, there were 5th years, girls and boys being belittled. You can't do that and expect loyalty. You have to lay down the ground rules and be persistent on them. Sometimes it even goes against your own nature. But once the students know the rules and that you are going to be fair, that's what they want.'

John Golds, Headteacher, Bishopsgarth Secondary School

It was only in the final third of the 20th century that educational processes – teaching, assessment and curriculum, as well as the attitudes of policymakers, leaders and teachers – were seriously and widely implicated in the creation of inequality in English schools (Ball, 2003; Dennis, 1980), During that period it became increasingly obvious that, at institutional and individual levels, the education service was not a neutral element in the chemistry of educational outcomes. The organisation of schools and their admissions policies, the content and assessment of the curriculum and the classroom practice of teachers are all capable of enhancing or limiting outcomes for young people from different backgrounds. So, accepting that 'professional behaviour' can contribute to differential standards is the first of the three necessary steps in raising the attainment of more vulnerable children. The other two are:

- believing that the behaviour should be changed; and
- understanding how that might be done.

Leithwood and Jantz (2009) remind us that synthesising those three steps is a relatively recent development, and that early attempts at managerial reform in education were 'something analogous to passing legislation holding medical practitioners accountable for curing all patients of cancer, even though a cure has yet to be developed – and imposing penalties on those who are unsuccessful!' (2009, p. 42). It was an initially naive assumption by policymakers that, if some schools were unusually successful against the trends, they must know why they were successful and others could readily learn from them.

High-leverage school leaders recognise the value of opportunities to be taken but also the potential of problems to be solved. One of us has described them as

> ... not prepared to accept a status quo they know does not do justice to their children and the families they serve. Nor are they content to stick to recipes and approaches to teaching and learning they know will not engage many families. Born out of a mixture of ambition and frustration they are determined to find new ways for schools to both provide services and engage their wider communities to improve educational outcomes for all.
>
> (Mongon and Leadbeater, 2012)

In this section we are focusing on high-leverage leaders' Acceptance that their organisation and its practices may be part of the problem as well as part of the solution. Simply put, high-leverage leaders believe that they and their staff are responsible for the outcomes from their work. They do not say 'what would you expect with people like this?', whether the 'people' concerned are their local community, professional staff or politicians (Mongon and Chapman, 2008a). In common with the school leaders in Togneri and Andersen's (2003) 'High Poverty Districts', or Fullan's (2006) 'Turnaround Schools', they start by putting right the weaknesses under their control: in effect, the weaknesses within the school. They accept that, to solve the problem or make the most of an opportunity, there are implicit and explicit features of the school which might need to be changed.

- *Implicit features* include the professional expectations and prejudices that staff have of one another, of the students and of the communities they serve.
- *Explicit features* are the working practices of the adults.

Implicit features

Although the research on teacher expectations has been stretched surprisingly sparsely over the last 40 years, high-leverage leaders know that these implicit aspects of school culture have to align positively with the school's ambitions for its students. The impact of expectation came to prominence in the seminal 1968 'Pygmalion study' (Rosenthal, 1968) and was quickly followed by Brophy and Good's (1970) demonstration of differential outcomes associated with the nuances of teacher behaviour towards students of whom they had different expectations. More recent research concludes that deficit views of working-class children and their parents continue to be ingrained in the teaching profession. Gazeley and Dunne, for example, found that a sample of teachers and trainee teachers defined underachievement in different ways and adopted different types of strategy to address it. These strategies appear to be influenced by the adults' perceptions and unconsciously stereotypical expectations of pupils, linked to their social class. The adults lack the personal experience and professional opportunities to reflect on the stereotypes in their own practice (2005, p.18). Andy Hargreaves, arguing that teachers' emotions are central and not peripheral to reform, describes how some teachers create a distance between themselves and some parents by inducing a sense of what he calls 'disgust':

> ... teachers who recalled negative emotion in relation to lower class or minority parents who challenged them, labelled them in inhuman terms as 'crazy', 'nuts', 'mad' and 'screamers', and described their actions in verbs of pollution when parents 'grilled' them, 'vented all over' them, and 'blurted' things into their face. These verbs of pollution are verbs of disgust and are means by which teachers as 'professionals' maintain their distance from lower class or minority parents, de-legitimize their actions and protests, and preserve their professionally distinct sense of what it is to educate and be educated.
>
> (Hargreaves, 2001, p. 35)

This is what one headteacher, quoted in West *et al.* (2005), calls the 'what do you expect culture' (2005, p. 81).

Much of the research has focused on the depth of this effect on individual students (probably not large) and its impact on groups of students (probably more significant) (Jussim and Harber, 2005). Attempts to identify how this effect is produced point towards teachers' classroom behaviour to students being associated with their expectations of them. A four-factor theory is often quoted as providing the dynamic (Tauber, 1998):

- *climate*: creating the socio-emotional mood or spirit;
- *feedback*: providing both affective information and cognitive information;
- *input*: tending to teach more to students of whom more is expected;
- *output*: encouraging greater responsiveness from those students.

Rubie-Davies found that teachers with a generally high expectation of their students (HiEx teachers) tended to have an approach that was distinctive compared to teachers with generally low expectations (LoEx teachers):

> Briefly, HiEx teachers had students working in mixed-ability groups, promoted student autonomy in learning activities, carefully explained new concepts, provided students with clear feedback, managed behaviour positively, and asked large numbers of open questions. LoEx teachers maintained within-class ability groups, directed student learning experiences, frequently gave procedural directions, reacted negatively to student misbehaviour, and asked mostly closed questions.
>
> (Rubie-Davies, 2010, p. 125)

Rubie-Davies has also shown that these differences are not only about the 'instructional environment' of the classroom (pedagogic technique) but also, as her research and that of others confirms, about the 'emotional environment' (social climate) (2007, p. 303).

There is an important caveat here: our research in an English context might have limited application in other cultures. Dimmock and Walker (2005) have shared an interesting perspective on the push towards school-based management and the movement of responsibility and power in favour of principals, teachers and parents. They conclude that societies in which power is distributed more equally would adjust rather more successfully to school-based management than societal cultures in which power is concentrated. They suggest that this is why the distribution of authority in some school system reinforces the power of the principal, while in others it leads to genuine participation by teachers and parents. They conclude:

> A central tenet of the restructuring of curriculum and pedagogy in many school systems is that students accept more responsibility for their learning. Accompanying this phenomenon is the espousal of goal setting at the

individual level and school development planning at the organisational level. Each of these tenets assumes the acceptance of responsibility for shaping the future ...

(Dimmock and Walker, 2005, p. 18).

Dimmock and Walker suggest a distinction between proactive and fatalistic cultures, one that might have some resonance outside schools in areas where fatalism is a pervasive consequence associated with long-term economic decay. It may also have resonance inside some schools where the staff culture lacks resilience. If organisational resilience is 'the organisational capability to anticipate key events from emerging trends, constantly adapt to change, and rapidly bounce back from disaster' (Marcos and Macaulay, 2008, p. 1), it is evidently dependent on the individual resilience of its staff members. This is, in effect, the extent to which they can bounce back in response to setbacks. It is to a large degree a measure of their shared self-belief, sense of purpose, optimism and adaptability.

This is certainly something we have recognised in high-leverage schools and which we referred to in Chapter 2 as 'locus of control' or 'self-efficacy'. This is typically an intolerance of the idea that events and outcomes are beyond local influence. It will also be recognisable to the reader that when we turn to Advocacy, later in this chapter, the wish of high-leverage leaders to develop their staffs away from managed dependency to collaborative professionalism follows the Rubie-Davies route from LoEx to HiEx practices. There is some evidence that teachers who are confident in their professionalism will have an approach to classroom management that appears 'intrinsic': relaxed, attentive, listening and quiet (Dimmock and Walker, 2005). This draws us into the explicit features of school life.

Explicit features

Schools and education services are not the only organisations that have to challenge existing practices, as one Scottish authority discovered when it compared notes on organisational change with a multinational oil company. Both found that one of their core challenges was 'to mobilise the workforce to accept the changes and clarification of problems to do with the challenge to traditional professionalism ...' (Boreham and Reeves, 2004, p. 7).

'We needed to find an approach which would encourage, allow, the children to want to learn ... The staff did not believe that they could do it so the pupils did not believe that they could do it, and the staff didn't believe that anyone could do it. Although I accept the framework of national accountability and strategies, we read them and fillet them for what might help the staff ...'

Elisabeth Corlett, Headteacher, Guildford Grove Primary School

One of the core tasks facing high-leverage leaders is to challenge existing practices. They know, as the National Audit Office in England drily confirmed (National Audit Office, 2006), that improving school leadership, teaching standards and behaviour management are three changes most associated with rising standards. Changing the last two, assuming that the school leader is the personification of the first, leaves some school leaders anxious about the effect on other people's lives (West *et al.*, 2005, p. 84). This is a challenge to existing values and beliefs that has potentially profound implications.

Advocacy

Navigation
Securing the vision, setting a direction and nurturing development
Advocacy: creating a 'living vision' and participating in focused workforce development to introduce sustainable change

Our proposal is that high-leverage leaders constantly Advocate the ethos, purpose and processes that they want for their school. They do this in part by promoting a well-grounded 'living vision', in part by modelling expected behaviour, in part through their persistent use of particular language, and above all by their commitment to learning and development for people of all ages and status.

Advocacy may be by far the most significant of the three Navigation activities in which the leaders with whom we have worked appear to have engaged. It is the one to which we will pay most attention.

There are few organisations that do not have their own vision or mission statement. In the global private sector, McDonald's stated mission is to be the world's best quick-service restaurant experience, while Google's is to organise the world's information and make it universally accessible and useful. The leading UK retailer Marks & Spencer talks about applying its core values of 'Quality, Value, Service, Innovation and Trust', and about achieving success 'by building a sustainable business for the long term, generating shareholder value through consistent profitable growth, whilst making sure that our customers can always trust us to do the right thing, the right way' (Marks & Spencer, 2010, p. 1). John Lewis, another leading retailer across much of the UK, is tied by trust deeds to its founder's wish to promote 'the happiness of all our members [i.e. employees] through their worthwhile, satisfying employment in a successful business' (John Lewis, 2011, p. 1). The Internal Revenue Service in the USA aims to 'Provide America's taxpayers top quality service by helping them understand and meet their tax responsibilities and enforce the tax law with integrity and fairness to all' (IRS, 2011, p. 1). The equivalent UK service, Her Majesty's Revenue and Customs (HMRC), is committed to making sure that money is available to fund the UK's public services, closing the tax gap, customers [sic] feeling [that] the tax system is simple and even-handed and being seen as a highly professional and efficient organisation. It is safe to say that no-one writes a vision which aims to provide second-rate services, to let down their shareholders, to disappoint their users, to be an exploitative employer or to be the second-best organisation in their field. Which begs the question: what are vision statements for?

The living vision

In the matter of vision statements, schools are not very different from other organisations. If there are striking and unusual examples of schools' vision statements, they cannot be easily found even though a well-known internet search engine produces about 100,000 hits for the phrase 'school vision statement', including plenty of advice, some apparently serious and some perhaps satirical, on how to write your own. An admittedly small sample of their suggestions for content tells us that most, like the following, are as ubiquitous and unobjectionable as parenthood and apple pie:

- to develop education which transforms lives and communities;
- to value the individual, to celebrate learning;
- to provide a happy, caring and stimulating environment where children will recognise and achieve their fullest potential;
- to provide a stimulating learning environment in which the team of highly-trained staff provides quality teaching in well-resourced buildings.

Corporate visions and mission statements are generally virtuous. No-one is going to argue about the agreeable purpose and direction they outline. That is the problem – visions of this kind are cameos, shadows without definition. The rhetoric in the examples above gives us, at face value, a nice set of ideas. The problems emerge when these have to be turned into real actions and outcomes. Who decides *which lives are to be transformed*, and how will communities know when that has been achieved? Does *the value of the individual* have any limits, at any cost to the community? Who knows, who decides *what a child's full potential might be* and whether they have achieved it? What is *a stimulating learning environment?*

It is no less clear what individuals have to do in order to turn the vision into reality. Visions of this kind focus more on the means, what we will do around here, and less on the ends, what will be different afterwards. It is not always evident that the well intentioned clichés about means lead necessarily to significant and improving outcomes. We might ask the creators of these vision statements: 'when the individual has been valued and learning has been celebrated, what enduring changes will have happened in young people's lives? What will they be able to do?' A clear answer is unusual. Similarly, we might all agree that a 'stimulating environment' is generally a good thing, but would we all agree what it should be or even what we expect it to achieve in different contexts?

The high-leverage school leaders we have met or read about use the 'vision thing' in a very different way. They use it to make a powerful, energetic connection between the moral grounding we wrote about earlier and the management attention to detail that we will talk about in the next chapter. To describe how that works we have borrowed the phrase 'living vision' from a development framework published by the Innovation Unit in the UK (Innovation Unit, 2009). We do so because that framework closely reflects the way our high-leverage leaders work.

In the Innovation Unit's model, a 'living vision' must have four important characteristics. It must be:

1 *focused*, creating an invigorating sense of purpose and the courage to set extremely stretching goals;
2 *feasible*, fuelling people with energy, passion and enjoyment;
3 *desirable*, offering an ending worth going for;
4 *imaginable*, enabling all the stakeholders to answer the question: 'what is it?'

Those characteristics emphasise the importance of connecting any overarching vision with the day-to-day work of an organisation.

> If leaders cannot imagine a preferable alternative to the status quo, why should followers follow them? Thus, if we ensure that utopias must be capable of realisation – that is concrete rather than merely abstract – then we can utilise the creative potential of the imagination and suffer from it or suffer from its absence.
>
> (Grint, 2001, p. 11)

A living vision, collaboratively created and celebrated, avoids platitudes and is specific enough to connect with the staff's and students' sense of their own destinies and to be tested in action. It is a compass for those who realise that change is needed, even if they do not immediately know how it can be done.

If a 'living vision' is written down somewhere, then it will be a little bit longer than those we quoted above – but not very long. It will not be written to be memorised, it will be written to be acted out. It is not a piece for recital, it is a call to action. It is likely to be articulated in the comments which staff make about their work and its purpose – comments which will not be identical but will be tightly clustered around a well understood set of phrases about 'the kind of place we are', 'what we do' and 'what the consequence is'. High-leverage leaders create this kind of culture using two predominant tactics:

- consistent personal modelling, especially of the learning expected of everyone; and
- consistent use of language that reflects and expresses the values and practices of the school.

Personal modelling: we are all learners here

Attitudes are rarely changed by publishing plans or organising structures. Rearranging deckchairs on the Titanic did nothing to save lives, but examples of individual bravery did. We are social animals, deeply influenced by the behaviour of others and in particular by the behaviour of those we respect and trust. Richard Elmore concluded that school improvement appears to be more successful when people internalise expectations, and that is achieved 'largely through modelling commitment and focus using face to face relationships and not bureaucratic controls' (Elmore, 2004, p. 82). Expected behaviour is constantly and consistently modelled by 'Dynamic leaders who lead from the front, set the tone and establish a "can do" culture' (DCSF, 2008a, p. 4).

Michael Fullan has written (2001) about an aspect of modelling which is recognisably similar to the high-leverage leaders' commitment to the communal and personal development of adults around the school. That commitment is a vital aspect of their approach and a recurring theme in our experience and in the wider literature. Fullan refers to this as the 'leader as coach', helping people to develop and invest in their capacity building (2001). This is particularly important, Fullan claims, at a time when the insecurity of change and the need for new skills can combine to create an 'implementation dip', a fall in morale and energy. This will be a familiar picture for leaders working in schools that are falling short of their own ambitions for young people who are not intuitive students. Countering 'the dip', Fullan argues and our research confirms, involves modelling learning, reflection, evidence-based enquiry and personal development for staff and, through them, for students. More recently, Fullan described two of the six secrets of change as 'Love your employees' and 'Learning is the work': 'The key is in enabling employees to learn continuously and find meaning in their work and in their relationship to co-workers and to the company as a whole' (Fullan, 2008, p. 11). This collaborative and sustained workforce development is consistently associated with positive effects on student motivation and outcomes and on teachers' commitment, attitudes and confidence. In contrast, workforce development that does not involve collaboration has been reported as producing a narrower range of changes and significantly weaker benefits for students and teachers (Cordingley *et al.*, 2003, 2005).

This commitment of high-leverage leaders is, in effect, another of Day's four basic leadership practices – 'Understanding and Developing People' by providing staff with intellectual stimulation (including CPD), individualised support and modelling (Day *et al.*, 2008). It is arguably the most influential aspect of their Navigation of the institution. The importance of this theme was confirmed in the review of international practice commissioned by the New Zealand government (Robinson *et al.*, 2009).

The reviewers concluded that, of the five dimensions of leadership practice which they discerned, this one – promoting and participating in teacher learning and development – has twice the positive impact of any one of the others (Robinson *et al.*, 2009, p. 38).

'We don't get experienced teachers applying for jobs here. We get NQTs who apply with an open mind and without negative experiences so they come with enthusiasm. The systems we have here support them well and they develop into good teachers … All of our teachers apart from myself and one other have started here as NQTs. Those who don't enjoy the experience move on quite quickly … We developed a Performance Management scheme for Teaching Assistants so that we could identify their INSET needs as well.'

Deputy Head, Castilion Primary School

Two other dimensions, 'establishing goals and expectations' and 'planning, coordinating, and evaluating teaching and the curriculum', have moderate impacts at about half the level of the teacher learning dimension. 'Resourcing strategically' and 'ensuring an orderly and supportive environment' have small effects. The review concludes that, in what we are calling 'high-leverage' schools, leaders participate more actively in teacher learning and development and are more likely to promote and participate in staff discussion of teaching and teaching problems.

Staff in those schools were more likely to see their leader as a source of professional advice, though not necessarily as a friend, suggesting that respect might be more important than comfort.

The leader doesn't stop at supporting or sponsoring their staff in their learning; they actually participate in the learning themselves – as leader, learner, or both. They do this in structured situations, such as staff meetings and professional development workshops, and in informal situations; for example, corridor discussions about specific teaching problems.

(Robinson *et al.*, 2009, p. 101)

Collaborative and sustained workforce development is consistently associated with positive effects on student motivation and outcomes and on teachers' commitment, attitudes and confidence (GTCE, 2009).

This approach has its roots in the leaders' sense of their school as a learning community. We will return to the 'community' aspect when we discuss Partnership in Chapter 5. For the moment we want to emphasise the learning aspect – what Southworth characterised as the school being a workplace which is also a workshop for teacher and staff learning (Southworth, 2004, p. 127). Chris Watkins illustrates this by drawing a distinction between schools that have a 'learning orientation' and those with a 'performance orientation' (see Table 3.1).

Watkins has used this distinction mainly to analyse the classroom experience of students in the UK's centralised and performance-oriented school culture. Our experience with high-leverage leaders suggests that their schools are permeated by a learning orientation for staff and students alike. Again, the medium is the message. In broad terms, Watkins's point is that the personalised and internalised

Table 3.1 Learning or performance orientation

Learning orientation	Performance orientation
←	→
belief that effort leads to success	belief that ability leads to success
belief in one's ability to improve and learn	concern to be judged as able, concern to perform
preference for challenging tasks	satisfaction from doing better than others
derives satisfaction from personal success at difficult tasks	emphasis on normative standards, competition and public evaluation
uses self-instructions when engaged in task	helplessness: evaluate self negatively when task is difficult
←	→
concern for improving	concern for proving

Source: Watkins *et al.*, 2007, p. 46.

strategies of a learning orientation have a deeper and more enduring effect on performance than institutionalised and externalised strategies in a performance orientation. International research supports Watkins's argument. 'Achievement press' is an index derived from students' reports on the frequency with which their teachers want them to work hard, tell them that they can do better and do not like their work. In 2002, the OECD reported that most of the 28 countries it surveyed showed a negative correlation (Kirsch *et al.*, 2002, pp. 134–5) between reading achievement or reading engagement and 'achievement press', and only two showed a better than 0.10 positive correlation. Our point is that Watkins's thesis is as true for the adults as it is for the young people in a school and that high-leverage leaders understand that.

The importance of this point is that high-leverage leaders are not only committed to the development of the adults at their schools, they express that commitment in ways which are absolutely consistent with the teaching practices which are likely to work best in classrooms. There is synergy and consistency in their creation of a learning community for everyone on site. Perhaps surprisingly, this learning orientation is not the default position of every school leader despite their being drawn from a profession for which a commitment to learning should be a central tenet. Timperley's (2006) study of a development project to improve literacy across 29 primary schools in New Zealand revealed how wrong it would be to assume that school principals could put their own learning and their staff's learning at the core of a development exercise. Most of the principals in the study appear to have acted primarily as conduits for information and as facilitators of collaboration. Learning, for themselves or for their teachers, was an incidental feature.

> 'Richard Schofield, headteacher, is committed to the learning of both the staff and students at Redbridge School in a difficult estate on the edge of

Southampton. The school invests heavily in staff development and of the 30,000 organisations with IIP status nationally, it is one of the handful which holds 'IIP Champion' status. In a quote which could apply equally to anyone, of any age, at the school, Richard says: "Increasingly we've recognised the link between learning and behaviour and we are all signed up to what goes into learning activities relating directly to what comes out in attitude and behaviour. An enormous amount of work has gone into learning styles and constructing pathways that better suit the needs and aspirations of the learner. In other words we are fitting the system to the needs of the learner and not the learner to the system."'

(Mongon and Chapman, 2008b, p. 45)

In contrast, high-leverage leaders are aware of what Timperley reports in a separate review: 'Teachers' daily experiences in their practice context shape their understandings, and their understandings shape their experiences' (Timperley, 2008, p. 6). In turn, the teachers' experiences shape their development. In a conclusion, in which her choice of the phrase 'student learning' is crucial, Timperley claims that 'Continued forward momentum also depends on an organisational infrastructure that supports professional learning and self-regulated inquiry. It is difficult for teachers to engage in sophisticated inquiry processes unless site-based leaders reinforce the importance of goals for student learning, assist teachers to collect and analyse relevant evidence of progress toward them, and access expert assistance when required' (2008, p. 26).

In effect, the high-leverage leaders we have observed are creating what Foucault calls the capillary transmission of power which 'reaches into the very grain of individuals, touches their bodies and inserts itself into their actions and attitudes, their discourses, learning processes and everyday lives' (1980, pp. 38–9). Brooke-Smith adopts a different metaphor and calls this the holographic or fractal nature of the institution. In a fractal system, he argues,

... the parts interact continually to recreate the whole and the operation of the whole affects the interaction and functioning of the parts ... behaviours, patterns, structures and processes will be similar at small group, department, divisional, and whole institutional levels. It is this repetition (and high level of redundancy) of patterned process that is able to give fit and context for mission and vision. Where there is little fractal self-similarity it is harder to create shared aims and goals.

(Brooke-Smith, 2003, p. 99)

For Brooke-Smith, this is at its most potent when it can permeate what he calls the 'shadow system', the non-legitimate counter-culture disconnected from official agendas and governed by the private rules of individuals. This, he says (2003, p. 88), requires leaders who can open up for discussion things that in a more rigid and defensive system would not be aired; allow comment that may appear critical of the aims and agendas of those in authority; open up for scrutiny power differentials and professional relationships and allow informal groups to form around new ideas and initiatives. This requires staff at all levels to exercise their leadership appropriately and everyone to see that they must shoulder some responsibility. Brooke-Smith's final conclusion – that it means having the courage of one's convictions while living with anxiety and not avoiding it – is echoed in our findings about self-efficacy amongst school leaders in England who are successful against the grain by raising the attainment of white working-class children (Mongon and Chapman, 2008a).

Language and conversation: talking the world into existence

One of the most powerful ways for leaders to nurture the fractal nature of their organisation is through the purposeful and careful use of language and conversation. This skilful oracy is a theme that will recur in every section of this book, as it does across respected international publications on effective leadership and across our own research. This is also elegantly illustrated in a very different genre, Bruce Chatwin's Australian travelogue *Songlines* (1986), in which the author develops his ideas about the relationship in Aboriginal culture between language and existence. Chatwin describes what Europeans used to call 'walkabout' as a way of spreading messages and singing the land into existence. The stories that the walker told or sung about the landscape had once, in the dreamtime, been part of creation and were now the means of renewing the environment and describing it to someone who had never passed that way. A key theme of the book is that the native Australians and their land are not simply inseparable, they are indivisible. The best singers can describe and see real places they have never visited but which they or their audience would want, eventually, to experience. Chatwin's work has its critics, with accusations of simplicity and colonialism among others, but it remains a stimulating exploration of how the words in our heads and from our mouths create and are created by the world we occupy.

'For example, we don't tell pupils what they have done wrong. We want the children to take responsibility for their own behaviour so we ask them to tell us which rule they have broken and whether this is what happens in good schools? You have to let the children know that you don't like what they have done, but you still like them.'

Jane Davenport, Headteacher, Hilldene Primary School

The analogy we want to draw is with the conversations and narratives which permeate every school and which simultaneously create and are created by that particular local environment. Davies calls this 'oral articulation' through 'strategic conversations' to distinguish them from the 'operational conversations' which carry the weight of day to day activity. One headteacher told Davies: 'We are constantly talking, large groups, small groups, individuals, a constant feast of two way conversations bringing people in line with where we are going' (Davies *et al.*, 2009, p. 17).

Stories and structures are interdependent: change one and it will go some way to change the other: change both and they will change everything. In England, the National College's enquiry into 'effective integrated leadership', leadership across services for children, reported that 'Where trust and belief have been established, a common language has been built up over time' (National College, 2009a, p. 15). Leaders in those settings had robust communication systems and created equity in conversations and mutual respect in relationships. 'A leader without a persuasive account of the past, present and future is unlikely to remain a leader for long' (Grint, 2001, p. 11).

One of the more relevant and accessible explorations of this theme is in Robert Kegan and Lisa Laskow Lahey's (2003) description of how our forms of speaking 'regulate the forms of thinking, feeling and meaning making to which we have access which in turn constrain how we see the world and act in it' (2003, p. 7). Kegan and Laskow Lahey propose seven language shifts that can change the way we speak, not just to others but also to ourselves. These are language shifts that change not only the way the world can be described but also the way the world appears to be. Our précis below of Kegan and Laskow Lahey's seven shifts serves to illustrate our point but does not do justice to their fuller and more interactive publication. The seven shifts are, in broad terms:

1 from the language of complaint (what we cannot stand) to the language of commitment (what we stand for);
2 from the language of blame (easily and reflexively produced) to the language of personal responsibility (drawing on the momentum of commitment);
3 from the language of New Year Resolutions (expressing sincere, genuine and weak intentions) to the language of competing commitments (expressing genuine countervailing and powerful commitments);
4 from the language of big assumptions that hold us (automatically produced without awareness and held to be the truth) to the language of assumptions we hold (creating valuable doubt and so the opportunity to question and explore);
5 from the language of prizes and praising (formulaic creation of winners and losers) to the language of ongoing regard (authentic personal appreciation);
6 from the language of rules and policies (intended to create order) to the language of public agreement (intended to create integrity);
7 from the language of constructive criticism (the hierarchical and brave exchange of bombshells) to the language of deconstructive criticism (a shared exploration of sometimes contradictory premises, beliefs and assumptions).

The stories which high-leverage leaders tell and the stories told about them have demonstrated to us that they are intuitively sensitive to the kind of language spectrum described above. They consistently try to adopt language that enhances the self-respect and therefore the learning of everyone around them.

This approach places these leaders in the style of what Lambert describes as 'constructivist leadership' (Lambert, 2009). She argues that constructivist leadership is predicated on learning that alters how actors think and act. This approach requires beliefs and assumptions to be evoked, new ideas and intriguing questions to be investigated. Sense can then be made of the contrasts and contradictions through dialogue that in turn reframes or reshapes actions (2009, p. 94). For Lambert a sense of community is a prerequisite of the reciprocity, purpose and learning that are the alchemy of constructivist leadership. Grint (2001) also emphasises the importance of community: 'Leadership is an essentially social phenomenon: without followers there are no leaders. What leaders must do, therefore, is construct an imaginary community that followers can feel part of ... Leaders, then, must spend at least part of their time constructing not just followers but a community of followers. Whether that community is held together by love of the leader or community, by hate of the 'other', by greed, or by honour is less relevant than that identity is an issue that successful' (2001, pp. 6–7).

These references to community are central to our recurring theme that what distinguishes high-leverage leaders from others is their community purpose – to make their school a community in its own right and an active member of the professional and neighbourhood communities around it. We will return to that theme in Chapter 5 when we consider Partnership. First, we will turn to Management, the role and activities that translate great ideas into effective practice.

4 Management

Role	Function	Activity
Management	Organising: problem-solving, creating order and providing consistency	Analysis: using data and other information to create a high-definition picture of how issues manifest themselves locally
		Action: emphasising priorities, and ensuring that change is explicit, funded and managed
		Application: relentless focus, in particular ensuring that the quality of teaching and learning – the basic compact between a school and its community – is first-class

Introduction

In Chapter 2 we introduced three key roles in which high-leverage leaders engage: Navigation, Management and Partnership. This chapter focuses on the second of those, Management. It explores how Management encompasses the three activities that we have called Analysis, Action and Application.

- *Analysis*: combining data, written material, local stories and other information to create a high definition picture of how well the school is working in parts and as a whole. High-leverage leaders understand the importance of the mass of numeric data at their disposal but also know the value of narrative accounts. Some of those narratives are written and some are oral; some are formally collected through performance management and through other purposeful enquiries or research; some, including narratives from pupils, might be less formal. High-leverage leaders then use their Professional Intelligence (a phrase we explain below) to translate the information collected into the language of informed judgements and professional ambition.

- *Action*: focusing directly on the target issue and selecting an appropriate style. If an activity is a priority for the school, high-leverage leaders ensure that it is explicit, funded and managed. They share, support and monitor the design and implementation of robust and targeted strategies. They use the open and collaborative cultures that we described in Chapter 3. Their intolerance of second-best for needful children becomes an inspiration for their staff. For a small number of staff this focus can be an uncomfortable and sometimes short-lived experience. Openness and collaboration do not prevent high-leverage leaders from being as determined and ingenious in their recruitment of good staff as they are in their development or detachment of underperforming staff.

- *Application*: applying themselves and their colleagues to ensuring that the actions happen and the outcomes are tracked. The core activity of a school is teaching and learning – this is the school's compact with its families and communities. If teaching and learning are not good or better than good, nothing else the school does will attract or deserve confidence.

Analysis

Management
Organising: problem-solving, creating order and providing consistency
Analysis: using data and other information to create a high-definition picture of how issues manifest themselves locally

Our proposal in this section is that high-leverage leaders combine numeric data and other information to create substantive and compelling evidence on which to base Awareness, Advocacy, Action and Application in their schools.

The first Management activity we consider, Analysis, is dependent on a supply of reliable information. This is a feature of the public education service in England that has been transformed over the past 20 years. We want to explore some of that transformation in order to illustrate the context in which high-leverage leaders now operate and how that context has developed even during the course of their own careers. In particular we need to reflect on how the compilation and scrutiny of attainment data and financial information have changed.

Attainment data often seems to be a very modern fixation, but few headteachers In England today would write, as one did about his summer break in 1967:

> Headmasters' wives dread the day when the whole family has to go about on tiptoe while the great man does a lot of nasty sums to prove that his school's results are 0.63, recurring, above the national average.
>
> (TES, 1967)

Although the core anxieties of school leaders when exam results are published seem to have persisted – they still want their school to be doing comparatively well – there have been two profound changes in the 40 years since that entry. Assumptions about the gender of headteachers have changed fundamentally, and the sums are being done in radically different ways. It is the latter which we need to explore here.

Number crunching is not what it used to be. That 1967 headteacher would have painstakingly calculated his 0.63 with long division and multiplication, using pen and paper. In the unlikely event that he or she had a calculator, it would have been mechanical, cumbersome and neither electronic nor electrifying. In contrast, every state school in England now has access to tools such as RAISEonline (Reporting and Analysis for Improvement through School Self-Evaluation: RAISE 2011) that rapidly and repeatedly generate complex analyses on the attainment and progress of pupils across each key stage. RAISE holds data about the attainment level of pupils at every state school in England at the national key stages for assessment – in particular at the ages of 7, 11 and 16. Alongside that it holds contextual data including the school size and, for pupils, the numbers of boys and girls, their ethnic background, special needs, care arrangements, free school meal entitlement, absence levels and attainment at the previous point of assessment. The interactive features of RAISE allow exploration of hypotheses about pupil performance, and use contextual information to make comparisons between schools nationally. Most local authorities in England also use the Fischer Family Trust data analyses (FFT, 2011) to support the processes of self-evaluation (using value-added analyses) and target-setting (using estimates) in schools. In addition to pupil attainment data, schools have access to data about attendance, the rate of exclusions and students' socio-economic circumstances. All these are collated and published nationally (DfE, 2011b). Locally, schools often collect their own data about accidents, behaviour and incidents of racism as well as information on parents' and pupils' views and levels of satisfaction with the work of the school.

Budget management is also not what it used to be. Our 1967 headteacher evidently worried about student outcomes, but it is unlikely that he would have been troubled about budget outturns. Just over two decades ago, financial information about each school would ordinarily have been confidential to a small number of local authority officers. In many cases, financial details would not even be shared with school leaders individually, still less collectively. The equivalent information is now not only at the fingertips of school governors, school leaders and bursars, it is 'their' funding. They, not local officials, have the authority to review, plan and deploy the school budget. National government in England can now publish a spending analysis for every one of the 25,000 state schools in the country, showing the total income for each and the total spent by each. This revealed for the first time, in January 2011, the amount each spent on staffing, administration, premises and learning resources (DfE, 2011c). In contrast to the decades when all that was really known about the economics of education was whether the local authority's education service budget balanced its bottom line at the financial year end, schools can now analyse and compare trends in their own spending and, if they want, associated benefits. All this is allowing analysts like those at the Centre for the Economics of Education to provide increasingly sophisticated interpretations of the return for investment in education.

The value of information about inputs (resources) and outputs (attainment) now available in England at national, regional, neighbourhood and school level is widely appreciated, even though irritation with data collection exercises is a frequent theme of teachers' blogging. The national inspectorate, Ofsted, recommends that using data is a first essential step for schools wanting to close gaps and reduce variation because '… it is critical to know and to use where they are now as a starting point' (Ofsted, 2008b, p. 18). However, official data collection has concentrated on politically high-profile and easy-to-measure outcomes. In response to pressure for constant but narrowly defined school improvement, the national system knows a lot about end-of-key-stage test scores or exam results, measured in terms of pupils' attainment, particularly at the ages of 11 and 16. Much less is known about the impact of schools on young people's sense of empathy, their emotional wellbeing, their social strengths, their ability to solve problems in a team or their inquisitiveness. Official narrative analysis is also limited. Inspection reports, for example, are constrained first by the questions that inspectors are required and allowed to ask and then by the variable quality of their analysis. While all those limitations have to be acknowledged, policymakers and service leaders do have incomparably more and better evidence on which to base their decisions than at any other time – if they choose to use it! Our experience is that high-leverage leaders use the full range intelligently.

> 'One of the key elements of our success is the fine detail tracking of the progress of individual pupils. You know, we sit around in groups on a regular basis and we demand data from heads of departments about progress of the pupils. That data comes to us, we collate it, we attach mentors, we attach extra work, extra lessons, whatever it happens to be. But we don't do it in a blanket way, you know, we get down literally to names and we will sit down and go through a list of names. However long that list needs to be is how long it will be and we will talk about each individual pupil.'
>
> Senior Leader, Cardinal Hume Secondary School

We have met school leaders who are wary of new knowledge and of numeric data in particular. They prefer to rely on their experience, intuition and wisdom, turning to the evidence only when *force majeure* requires it. In contrast, we have also met school leaders who are entranced by spreadsheets. They assume that knowing what the numbers say is the same as understanding what they might mean. High-leverage leaders are in neither of those camps: their professional intelligence informs how and when to use data that in turn enhance their professional competence. From high-leverage leaders, we have learned that:

- *Analysis* satisfies ambitious curiosity;
- *Analysis* is an aid to accountability;
- *Analysis* is now relatively easy.

Analysis satisfies ambitious curiosity

High-leverage leaders and their colleagues are impelled by curiosity – by the need to understand what works so that their practice can be improved. That impulse leads directly to an enthusiasm for personal and communal learning that adults can share with one another and convey to their students. Analysis is therefore the essential foundation of the commitment to professional development that, in Chapter 3, we described as essential to Advocacy. High-leverage leaders are not just personal users of information; they draw their staff into a shared and healthy relationship with information. They understand that, without robust evidence, at best there are only opinions and perhaps only prejudices. They use robust evidence to inform their personal learning and operational judgements. High-leverage leaders also understand that robust evidence is the ideal medium for sharing, comparing and contrasting experience and learning within and between organisations. Analysis is therefore the robust guarantee for three key elements of their curiosity:

- that outcomes for students are the focus of any action;
- that the appropriate action is being taken; and
- that the right children are in the frame.

High-leverage leaders and their colleagues move seamlessly between the roles of practitioner, researcher and learner. Those roles might be formally recognised in job descriptions or in the accreditation of professional learning; on the other hand, research and learning are often no more than an informal, though vitalising, thread in their day-to-day work as practitioners. Across all three roles, they combine numeric data and accounts of practice to produce reflections on activity and impact. The robust evidence they produce makes an inestimable contribution to the quality of teaching in high-leverage schools. It provides the core for practitioner knowledge that is a characteristic of other professional services but is less well defined in the teaching profession. It provides an impetus for professional development that in turn drives improvement. Analysis is the means for producing robust evidence.

It is not uncommon to meet school leaders who seem to lack confidence in their understanding of evidence collection and analysis. In particular they may doubt their mathematical skills and grasp of statistical concepts. That is usually a misplaced concern. Although inquisitiveness and insight are crucial to the effectiveness of Analysis, that is far from expecting that every leader must have degree-level skills in numeracy and spreadsheet manipulation. We can use the metaphors of maps and X-rays to illustrate this point. A team which plans a trip, decides on a destination, forecasts the weather, plans the meals and packs the bags will not all be great cartographers and may not include a cartographer at all. Someone will need to be able to find the right map, read it and ask the right questions of it, but they don't have to make it. The team that repairs a damaged body, diagnoses the broken bone, prepares the plaster cast and provides the physiotherapy will not all be radiographers. Someone will need to be able to source the right X-ray, read it and ask the right questions of it, but they don't have to produce it themselves. The critical factor is that the team understands the potential value and purpose of the tool (be it map or X-ray) and knows someone who can provide one. Cartographers and radiographers have their vital places in journey planning and medicine respectively. Their contribution has to be respected and accessible. By analogy, data analysis is now a vital part of school leadership activity, familiar to everyone in the leadership team but not necessarily part of everyone's advanced skill set. High-leverage leaders know the importance of creating teams which complement and respect one another's skills.

One important aspect of Analysis is the opportunity it offers high-leverage leaders to create transparency and encourage professional conversations. Our experience with high-leverage leaders confirms Michael Fullan's (2008) claim that there is no way that continuous improvement can occur without continuous transparency fuelled by good data.

> When transparency is consistently evident, it creates an aura of 'positive pressure', pressure that is experienced as fair and reasonable, pressure that is actionable in that it points to solutions, and pressure that is ultimately inescapable.
>
> (Fullan, 2008, p. 14)

Similarly, in her study of distributed leadership in seven New Zealand elementary schools, Helen Timperley claims that 'leadership activity, together with the artefacts and relationships that form an integral part', are the critical factors (Timperley, 2005, p. 398). She is making the point that what leaders do is the only way we can make sense of any connection between leadership models and outcomes for students. Our proposal about Analysis connects with Timperley's description of achievement data as one of the integral 'material artefacts in a school'. It is a device which leaders can use to represent an idea or a concept, and which is then capable of enabling or constraining practice. Timperley found that the different ways in which the data were presented and worked on across the seven schools was associated with the gains in achievement that followed. She concluded that, to be effective, 'the forms of material artefacts need to be different for [the staff] with different task responsibilities' (2005, p. 416). Classroom teachers needed information about individuals to inform their daily practice, school leaders needed to understand the overall picture. If we return to our map metaphor, some people in the school need a scale of 1:250 and some need a scale of 1:25,000; some need the road map version and some need the landscape version. The required versions of the maps, for which read school data, can be produced by the specialists. Timperley concluded that the need to modify data artefacts to meet the requirements of people in different roles might appear obvious but it was not apparent in every school. What is required of the potential users is that they can explain what they need to understand and what they think they might want to do. (However, ignorance allied with confident inquisitiveness should not be underestimated for their ability to provide unexpected and unlooked-for insights for people prepared to 'play' with the artefact.)

Confirmation of the importance of Analysis surfaced in Copland's study of schools from The Bay Area School Reform Collaborative (BASRC) in San Francisco (Copland 2003). BASRC's large-scale system reform was predicated on two main principles: commitments to distributed leadership and to continual enquiry. Copland describes the distributed leadership, in broad terms, as an emphasis on collective activity, focused on collective goals, spanning traditional organisational roles and based on expertise rather than hierarchical authority. It leads, in his description, to 'communities of practice built around cycles of enquiry' (2003, p. 379), in effect around what we would call Analysis. As trust and confidence grew, Copland observed a trend for schools to move through three stages of inquiry and therefore of data use. The movement was not linear or static: there were ebbs and flows. Copland represented those fluid stages in Table 4.1.

Copland (2003) explains the movement through these stages by reference to the increasingly distributed style which the leaders adopt. His 'Cycle of Enquiry', akin to what we call Analysis, becomes locked into a self-serving virtuous circle:

> ... a critical component to developing vision, giving credence to shared leadership structures, and constructing a culture of data ... The use of an

Table 4.1 School stages of inquiry

School stages of inquiry	*Stage defining characteristic*
Novice	• Learning the value of data and learning, and struggling with how to use data • Experimenting with the inquiry process and becoming comfortable with procedures • Valuing and using data; trying to seek out the best data; sometimes struggling with how to do so
Intermediate	• Inquiry process shifts closer to teaching and learning; may require changing directions to get close to core concerns of the school; 'competency traps' possible if school become complacent • Managing data is no longer a struggle but instead the norm for making decisions
Advanced	• The inquiry process is an accepted, iterative process involving the whole school and connected to the classroom level • Actively pursuing sustainability of the reform

Source: From Copland, 2003, p. 384.

> inquiry-based approach builds a common vocabulary, enables articulation of the one or two key issues that the school aims to address, and is a key vehicle for building distributed leadership.
>
> (2003, p. 387)

> These principals are engaged in asking questions, exploring data, and engaging faculty and the broader community in questions that can move the school forward.
>
> (2003, p. 391)

Copland concludes, with a flourish, that the power of enquiry is '... the engine to enable the distribution of leadership, and the glue that binds a school community together in common work' (20003, p. 391).

Qualitative information makes some leaders nervous: they suspect that it is less valid and therefore less useful than numeric data. The stories that people tell, which are, after all, the basis for much of our qualitative information, can be invaluable. When properly collated, presented and weighed in the balance, they have a validity of their own and provide insights below the numeric surface. High-leverage leaders tend to agree with Ofsted that numbers are not the only, and certainly not always the best, information for analysing issues around their school.

> No single kind of data or analysis can tell the whole story about a school. ... to achieve a rounded and comprehensive picture of a school's recent performance, a range of different kinds of data and analyses is required.
>
> (Ofsted, 2008b, p. 10)

Despite the alleged dependence of its inspection teams on numeric attainment data, the above Ofsted summary concluded that, for self-evaluation and planning for improvement, a more detailed analysis (than that for external reporting) is required, enabling the school to identify the strengths and weaknesses of its performance not only across phases, subjects and groups of pupils, but also class by class, pupil by pupil and question by question.

High-leverage leaders use qualitative as well as quantitative Analysis to diagnose the variations in performance, to identify priorities for improvement, and to plan the actions and put in place the support to bring about that improvement. The value of that breadth was illustrated in an evaluation by England's Training and Development Agency for Schools (TDA) to which we contributed (TDA 2009). The evaluation was of a programme to reduce in-school variations (ISV) in performance by improving the performance of low attaining groups of students or staff. The TDA report listed a wide range of measures used to gauge success and inform the next steps. These included student feedback, attendance and behaviour data, assessment for learning outcomes and wider well-being indicators. The report confirmed that qualitative information has an important part to play in what we now call Analysis and can come from sources as varied as records of lesson observations, analyses of schemes of work, differences in approach to individualised learning, the uses made of formative assessment and the use of resources etc. Qualitative information, the TDA report concluded, may also help to assess how effective an activity has been in creating changes in working practices, attitudes and professional standards across a school.

High-leverage leaders therefore use 'information analysis' rather than 'data analysis' to create the high definition picture they need. They weave narrative and other qualitative, non-numeric material in with the statistical analyses. They are not mesmerised by numbers – unlike some policy makers and some of their peers. They know that spreadsheets are only one perspective on the world and that writers, novelists, playwrights, musicians and artists have all provided inspirational insights into the human condition. They understand that numbers provide a powerful lens through which to look at their work, but not the only one.

> 'We've been trying to get a more confident understanding, drilling down the data on individual students. We don't want quick fixes. So looking at a range of variables, single parents, gifted and talented, FSM, SEN, we found that the big dip is for students for whom we have limited or no contact or details for parents at home. There's more to do, some of the information is dated and we need to check against what we know about attendance at parental meetings.
>
> 'We've then identified all the extra provision we offer to Year 11 and which of the students attend. And it is stark, the disengagement of this group. We are at the early stages but there are definite links between the students' disengagement and parental disengagement. We wonder if they're repeating the experiences of their parents and grandparents.
>
> 'Our hypothesis at the moment is that parental contact is the most important variable … but … How does that then feed into the student's experience – what creates the effect?'
>
> Teacher Researcher, Elizabeth Garrett Andersen Secondary School

The three obvious sources from which high-leverage leaders draw qualitative data are their students, staff and parents.

The student body always has the potential to provide the richest seams of information for high-leverage leaders. No-one has more contact with or more to say about teaching and learning than the students. When young people are taken seriously and feel their views make a difference, they become more engaged with the school, feel more positive about themselves and manage their own progress better. Consulting with pupils also helps teachers to understand how to support pupil engagement and to build more collaborative and communicative relationships with their pupils (GTCE, 2005).

The Harris Student Commission on Learning was launched in 2008 to create significant changes to teaching and learning and a step-change in student engagement, motivation and learning across a group of South London schools. The Commission is an ambitious enquiry, co-led by students and staff, into the most effective learning approaches in the UK or abroad.

'In a school where there has been a lack of confidence and aspiration, student commissioners have given their peers the confidence to demand more and better learning.'

Terrie Askew, Principal, Harris Academy Falconwood (Harris, 2011)

Staff in a school can create narratives of school life in a variety of ways including 'behaviour trails' or 'audits'. In England, the Centre for the Use of Research and Evidence in Education has produced a brief *aide memoire* to support this kind of enquiry (CUREE, 2009a and 2009b).

These exercises are highly effective devices for promoting the conversations and shared language that, in the previous chapter, we described as powerful aspects of Advocacy. They are about high-leverage leaders using language and conversation in different formats and contexts. We said that they use conversation as a powerful device for creating and telling the narratives of their schools and, through that medium, they change the expectations and eventually the behaviour of the staff and students.

'Just recognise the power of the grapevine.'

Dave Dunkley, Headteacher, Coleshill Primary School

Parents and the community always have stories to tell about the local school. The question for high-leverage leaders is whether those stories are left to fade away in the supermarket queue – or worse, left to fester as they are passed around – or whether they are methodically captured, considered and used by the school.

Analysis is an aid to accountability

High-leverage leaders are sensitive to the demands of accountability and target setting. We will explore their attitudes and approaches to this in full in Chapter 7. We will show that they are not just comfortable with having the detail of their work surveyed and checked; they use external oversight much as wrestlers use the impetus of an opponent – to their own ends and to support their own momentum. In this chapter we need only a brief reminder that, in England over the past two decades, politicians and professionals have been gripped by numeric accountability and target setting. Politicians have used statutory powers and emotional leverage to impose on the system increasing demands for numeric performance data. Professionals have not generally had the political strength or overall the Professional Intelligence to resist that or to offer convincing alternatives. This has meant that, although knowledge about the system has increased exponentially, understanding has not developed in step and, to some degree, resistance to data collection and use is therefore common.

High-leverage leaders occupy a particular place in this context. They use Analysis actively, not passively. Data and, even more so, Analysis are not something they grudgingly create and reluctantly provide for external agencies, or sceptically receive from outside bodies. They analyse for their own benefit and curiosity, for their colleagues and for their students. In turn, this helps them to shape the terms of their accountability through:

- describing individual and collective performance (using some criteria which are nationally designed and others which are locally selected for local purposes);
- comparing performance with expected standards (some of which are individual, some collective, some local, some national);
- providing a contextual commentary on, but not excuses for, individual or collective performance (in order to understand where and how to focus the energy for improvement); and
- selecting the local outcomes by which they, their staff and students are prepared to be judged alongside the national requirements (because national targets are not the only worthwhile targets).

We will expand on these points in Chapter 7.

Analysis is now relatively easy

High-leverage leaders are varied in their enthusiasm for new technology: not all of them design, still less complete, their own spreadsheets. However, in England, the analysis of data, particularly in its narrow, numeric sense, is no longer an intrinsically long-winded or difficult exercise. Much of the numerical material is collected by national agencies and then made available in formats that can be easily manipulated in schools. E-technology can now rapidly accumulate and analyse information that would once have been redundant before it could be compiled. Any young researcher or school leader looking back at the paucity of data with which their predecessors were working, even towards the end of the 1980s, would wonder how policy decisions at any level could have been well informed. Perhaps they were not. There are very few schools now where there is no-one who knows the difference between mean, median and mode, or who can spot a trend when they see one. Many secondary schools appear to have a member of staff with particular responsibility for this work. 'Developing the use of data as a tool was one of the easiest areas in which to make progress', reported schools participating in the national in-school variation trial for the Training and Development Agency in England (TDA, 2009, p. 11). These schools found that sound data and tracking systems at individual, key stage, year group and departmental levels were '... key tools for identifying where ISV occurs and prioritising the areas where a reduction in ISV is most significant' (TDA, 2009, p. 11).

School leaders have drawn our attention to the use of maps and X-rays as metaphors:

> We tried to envisage data analysis as an X-ray of the school – something that would give us a real insight into why and how we were seeing the variations we had identified.
>
> (National College, 2010b, p. 1)

It might help to return to that metaphor. The X-ray is an image on radiographic film of the denser material in a limb, in effect a picture of the skeleton. The map is a technical representation of an identified area to a given scale, in effect a picture of the landscape. The value of both is in the end user's ability to interpret a picture produced by a specialist in that form of picture production. The added value is in the analysis, interpretation and conclusions reached to inform action on the basis of the evidence. A skilled medical specialist will look at an X-ray and have a picture in mind of the anatomy and pathology it represents. A skilled navigator will look at a map and quickly have a colourful 3D image in mind of what the terrain would look like from given points.

High-leverage leaders use data in a similar fashion, to create a picture of what is happening to a child's learning, the progress of a class or the development of a school. A sheet of data, like an X-ray or a map, may to some beholders be a thing of beauty, but it is never an end in itself. It is a means to an end. Like the X-ray and the map, educational data offer a description of what is there, some insight into how that came about and information to help decide what might be the best thing to do next.

Action

Management
Organising: problem-solving, creating order and providing consistency
Action: emphasising priorities, and ensuring that change is explicit, funded and managed

Our proposal in this section is that high-leverage leaders focus change in their schools by emphasising a limited number of critical priorities and ensuring that the importance of those priorities is evident in the resources they are allocated, not least management interest and time.

We have been describing how high-leverage leaders contribute to setting the scene and establishing the mood for their organisations. Their focus on what we have called Awareness, Acceptance, Advocacy and Analysis has its main impact through the attitudes, aspirations and ambitions they nurture across their school communities. These are the necessary features of high-leverage leadership, but they are not sufficient. They appear to create the energy which high-level performance requires, but they do not provide the focus. We turn therefore to Action, the activity through which high-leverage leaders begin to demonstrate that they are not just good at talking the talk – they can also get the work done. In this section, we reflect on how these leaders move from Advocacy to Action, focusing their concentration and that of their colleagues on a limited number of priorities and making sure that those priorities are supported with the capacity and capability that they demand.

It is axiomatic that, unless the energy of any improvement programme, in effect the effort of the people involved, is focused on a limited range of agreed priorities, then the collective endeavour will dissipate and fail to meet its potential. 'A clear focus on a limited number of goal has been identified as a key characteristic of effective and improving schools' (Muijs *et al.*, 2005, p. 94).

This is what Davies calls aligning the people and the organisation to the strategy by changing the mindset and behaviour of the people within the organisation (Davies, 2009). School leaders in Davies's research often achieved this by using 'conversations' with their colleagues. These conversations developed increasing depth and engagement, first with a tentative exploration of ideas, then with greater knowledge and participation. Then came increased motivation, commitment and ambition and, finally, they built personal and organisational capability. Davies observed a transition from Advocacy to Action, though the process is neither simple nor linear.

> 'We have a rigorous programme for evaluating the quality of our teaching and learning. We include lesson observations, work sampling, questionnaires, interviews and data analysis. We translate that into priorities for the development plan and specific roles and responsibilities for each member of the leadership team.'
>
> Headteacher, Stoke Hill Primary School

We have already written about conversation as an essential feature of Advocacy, and we will make the same claim for Action.

> We are constantly talking, large groups, small groups, individuals, a constant feast of two-way conversations bringing people into line with where we are going.
>
> (Davies, 2009, p. 19).

Davies also adds the necessary though often overlooked skill of 'strategic abandonment' to the critical list of knowing what, how and when to change. Davies writes that something has to stop if new things are going to start, and 'strategic abandonment' is an echo of what Peter Drucker calls 'systematic abandonment' – deliberate and regular decisions to end some activities are just as important as decisions on what new or different things to do. Activity which no longer fits the overall purpose or mission, which no longer conveys satisfaction for the service users or no longer makes a superior contribution, should be systematically abandoned (Drucker, 2007). The decision to downgrade the importance of an activity and its demand on time or other resources is less difficult when it is obviously not working or is unpopular. The greater challenge for school leaders, Davies writes, is when 'the school has to give up acceptable current practice to make capacity available for future improved practice' (2009, p. 22). Sometimes activity has to be abandoned not because it is flawed in its own right but simply because it has become less important than other, often newer, activities.

Judgements by high-leverage leaders to strategically or systematically abandon activities are vital to the avoidance of overload that will bring an organisation to its knees. These are also judgements that are vital to maintaining momentum. They are judgements that become more difficult if the leadership has limited influence or even lack of control over aspects of working practice. For example, the classroom habits of individual teachers in primary schools and the habits of individual departments in secondary schools – especially those which occupy their own specialist area – have historically been privileged spaces in some schools. In those circumstances, much then depends on the capability of leaders to embed their Advocacy, Analysis and, we shall see shortly, Application deep into the school's systems. Without strategic, systematic abandonment of current activity, workload just piles up and proposed changes skim the surface of effectiveness. Workload is, of course, an issue in the schools we have worked in, though we are constantly told by leaders and other staff alike that is not the critical factor. Success and appreciation, themes that are constantly promoted by high-leverage leaders, appear to be far more influential on staff's endurance than a calculation of hours and weight of work.

High-leverage leaders consistently tell us – and the literature confirms (Fullan 2008) – that an open and collaborative culture is the best way of producing the momentum necessary for improvement. Mulford (2010, p. 193) describes this as a view of organisation as a process characterised by constant adaptation and growth in response to a strong desire for learning and survival. He contrasts this with transactional, command and control forms of leadership in which supervision is tight, pedagogy prescribed and decisions centralised. Leaders who are determined to draw attention to differences in adult or student performance require enthusiasm and sensitivity as well as determination. In England, the Teaching and Development Agency (TDA) has confirmed that school culture is important to the reduction of in-school variation (ISV) of the kind we discussed above:

> A high degree of collaboration and openness that draws people together and enables the ready sharing of best practice across the school will most effectively secure benefits. Schools are likely to gain the most from designing ISV programmes that reflect the extent of trusting relationships and collaboration within their existing culture. Where trust is at lower levels and collaboration is not well-developed, smaller steps will be required during the initial stages.
>
> (TDA, 2009)

To guarantee that vulnerable children are offered nothing less than the best available teaching, to say nothing of other provisions, demands an implacable focus on nurturing and delivering high-quality service. In our experience, high-leverage leaders achieve this by joining, supporting and monitoring the design and implementation by their colleagues of robust and targeted strategies. Difficult decisions are then necessary if any of the adults cannot use collegiate support effectively. That is the aspect of high leverage-leadership we will explore in the following section, Application.

Application

Management
Organising: problem-solving, creating order and providing consistency
Application: relentless focus, in particular ensuring that the quality of teaching and learning – the basic compact between a school and its community – is first-class

Our proposal in this section is that high-leverage leaders are relentless and implacable in ensuring that the school's priorities and common processes, always including the quality of teaching and learning, are accepted and applied by everyone involved.

Once Analysis is as complete as it can be and a course of Action has been decided, then high-leverage leaders Apply themselves and their organisations to ensuring that the activity takes place and the expected improvements are delivered. In this section we describe how these leaders establish the systematic approaches that draw the school community together, working as a unit around the actions that have been decided.

> 'It's consistency, it's no good having all of these like purges or we're going to do this and then nothing else happens or we're going to do that … it's having the consistency over all of the little things I think that happen all the time.'
>
> Middle leader, Cardinal Hume Secondary School

Application in schools, as it would be in any service industry, means ensuring above all that the organisation's core activity is of an unremittingly high quality. Healthy outcomes, community cohesion and safeguarding for children are all important, arguably essential, matters for high-leverage leaders. They are not their core business. The core compact of every school with its pupils, families and community is that children will learn. The core business of every school is learning and the core activity is teaching. Through learning and through the ways in which teaching is organised and delivered, schools can enhance the health and well-being of their students. It is widely understood and, we think, accepted that schools are designed to work that way round and not the reverse Therefore, high-leverage leaders will always apply most of their energy and expend most of their emotion on the quality of teaching and learning.

Educational attainment is of central importance for these leaders not just because of political pressure or professional pride, though those count for something. Educational attainment is centrally important because high-leverage leaders are committed to meeting the expectations that families and pupils bring into school. In our conversations with these leaders we repeatedly hear them challenge the allegation that low aspiration is the default position of any family. They are more inclined to think that low aspiration is a learned attitude that can be unlearned. We noted earlier that these leaders were attracted to work in the education service because of a moral dimension they bring to their professional lives. We have also noted that the moral dimension counts for little if it is not reflected both in the way these leaders treat the people around them and in the impact their work has on the attainment and achievement of young people.

High-leverage leaders understand that employers ask young people how many GCSEs they have or at least how well they read, write and calculate numbers. Employers do not ask young people about the value-added scores of their schools or whether they were happy there. High-leverage leaders do not use the sometimes uncomfortable truths about employment as an argument that attainment is more important than health or wellbeing, but as a reminder of the interdependence of all three in children's lives and of their own predominant role in promoting attainment. High-leverage leaders tell us that, without a successful core of teaching and learning, and therefore of students' standards and outcomes, their schools would haemorrhage credibility with families, communities and governors. They would also be under pressure from local and national authorities to improve their performance. Any ambition they have to improve outcomes outside the golden circle of attainment, especially by engaging more with the local community, would be decisively undermined if the quality of teaching let them down (Leadbeater and Mongon, 2008, pp. 23–6). High-leverage leaders are risk takers, but they are not rash. At times when they do have their attention and personal effort drawn outside the emphasis on teaching and learning, they need to be confident that someone in their leadership team has the capacity and capability to take good care of that core work.

'I and the leadership team have had to be decisive in tackling under-performance when a teacher has not responded to support and guidance. It is really not comfortable but our pupils can't afford for us to tolerate anything second-rate.'

Headteacher, Parkside Primary School

The relentless emphasis on teaching and learning as a key component in the leadership of effective schools permeates the literature as well as our own experience with high-leverage leaders. The emphasis is important because the quality of teaching has more impact on core business, the attainment of students, than any other factor under the control of the school. High-quality teaching is the bedrock on which attainment is built and the only underpinning capable of sustaining a school's ambition to contribute to other outcomes in children's lives. Everything else implodes without it. High-leverage leaders have to tackle teacher quality within and across schools because, as the following summaries of studies in three different countries show, variations in teacher quality and the impact of those variations are critical to success.

A study over ten years in two adjacent North American School Districts found remarkable differences in student outcomes associated with the quality of their teachers: '... a one standard deviation increase in teacher quality raises reading and math test scores by approximately .20 and .24 standard deviations, respectively, on a nationally standardized scale' (Rockoff, 2003, p. 14). Rockoff's work also provided evidence that more experienced teachers were associated with higher student reading test scores – a conclusion with interesting implications for teacher deployment (2003, p. 15). In a long-term study of the effect of teachers on student attainment in Tennessee, Sanders and Rivers (1996) reported a difference of 50 percentile points after only three years as a result of teacher effects. The study used a 'statistical mixed process model' to allocate teachers to quintiles according to their effectiveness over a period. Students who worked with highly effective teachers over three years showed 'dramatic' differences in performance compared with students who worked with the least effective teachers over three years. Where students worked with a mix of teachers over the three years, the researchers concluded that '... the residual effects of relatively ineffective teachers from prior years can be measured in subsequent student achievement scores' (1996, p. 4). In another study of the test scores across Grades 3 to 7 for three cohorts totalling one and a half million students in 3,000 Texas schools, Rivkin *et al.* (2005) concluded that, although overall school quality is an important contributor to student attainment, the most important predictor is teacher quality. Rivkin and colleagues also suggest that much of the variation in teacher quality exists within, rather than between, schools (2005, p. 421) and is deeply influenced by 'effective hiring, firing, mentoring, and promotion practices' in schools (2005, p. 450).

An Australian study using a dataset covering over 10,000 Australian primary school teachers and over 90,000 pupils concluded that:

> The differences between the best and worst teachers in Queensland are considerable ... In terms of literacy and numeracy test scores, a 75th percentile teacher can achieve in three-quarters of a year what a 25th percentile teacher can achieve in a full year; while a 90th percentile teacher can achieve in half a year what a 10th percentile teacher can achieve in a full year.
>
> (Leigh, 2007, p. 21)

In a context where it is increasingly evident that there is a high price to pay for underestimating, still more so neglecting, the importance of teaching and learning, Muijs and Reynolds have argued that:

> ... the research that has been done since the arrival of the new statistical 'multi-level' methods in the mid-1980s into the contribution of the different factors of LEAs, schools, teachers and indeed the pupils themselves to their educational achievements has suggested that the behaviours of teachers in classrooms is the most important factor of all.
>
> (Muijs and Reynolds, 2005, p. 6)

One study (Sammons *et al.*, 2008), government funded, across 125 English primary schools concluded:

- First, it is possible to classify teachers in Year 5 (age 10) classes into groups according to differences in their overall Teaching quality across a range of different dimensions of classroom behaviour and practice.
- Second, overall Teaching quality is a significant predictor of cognitive progress for children across the period Year 1 to Year 5. Children in schools where Year 5 overall Teaching quality was observed to be High do significantly better in both Reading and Mathematics than those attending schools where Year 5 quality was observed to be Low.
- Third, the overall quality of teaching as measured in the study had a consistent influence on children's academic progress but not on children's social/behavioural development. None the less, more specific aspects of classroom processes were found to predict both better social/behavioural development and better cognitive progress.

High-leverage application

High-leverage leaders understand that the impact of teaching quality becomes even more important when, for better or worse, it affects children from the most disadvantaged backgrounds. It is an international phenomenon that students in socio-economically poor areas often have poorer school experiences than their financially better-off peers. Rivkin and his colleagues, in the study referenced above (2005), reported that disadvantaged students were more likely to experience teacher turnover in their schools and to be taught by inexperienced teachers, both of which were factors that their research had associated with less effective teaching. Also, writing about the USA, Biddle (2001) concludes:

> ... on average, where students from low-income backgrounds are concentrated, the investment of resources and the quality of educational learning opportunities are substantially lower than in schools serving more affluent, mainstream children ... Closely linked to this pattern is the distribution of teacher qualifications with schools serving the greatest concentration of

children from low income families staffed by teachers with lower levels of preparation for their work.

(2001, pp. 175–6)

This is a pattern repeated across the English system too. In successive Annual Reports, Ofsted, the national inspectorate, has confirmed the 'strong association' between deprivation and poor provision (Ofsted, 2010a, p. 37). Reporting on observations of teaching in Year 5 classes (pupils age 10) and using free school meal (FSM) entitlement as an indicator of deprivation, Sammons and her colleagues concluded:

> In addition, the current research indicates that observed teacher behaviour varies according to FSM context. It is found that on aspects such as 'Basic skills development', 'Depth of subject knowledge', 'Social support for learning in Mathematics', 'Pupil engagement' and 'Classroom routines' in Literacy, observed scores were lower in classes in more disadvantaged contexts. Overall, observed scores for 'Pedagogy' in Literacy and 'Subject development' for Numeracy tended to be lower in Year 5 primary classes in schools with high levels of FSM. *It appears from the observations in Year 5 classes that the quality of teaching tends to be poorer in schools with higher levels of disadvantage, while the behavioural challenges in terms of pupil behaviour in class tend to be greater.*
>
> (Sammons *et al.*, 2006, pp. ii–iii, emphasis added)

Overall, high-leverage leaders do not need international research to persuade them of the importance of teaching quality and will tend to agree with Dylan Wiliam's analysis that the quickest way to improve pupil attainment is to improve the teachers already available, not because they are not good – though some are not – but because they could be better (Wiliam, 2009). Replacing teachers is an important but slower option, so Wiliam proposes that the changes which make a difference to student performance are changes in the practice of existing teachers. High-leverage leaders achieve this in the main through Advocacy and their commitment to professional development. Focusing on those fundamental changes in behaviour is not an easy matter. So, in the absence of a well-thought-out national approach to either the professional development of teachers or, even more so, the strategic deployment of the best practitioners – both of which would be features of most private-sector businesses with a national profile – the leaders we have worked with take the matter of teaching quality assertively into their own hands. We have already written about high-leverage leaders supporting the development of their existing staff through Advocacy, and we will write in Chapter 5 about how they build a strong sense of community through Association. Here we want to make reference to some of the Action they take to regenerate their teaching force by replacement and recruitment.

In our report on leaders who are successful at raising the attainment of white working-class pupils (Mongon and Chapman, 2008a), we wrote about recruitment being a challenge and a vital priority. The international nature of this issue is illustrated by this American source:

> In larger urban districts, in particular, where the children of poverty are generally concentrated, recruitment and hiring processes are often cumbersome, untimely and inefficient: good teaching prospects are often snapped up by more efficient districts (typically those that serve a more affluent clientele) or by non-public [private] schools.
>
> (Knapp, 2001, p. 198)

So, like other high-leverage leaders, those we have worked with are both methodical and imaginative about filling staff vacancies. The conviction that their students are entitled to the best teachers and their staff to the best colleagues has led them at times to personal head hunting, arm twisting and calls on the loyalty of friends. Their uncompromising and resourceful approach to the 'hiring and firing' that Rivkin described above is not to be found in the human resources department's manual of best practice. In some cases it may even skirt the borders of legality. It does, however, contribute significantly to the aim of putting high-quality teachers in front of the students.

The literature on teaching quality repeatedly confirms our experience of high-leverage leaders applying a hard edge of Professional Intelligence alongside their commitment to nurturing through Advocacy and community building through what we will later describe and explain – in Chapter 5 – as Association. The following examples from the literature illustrate that point.

Henchey's study of 12 effective schools in low-income areas in Quebec concluded that these schools had a particularly strong focus on core instructional processes (Henchey, 2001). Henchey wrote that there was a lot of romance and pie written about the role of a good principal, but that the practice is very different (2001, p. 64). In reality, the principals in his study spent a lot of time paying attention to detail, maintaining systems and solving problems. Much of that effort, he concluded, was directed at ensuring consistency of teaching quality. One leader in another study introduced a rule that at least 50 per cent of regular meeting time must be committed to the development of teaching and learning – a tactic which not only emphasised its central importance but gave staff 'a language to talk about teaching and learning' (Hopkins, 2001, p. 4). Aligning resources with the teaching mission, monitoring student progress, supervising instruction, and buffering staff from distractions to their core work come together in what Day's research confirms as one of the four 'basic' practices in the recurring 'repertoire' of leadership – 'managing the teaching and learning programme' (Day, 2007, p. 183).

Englefield's (2002) study of 14 successful primary schools in varied but challenging contexts concluded that the headteachers *intensively* (our italics) emphasised: ensuring rigorous and accurate assessments of pupils' progress in order to set challenging tasks and targets, measuring, analysing and celebrating pupil progress rigorously, and high expectations where staff and pupils work well together. A broad-ranging review of international research on school improvement in socio-economically disadvantaged areas concluded that the most effective leaders exceeded normal efforts, focused on teaching and learning and applied an indirect but powerful leadership influence (Muijs *et al.*, 2004). Ofsted (2008a) reported on the work of schools that are successful in raising the attainment of white boys from low-income backgrounds. Features of those successful schools included rigorous monitoring systems to track performance against expectations, realistic but challenging targets with frequent reviews of performance against targets, a highly structured step-by-step framework for teaching and a tightly structured curriculum. A government-led study of 50 very successful schools from some of the most deprived areas in England discovered much the same thing, reaching the conclusion that, 'Unsurprisingly, they are all excellent schools, and they do all the things that good schools do' (DCSF, 2008a, p. 4). Our experience, like the experience in that study, is that high-leverage leaders do the things that others do but with a passion and an application which goes the extra mile.

In particular, high-leverage leaders are prepared to challenge inconsistency and variation in performance within their school. Their primary tools for doing that are the pursuit of the shared learning culture that we have repeatedly described. That does not always work perfectly, certainly not across schools in England overall where what has become known as in-school variation (ISV) overwhelms between-school variation as a factor in children's attainment. The OECD has reported that the consequences of ISV are four times greater in the UK than between-school variation, and higher than in almost any other OECD country (OECD, 2001). A DfES study in 2003 is quoted by Hopkins *et al.* (2005) as having discovered that ISV in England is even greater than the OECD found. In value-added terms, key stage 2 within-school variance appeared to be five times greater than between-school variance and for key stage 4 14 times greater (Hopkins *et al.*, 2005, p. 18). A later study by one of the same authors, of performance in the 65–75 percent of secondary schools where pupils' progress in key stage 3 was roughly in line with national expectations, concluded that over a three year period half of them had at least one subject where progress would put them in the top 20% nationally for the subject/year concerned (Reynolds, 2007, p. 3). In effect, if every school in England could bring the average performance of its lowest-attaining pupil groups and least effective teachers up to the level of its own best, the landscape of educational achievement and attainment would be transformed. This is an area of performance that falls most directly within the remit of school leaders and has been addressed assertively by high-leverage leaders across the decade in which we have been working with them. Their behaviour tends to support Reynolds's maxim that every school has practice that is relatively more effective than elsewhere in its organisation and that, therefore, every school can look internally for generally applicable good practice (2007, p. 3).

An approach taken by many high-leverage leaders to within-school variation and which distinguishes Application from Advocacy or Association is the introduction of what are becoming known as 'standard operating procedures' (SOPs)

(National College, 2006b). In some schools, this has meant the introduction of 'tighter specification of systems, procedures and responses to ensure consistency, reduce the isolation of individual staff or departments and to clarify expectations of pupils across the school' (Reynolds, 2007, p. 15). In effect, this means agreeing and applying key aspects of practice uniformly across the school. 'Key aspects' is an important qualification in this context because some variety in procedure is necessary and some is desirable. Not every subject area, not every teacher and not every pupil can be pressed into a single mould. Standardisation reportedly works when it is applied to data and monitoring and some core aspects of lesson planning. It benefits from a shared understanding not only among staff but also by students and parents. The best SOPs ensure that effective practice becomes universal and manage to avoid being numbingly rigid. They meet an important, dispersed and persistent need clarified by staff and students who have also been involved in designing the procedures, given the opportunity to understand them and, if necessary, trained to apply them.

> 'Everything is driven by clear, simple systems which everybody can under-stand and operate. We're aware of the impact that assessment for learning can have on attainment; forget jargon, we mean "students understanding what they do to improve their learning". So every classroom has a green sheet on the wall with five basic questions: what have I learned this lesson; how have I learned it; where am I going next; what do I need to do; how will I do it? It's not rocket science, it's dead simple.'
>
> Deputy Head, Redbridge Secondary School

SOPs have to be constantly monitored, reviewed and challenged so that they are a basis for professional learning and not an excuse to avoid personal responsibility. Where they are flawed they need to be changed quickly and the people who identified the flaw need to be publicly celebrated (Stringfield *et al.*, 2008; National College, 2010c).

Conscientiousness

In our research into leadership that successfully raised the attainment of white working-class pupils in England (Mongon and Chapman, 2008a), we commented on the leaders' remarkable attention to detail. That attention was applied above all to the quality of teaching and learning – as we have described above. It extended, however, to every aspect of the school's life including, for example, the students' dress, the appearance of the buildings and the quality of the school meals. We described this as a personality trait of those high-leverage leaders and chose Conscientiousness as the word to describe it. We did not adopt Conscientiousness in a strict clinical sense where it is one part of a Five-Factor Model often used in psychology to describe personality traits – the others are openness, extraversion, agreeableness and neuroticism. We adopted it because it seems to us to be a word whose meaning is sufficiently the same in clinical and lay terms for it to make sense to a wide audience. Conscientious individuals tend to be painstaking, self-disciplined, organised, careful before acting and striving to achieve. They are generally hard working and reliable, sometimes even perfectionist, often compelling and irresistible. They are engaged in an incessant struggle, familiar to most school leaders, to achieve more and more in the minimum time. Describing their observations of this phenomenon, Engels *et al.* (2008) used the phrase Type A Behaviour. We recognised something of that in some of the high-leverage leaders we know. Overall, though, we feel that Type A Behaviour is a phrase too often associated with competitive aggression to reflect the disposition of our leaders properly or fairly. We prefer Harris and Chapman's (2002) phrasing, 'the confidence to be contentious and to deal with conflict, highly pragmatic, resilient and determined' (2002, p. 3), or the DfES's 'not shying away from making decisions [and having] a passion for order and thoroughness ... an insistence, persistence and consistency about certain non-negotiables' (2007, p. 11). High-leverage leaders are not usually aggressive although they can be assertive; they are not usually competitive in ways that require other people or schools to be defined as losers, though they are ambitious for their staff and students to be winners. The ambition and sense of perfection with which high-leverage leaders constantly struggle is best characterised by the quality of the relationships they create around them and by the student outcomes with which they are associated.

5 Partnership

Role	Function	Activity
Partnership	Modelling partnership: treating partners with equal esteem and deep respect	Association: being socially aware: nurturing the school as a community in its own right, as a member of its neighbourhood community and as a unit in a wider professional community
		Alignment: improving the alignment of the students' home and school experiences – without prejudice to what changes and where
		Area focus: engaging with the wider community in a partnership role because there is no 'one size fits all'

Introduction

In Chapters 3 and 4 we focused on two of the three key roles in which high-leverage leaders engage, Navigation and Management respectively. This chapter focuses on the third, Partnership and describes how Partnership encompasses the three activities that we have called Association, Alignment and Area Focus.

- *Association*: High-leverage leaders have a core disposition towards *Association*, a particular approach to the relationships they promote within their school and which they translate seamlessly into their work outside the school. Their disposition is founded on two beliefs:
  - that the school is a community where outcomes will improve if relationships allow everyone to learn together; and

- that the same is true both for wider professional communities and for neighbourhood communities.

High-leverage leaders use what, in Chapter 2, we called their Social Intelligence and Contextual Intelligence to become intuitive community builders and investors in social capital.

- *Alignment*: The point of education for high-leverage leaders, one of them told us, is working out how we can all live together with dignity and in harmony. Their task is to ensure that every child has the opportunity to become a dignified adult in a harmonious community. They know that their pupils' academic attainment is a critical contribution to those goals. They do not accept that attainment is the only important contribution and they do not allow it to overwhelm other outcomes. Because they believe that process is directly related to product, they align the ways in which they and the people around them behave with what they are trying to achieve. That is as true for the school's relationship with the communities and families it serves as it is for the leadership's relationship with staff and students in the school.

- *Area focus*: High-leverage leaders adapt and localise national policy and external demands so that they enhance rather than inhibit the local focus of their work. They know that the lives of their students and staff in school are inextricably interwoven with their lives outside school. Inevitably, the effects of one pass on into the other. These leaders enter into partnerships with their neighbourhood and professional communities because they recognise the power of Association.

In the following sections we will show how high-leverage leadership uses Association, Alignment and Area Focus to build close and effective partnerships with students, families, neighbourhoods and other services. Like any healthy community, those partnerships share rights, privileges and interests. We will explore where the impetus and material for that kind of partnership comes from and how they are sustained.

> 'Remember your social responsibility as a leader. It is your duty to consider what you can do to support the community so that it can begin to thrive, and then support itself. You need your staff to understand that they are serving the community, not the other way around.'
> Sheila Audsley, former Headteacher, Clifton Green Primary School

Association

Our proposal is that high-leverage leaders influence the way that the people around them feel about one another. This is one of the key tactics through which they promote and sustain change in the way people work together.

We have called this approach Association. We needed a word that is less taken for granted and has less baggage than either community or partnership. We

> Partnership
>
> Modelling partnership: treating partners with equal esteem and deep respect
>
> Association: being socially aware: nurturing the school as a community in its own right, as a member of its neighbourhood community and as a unit in a wider professional community

were looking for a word that could encompass and provoke curiosity about the personal, emotive connections which high-leverage leaders activate. We want to use Association in its original sense of connection through friendship and companionship because high-leverage leaders tend to employ approaches which have deeply affective dimensions and which transcend the functionality of many workplaces and working partnerships. The high-leverage leaders' approach to Association is informed mainly, but not exclusively, by what in Chapter 2 we called their Social Intelligence:

> This behaviour is rooted in a value system and sense of moral purpose, a clear view about how people should behave towards one another ... They drive high expectations without losing their sense of empathy or eroding anyone's dignity.
>
> (Mongon and Chapman, 2008a, p. 9)

The theme of Association crystallised during an enquiry into schools that had contributed successfully to community cohesion (Mongon, 2010). The interviewed leaders littered their conversations and accounts with the word 'community', either as a noun or an adjective. 'Community' was evidently a significant lens through which they looked at their work. They made repeated reference to their membership of three communities:

1 *The school community:* a place where everyone is a learner and contributes to the learning of others.
2 *The neighbourhood community:* a locality within which adults can be offered learning opportunities and can contribute to the learning of their children.
3 *The provider community:* the network of voluntary and statutory services whose members can learn from one another and contribute to one another's learning.

Those leaders spoke very clearly about what it meant to be a member of each of those communities and to be one leader amongst many leaders, inside as well as outside their schools. We recognised this as a feature of other work we had done with high-leverage leaders who promote parity of status and a commitment to shared learning in the school, neighbourhood and provider communities. They bring those attributes without shedding their confidence, sense of personal responsibility or conscientiousness. This disposition to 'community building' and 'partnership making' is what we mean by Association.

High-leverage leaders weave Association into the continuum of their influence from classrooms to community centres and from pre-school pupils to world-weary adults. During the Networked Learning Communities Programme on which we worked, John West-Burnham and George Otero described leaders like these building 'relational trust' (derived from Bryk and Schneider, 2002) which consisted of:

- *respect*: acknowledging one another's dignity and ideas;
- *competence*: believing in each other's ability to fulfil responsibilities;
- *personal regard*: caring about each other enough to go the extra mile;
- *integrity*: trusting each other to put children's needs first even in the face of tough decisions.

West-Burnham and Otero concluded that leaders who have this bridging disposition inside their schools will be well placed to integrate the differences that are endemic in complex systems, partnerships and communities (West-Burnham and Otero, 2006).

Andy Coleman, in his study of school-based partnerships (Coleman, 2011a), distinguishes between:

- *ideological trust*: the underpinning values and ethics of a potentially trusted individual;
- *behavioural trust*: the ways in which individual values and beliefs are evidenced in the behaviours and approaches of leaders;
- *perceptual trust*: how the trustor views the trustee, how leaders are *seen* to be or act, and how followers interpret and construct meaning from a leader's action.

Coleman argues that perceptual trust is an underestimated factor, and found that the leaders viewed as most trustworthy recognised the significance of even the most mundane action in promoting positive relationships with others – a profound echo of what we have called Advocacy.

Association in or outside schools draws deeply on aspects of the approaches we wrote about when we described the three elements of Navigation.

- *Acceptance*, we wrote, is their ability to accept, when necessary, that the school's practices might be regarded as a problem by other partners. That is not to say that these leaders always agree with the partners – though they build Association by treating partners' views with respect, seeking to understand and respond thoughtfully.
- *Advocacy*, we argued in Chapter 3, requires 'constructivist leadership' and the promotion of a 'living vision'. By taking personal modelling, professional

development, a learning orientation, a concern for improvement and the careful use of language from within to beyond the school, high-leverage leaders generate a strong sense of Association across local partnerships.

- *Awareness*, we wrote, means constantly anticipating the issues that need to be addressed. Just as in school, high-leverage leaders contribute to this in their other communities by helping to define and to hold the moral ground around which the shared activity is designed. They build Association by sharing responsibility with other leaders for scanning the political horizons so that collective work is not ambushed by initiatives and policy shifts.

Key approaches adopted by school leaders in the community cohesion enquiry (Mongon, 2010) can provide a framework for exploring how high-leverage leaders develop Association within their schools before they employ it more widely. These are:

- *a strong sense of purpose* with the quality of teaching and learning as the core contract with children and families;
- *an inextricable commitment* to both 'hard' and 'soft' outcomes, to children's attainment and to their well-being;
- *a seamless approach* to work inside or outside the school;
- *a sense of respect* without condescension for pupils and students;
- *a belief that the medium is the message* – the way that adults are treated and treat one another cannot be different from the way in which pupils are treated and are expected to treat one another.

A strong sense of purpose: teaching and learning

We have already identified 'sense of purpose' as a fundamental feature of the high-leverage leader's approach to their Navigation and Management roles. We want to reflect on how 'sense of purpose' works like a kind of gravity, invisibly holding the disparate elements of a group together and contributing to Association.

> 'The most important thing for the students is to have a good teacher in front of them, someone they can respect and who respects them, so that teaching, learning and behaviour improve hand in hand.'
> Paul Grant, Headteacher, Robert Clack School

High-leverage leaders are good at identifying the common purposes around which Association can develop. We have already proposed that in schools the common purpose is invariably and deeply rooted in the quality of teaching and learning. In our experience and research, the most effective school leaders have regarded teaching and learning as their core compact with the families and children to whom they are offering a service. It is less often and less well recognised that it is also the core of their compact with their adult colleagues and even with the providers of other services who depend on schools to do this well. For the adults and young people in the school, teaching and learning is the common, daily expectation that binds them together, even though other social or financial motives might contribute to the attraction. High-leverage leaders know that there are inputs other than direct teaching that can enhance learning and there are outcomes other than attainment which are evidence of good teaching. However, unless teaching and learning are good or better than good, these leaders know that their school is in breach of its compact irrespective of how creative other inputs are and however remarkable the other outcomes might be. These leaders repeatedly tell us that, in the economically poorest communities just as in the wealthiest, the majority of families will judge their school first by what happens in its classrooms and only secondly by anything else it achieves or to which it contributes. High-leverage leaders, we will show in Chapter 7, care a great deal about the formal judgements made by national and local government agencies, but they care at least equally about the informal verdicts reached by their local audience, the associate partnership composed of families, other community members and partner services.

Defining a 'common purpose' is likely to be more difficult when a partnership is more broadly based. A strength of high-leverage leaders is their preparedness to explore and to negotiate the purpose of external associations rather than to dominate them. They understand the need for what Huxham and Vangen (2005) call a formative approach to the purposes of partnerships. They understand the fundamental paradox at the heart of partnerships:

> The possibility for collaborative advantage rests in most cases on drawing *synergy from the differences between organisations*, different resources and different expertises. Yet these same differences stem from different organisational purposes and these inevitably mean that they will seek different benefits from each other out of the collaboration.
>
> (Huxham and Vangen, 2005, p. 82; our emphasis)

An inextricable commitment: both 'hard' and 'soft' outcomes

High-leverage leaders believe that 'hard' outcomes (predominantly students' measured attainment when they leave the school) and 'soft' outcomes (predominantly health and well-being) are inextricably linked. One of them, wondering why anyone would apply a greater priority to one than to the other, told us: 'Our commitment has to be to the whole child, helping them to become accomplished and comfortable with themselves' (Mongon, 2010, p. 3).

In Chapter 7, when we explore governance and accountability, we will consider in more detail how high-leverage leaders adapt external demands for 'hard' outcomes and also adopt broader outcome measurements for some of their work. Here, we want only to acknowledge the importance of this breadth in their work. They are pre-occupied with student attainment against national measures – they know that their licence to operate on a wider range of processes and outcomes depends on producing good results in those areas. But they are not overwhelmed by those measures. They do not lose sight of the complex connections between educational attainment, economic security, emotional wellbeing, personal lifelines, professional attitudes and neighbourhood experiences. They are constantly working on the items in that list that are within their direct sphere of influence and to mitigate the effects of those they cannot directly influence.

A seamless approach: inside and outside school

High-leverage leaders combine their commitment to the development of a young person in school with an interest in his or her experiences outside school. They see work with the community of parents and the wider neighbourhood as a natural and inevitable consequence of their work with the local children and young people. They have no sense of Association being an addition, still less an imposition. They understand that schooling is as much an intervention in family life as health or social care services. Schooling is a universal, taken for granted, continuous and less crisis-prone intervention but it is none the less an intervention. The lead on children's education is initially with their parents. Legally, ethically, and in practice, the school exists to help. High-leverage leaders know that schooling (compared to educating) can be a narrow enterprise and that educating (compared to schooling) is inevitably a joint enterprise. They see the school, parents, neighbourhood and other services as associate partners in the service of education. The associates each contribute time, venues, placements or other resources to create a curriculum, or indirectly influence the attitudes and ambitions of the children and young people. High-leverage leaders approach the creation of associations in ways which reflect their local circumstances but which contain the common threads being described here

> 'Working with parents and the community, is how you create the right atmosphere. It's not just the encouragement parents will then give their own children, it's the contribution different adults make, in different kinds of ways, to our curriculum offer.'
>
> Keith Whittlestone, Headteacher, Joseph Leckie School

A sense of respect for children: without condescension

Being a school community is synonymous, for these leaders, with treating pupils with constant respect. In our conversations we often struggled to work out whether high-leverage leaders were talking about children or adults or both. The moral ground they hold is a deep sense of shared humanity; their values embrace respect for other people whatever their age or status; their behaviour reflects those beliefs as consistently as they can manage and they have a profound belief in the potential for everyone to learn. Pupil voice, student councils, pupil self-evaluations, pupil lesson evaluations, student leadership, student evaluations of the service on offer – these are the descriptions of activity which we encountered frequently and which are also regularly acknowledged by school inspections for their positive impact. Valuing and nurturing the students' contribution to their own learning and to the development of the organisation permeates each of these schools, whatever the age or abilities of the young people.

> 'There is a good sense of control and they let you know they are in charge but they also care, celebrating what you do well and doing things outside the class for you and it makes you feel part of something.'
>
> Pupil at Robert Clack Secondary School

> 'Be respectful, don't be bossy. Listen, treat everybody equal not high rank and low rank, listen and pull people together. That's it for everybody here.'
>
> Pupil at Redbridge Secondary School

A belief that the medium is the message: do as you would be done by

Being a school community means, for these leaders, that the medium needs to be the message. The way that the adults are treated and treat one another cannot be different from the way in which they are expected to treat the pupils. Their care for the staff does not prevent these leaders having high expectations of their colleagues and some staff who cannot improve to an acceptable standard with the available support are helped, or even required to move on. However, it appears that the very large majority of the staff inherited by these leaders stay in post, working effectively, in some cases even more effectively than before. High-leverage leaders acknowledged the contribution and value of their colleagues. Their fundamental respect and concern for staff showed itself in many different ways from the school-funded end-of-term lunch (for adults once the pupils had left), through formalised lifestyle policies, and on to a professional development commitment that was common across the schools.

Beyond distributed leadership?

The five key features we have just described take high-leverage leaders beyond 'Distributed Leadership' – what Harris and Spillane (2008) have called 'the leadership idea of the moment' (2008, p. 13). Harris and Spillane describe Distributed Leadership as a perspective recognising that there are multiple leaders within and between organisations (p. 12). It acknowledges, they write, the work of all the individuals who contribute to leadership practice, whether or not they are formally designated or defined as leaders. Distributed models of leadership focus upon the interactions, rather than the actions, of those in formal and informal leadership roles. By that definition, high-leverage leaders certainly appear to be promoting some form of distributed leadership across their schools and the associated partnerships. We need, though, to be clear about what this means. Despite its current popularity in school leadership discourse, it seems to us that school leaders and some observers confuse distribution with delegation. A lack of conceptual clarity in some explanations and some contexts leads school leaders to believe they are distributing leadership when they are only delegating accountability. Our experience with high-leverage leaders has been very different.

It is tempting to describe high-leverage leadership as 'dispersed' rather than 'distributed'. John MacBeath (2008) has wondered whether 'dispersal' better represents the idea of a 'fertile environment' in which:

> … people, irrespective of status or rank, are prepared to assume responsibility according to the nature of the task, are able to take the initiative and respond creatively to meaningful change.
>
> (MacBeath, 2008, p. 42)

However, both 'dispersed' and 'distributed' imply that there is a clearly identifiable entity (leadership) that someone can either deal out (in the case of distribute) or scatter (in the case of disperse). We accept that there is a recognisable set of leadership and management activities and that there are circumstances in which those activities are dominated by a limited number of senior people. We will deal with that in more detail when, in Chapter 6, we consider the pathology of schools and the variations that different contexts can demand of the relationship between Navigation, Management and Partnership. We will suggest that high-leverage leaders will tend to disperse or distribute those leadership activities towards staff and students across the school, even though in some circumstances their initial approach has to be more directive and controlling. High-leverage leaders tell us that the improving health of a school can be measured by the movement of leadership across the school and its partnerships towards being a more 'intuitive, assumed, organic and opportunistic' activity. At that point, it appears to us, there is a step change in how leadership works which is beyond 'distribution' and 'dispersal'. Association, it seems to us, is closer to what MacBeath calls 'cultural distribution' (2008, p. 52).

Distribution becomes cultural, MacBeath writes, when people exercise initiative spontaneously and collaboratively, when the demarcation between leaders and followers becomes unclear (2008, p. 52). He uses 'symbiosis' to describe these reciprocal relationships in which there is an implicit give and take and a level of mutual respect. 'While delegation is expressed in "giving" responsibility to others or allowing responsibility by structural default, symbiosis has a more organic quality' (MacBeath, 2008, p. 53).

This 'intuitive, assumed, organic and opportunistic' approach matches our observations of how high-leverage leadership works. MacBeath writes that this might also be similar to the concept of social capital which Szreter (2004) calls 'bridging capital' in contrast to 'bonding capital':

> Whereas 'bonding' social capital tends to emphasize strong internal and mutual links, which can often be exclusive and become inward looking,

bridging social capital is characterized by many and weak links, a fluidity of relationships which is always alive to something new and challenging. In open, boundary-less relationships leadership moves fluidly and un-self-consciously among people.

(Szreter, 2004, p. 52)

In our view, MacBeath underplays the importance of what Szreter calls a special case of bridging capital, 'linking capital', which operates in contexts of which schools might be one example – where vertical, unequal power relations are inherent.

Linking capital takes on a democratic and empowering character where those involved are endeavoring to achieve a mutually agreed beneficial goal (or set of goals) on a basis of mutual respect, trust, and equality of status, despite the manifest inequalities in their respective positions.

(Szreter, 2004, p. 579)

To distil some insight from our observation of high-leverage leaders, we will build on what MacBeath (2008) calls 'collective intelligence and collective energy'. 'Distribution culturally sees the strength of the school as located in its collective intelligence and collective energy' (2008, p. 53). Alongside cultural distribution, collective intelligence and collective energy form recognisable features of what we are calling Association. Quite simply, they represent the sense of shared and focused insight, applied with purposeful excitement, which characterises the high leverage schools. To understand that, we want to consider:

- how 'collective intelligence and collective energy' emerge from the activity of high-leverage leaders;
- how the commitment of high-leverage leaders to Association helps them to move beyond either 'transformational' leadership based on charismatic individualism or 'managerial' leadership based on systems and structures;
- how high-leverage organisations move beyond distributed or dispersed leadership towards symbiotic leadership characterised by a web of associate partnerships.

Our exploration is influenced by writers – amongst them Peter Gronn (2000) and Gabriele Lakomski (2005) – who have asked radical questions about models of leadership which are based on heroic individualism or techno-structural managerialism. In broad terms, their argument is that, irrespective of what designated senior post-holders do or say, activities described as leadership are, in reality, always widely spread across any organisation. They claim that ideas about centralising or spreading leadership as if it were in the gift of one person or a small band of people need to be reconsidered.

Lakomski declares that her objective is '... to drive a wedge between people's every day, taken for granted understanding of leadership ... and to ask whether this understanding really squares with how leaders really work given what we know about human cognition and information processing' (2005, p. 139). She asks whether leadership is a distinguishable feature of organisational activity, even though she acknowledges the existence of exceptional Chief Executives: '... of course these gifted individuals do exist, or the idea of leadership would not have got off the ground in the first place' (2005, p. vii). Lakomski questions why so many of us readily believe in a causal link between organisational functioning and formal leadership when our own experience tells us that organisations are messily complicated and that those in positions of leadership are neither infallible nor omniscient. She links organisational change fundamentally to the durability of an organisation's cultural meanings and practices. Formal leaders may be as deeply embedded in these practices – in effect bound by them – as any other actors. Organisational culture, she writes, '... happens as the result of human interactions and shared experiences over time' (2005, p. 13). It is not independent of activity inside and across the organisation. Leadership, Lakomski argues, is therefore the emergent, self-organising property of complex systems dependent on distributed cognition to produce collective activity. The introduction of cognition into this argument points directly, of course, to learning as a key factor in leadership, a direction which Lakomski endorses. For us, that appears to be a significant echo of the importance attached by high-leverage leaders to the learning of everyone in their schools and what we described above as their creation of a 'learning zone' around their associate partnerships.

Gronn (2000) recognises merit in both individual (charismatic) and structural (managerial) perspectives on leadership, but argues that the tension between them is false. Although the personal and the systemic can be analytically distinct, they are fundamentally intertwined. Activity, what so-called 'leaders and followers' actually do, is the bridge that connects, and then can explain the connection between, the two. Gronn claims that, when people around schools talk about leadership, more often than not they are talking about 'headship'. They are then confusing influence (akin to what we have called Advocacy) with the exercise of formal authority (what we have called Application) by the most senior post-holder in a managerial hierarchy.

> ... the head individual who exercises overall responsibility becomes vested with a monopoly of influence. Thereafter an expectation solidifies that the chief authority figure or head is also, by definition, the leader.
>
> (Gronn, 2000, p. 33)

Gronn (2000) argues that leadership should be disentangled from any presumed, automatic connection with headship and that activity theory provides a means of tracking influence and leadership across an organisation. 'The activity system model at the heart of this approach forms a helpful and useful bridge between organisational structures and the actions of agents' (2000, p. 334). He is cautious about arguments that propose that organisations can be reduced to networks of distributed cognition or collective learning. These are important features, but not so important that they override other considerations. This is not least, Gronn writes, because of the need to resolve a profound paradox around what he calls:

> ... articulation and rearticulation ... coincident with the process of differentiating tasks into their subcomponents is the simultaneous requirement that these be reintegrated by means of coordination and control mechanisms. Task integration is a precondition of cooperative effort and effective conjoint activity, yet none of this work is called into play automatically.
>
> (Gronn, 2000, p. 334)

He concludes that it would be premature to remove leadership from the analytical equation, although it can be relegated to a contributory role while the foreground should be occupied by organisational work and labour.

High-leverage leaders intuitively harness the processes which both Lakomski and Gronn outline. They understand that, while personality-based leadership and techno-managerialism might be necessary processes, they are not sufficient to create sustainable momentum. Our earlier sections on Navigation with its strong personal features and Management with its strong systemic features illustrated their use of both those tactics. High-leverage leaders, using their Professional and Social Intelligence, Conscientiousness and Rapport, adopt tactics from personality-based or techno-managerial repertoires as circumstances require. Above all, they understand that, if new processes are not 'owned' by the large majority of the people being asked to apply them, they will be subverted and perish. No amount of charisma-fuelled 'followership' or target-driven servility can provide sustainable, positive development for an organisation. Their tendency towards Association is the medium through which they make leadership an explicit, permeating, cultural phenomenon and therefore an enduring contribution to the quality of processes and outcomes at the school.

High-leverage leaders are not disposed to treat leadership as something that can simply be given or taken away, either from adults or from children. They know that every member of the staffroom and every child in the playground is the leader of his or her own life and an influence in the lives of those who know them. Everyone has a hand in leadership by default. Design cannot take that away. High-leverage leaders know that widespread leadership can be overwhelmed (by personality) or overcome (by systemic management). They know that, even when that might be necessary, it is an exhausting and self-limiting tactic which cannot be maintained into the medium or longer term. High-leverage leaders therefore work to shift the culture of organisations from strongly held traditional views of headship towards distributed or dispersed leadership. They then nurture activity that leads both staff and students into cultural leadership and towards Association. They instil a belief that leadership is not something that formal post-holders have and can somehow allocate to other people if they choose. They develop Navigation and Management by allowing people to exercise the twin pillars of leadership – responsibility for their own lives and influence over other people's.

Alignment

> **Partnership**
>
> Modelling partnership: treating partners with equal esteem and deep respect
>
> Alignment: improving the alignment of the students' home and school experiences – without prejudice as to what changes and where

Our proposal is that high-leverage leaders minimise the dissonance between students' experiences in school and their experiences in the families and communities within which they spend the other 85 per cent or so of their time, as well as that between different providers working with children and their families.

High-leverage leaders recognise that the school, families, communities and other providers of services for children have potential to add value to one another's contributions while having their own limitations. They do not assume that the school has the best solutions to every question, though they might claim that '... schools are one of the few public institutions with both the capacity and the opportunity to generate social capital within the communities that they serve' (Flint, 2010, p. 4).They are open-minded enough to adapt their approach in pursuit of better outcomes. In our terms they are using their sense of Acceptance to begin creating Alignment across these different experiences.

Recurring evidence of the correlation between students' backgrounds and educational outcomes does not provide solutions to help practitioners break the negative connections, especially when commentators reach different conclusions about the causes. In England, most commentators in the quarter century after 1944 described the practices and cultures of some families as pathological, while schools and schooling were a taken-for-granted and generally virtuous factor in the equation. A second wave of explanation in the 1970s and into the 1980s focused on the practices and cultures of schooling as problematic and on schools as places where inequality was actively nurtured. A third, more recent wave focused on school effectiveness and school improvement. That approach has attempted to understand how the best schools work and to transfer their practices across the system so that every school can be successful. Over time this has been a journey that has put school leadership under increasing scrutiny.

In England, despite some improvement – fewer schools in difficulty, higher pupil attainment on average – there is still a disproportionate number of students from particular groups who are adrift of the national averages and a long way behind the highest attaining groups. For the interested reader, there is a large body of research exploring the different genetic, family, contextual and social factors which might contribute to creating gaps between those groups and others (see, for example, Sammons, 2007; Raffo *et al.*, 2007; Feinstein *et al.*, 2004; Rubin and Silva, 2003).

Although some of the identified factors are beyond the influence of individual schools, others are intrinsic to schools, either under their direct influence or even created by them. High-leverage leaders are fascinated by factors within and close to schools that they believe they can influence and of which the following three are illustrative:

- teachers' attitudes;
- parental engagement;
- the ambitions of young people.

Teachers' attitudes and expectations have been offered repeatedly as explanations for differential outcomes between economic and ethnic groups. The Pygmalion study (Rosenthal and Jacobson, 1968) gave iconic impetus to this field of research, but more recent work continues to find that deficit views of working-class children and their parents are deeply ingrained in the English teaching profession (Gazeley and Dunne, 2005, p. 18). Stereotypical expectations of minority ethnic children and the organisation of schools around majority norms also appear to be significant contributors to black students' disproportionate entry on vocational courses and to their higher exclusion rates and lower exam attainment (Gillborn, 2008).

Parental engagement with education is generally associated with higher outcomes for young people though there is some debate about what is meant by 'engagement' and how the dynamics of that lead to better outcomes (Feinstein *et al.*, 2006; Hills and Stewart, 2005). Parental support for education is generally strong, but many parents feel inhibited by their own lack of confidence and by the inaccessibility of schools, particularly secondary schools (Moon and Ivins, 2004). Because nearly all parents have positive general aspirations for their children (Cuthbert and Hatch, 2008, p. 3), it has been an act of faith for many school and children's service leaders to believe that a closer connection with families would lead to better outcomes for young people. The evidence is more tenuous. 'Spontaneous' parental involvement (in crude terms, a 'good home') is associated with positive outcome. In contrast, the evidence from 'enhanced' parental involvement (in crude terms, programmes to involve parents) is at best inconclusive, albeit showing high levels of appreciation from the adults involved (Desforges and Abouchaar, 2003). Desforges and Abouchaar (2003) conclude that this does not mean that parental involvement cannot be promoted: on the contrary, they write, if the best of what is known about parental engagement is applied, then real progress is possible.

The ambitions of young people are generally optimistic, irrespective of their ethnic or socio-economic background (DCSF, 2008b). Ambition, however, is woven from two threads: aspiration (what is hoped for) and expectation (what is realistically anticipated). For some young people these can become unhelpfully separated and low expectation often begins to dominate. This phenomenon has been explored in some detail by Cuthbert and Hatch (2008), who revealed its particularly corrosive implications during teenage years and, in England, within longstanding communities whose industrial economic base has disintegrated.

The recurring evidence is that young people without the material, cultural or symbolic (mainly adult and peer role models) resources to sustain success at school, manage that situation by lowering their requirements and needs. Their experience seeps into their attitudes and emotions (Jackson, 2006; Goldthorpe and McKnight, 2004; Raffo *et al.*, 2007; Sutton *et al.*, 2007; House of Commons, 2008, Para. 58; Wright and Weekes, 2003). Cuthbert and Hatch (2008) found that '... deprived communities are not all the same: young people in some very deprived communities have high aspirations' (2008, p. 7). They concluded that close-knit social networks, a sense of isolation from broader opportunities and a history of economic decline appear to be associated with low aspirations. The development of information, inspiration, self-esteem and self-efficacy for young people are, they write, the required solutions.

High-leverage leaders are implacable in their efforts to challenge low expectations, remove the barriers between schools, families and communities, enhance the mutually valuable connections between them and raise ambition across the threesome. In previous chapters we have described how they approach this with their professional colleagues. It is an approach that also requires the active participation of parents as complementary educators and of students as active learners. For high-leverage leaders, 'parents and students are agents, not consumers: their actions help constitute education as a public sphere' (Martin *et al.*, 2000). One of us has characterised this as a 'new story for education' (Leadbeater and Mongon, 2008). Martin and colleagues adopt a similar perspective:

> ... *a new professionalism*: evident, for example, in the pedagogies of active learning, the organisation of 'positive' approaches to school discipline and the reconstruction of the teacher's authority in respect of relationships with students, parents and community and colleagues.
>
> (Martin *et al.*, 2000, p. 127; our emphasis)

They conclude that leadership in these circumstances is characterised by '... the recognition of difference and the commitment to decision making through dialogue and shared understanding regarding the conditions and purposed of learning' (2000, p. 127). This sounds very much like what we would call Association, Advocacy and Alignment.

If that sounds self-evident or 'bog-standard' to some school leaders and researchers, it is because we cannot claim that high-leverage leaders have found a radical new approach to these issues. They are in tune with an approach that is available to, but not effectively adopted by, every school leader:

> ... diverse strategies and interventions are required that are based upon the particular needs and experiences of specific groups of boys and girls in particular contexts ... there is a need for educational interventions that are tailored much more directly to the particular needs and concerns of pupils in specific classes and schools.
>
> (Connolly, 2006, p. 16)

Connolly's conclusion echoes the findings of another study to which one of us contributed and which reported that the strategies adopted by schools which were improving in challenging circumstances '... were not a great departure from those adopted more widely in disadvantaged areas and are not restricted to schools in challenging circumstances' (Harris *et al.*, 2006, p. 419). In that study it was the selection and application of a combination of strategies tailored to local develop-mental need, context, and pupil configuration that proved critical. Each successful school had its own differentiated approach to deploying the common tactics.

This is not rocket science, but it is Alignment: high-leverage leaders sponsor creative and flexible engagement that makes staff, students and families feel valued and valuable. They repeatedly iron out the discontinuities between pupils' home and school experiences. Because Alignment is essentially based on Association, the practice that follows it will be contextually varied. A recent enquiry into parental engagement concluded that it was as varied and as diverse as the schools involved (National College, 2010d). However, the variation disguises some key operational principles. From 2008 to 2010, we worked with other researchers and a group of eight school leaders in an enquiry funded by the National College to explore the relationship between schools and their wider communities (reported fully in Mongon and Leadbeater, 2012). In addition to 'managing resources internally', which was held to be a foundation without which any other work haemorrhages credibility, that project identified four key tasks which we have also observed permeating the work of other high-leverage leaders:

- attracting more resources from within the community;
- dispersing resources into immediate social networks and families;
- investing resources to create social capital and capacity;
- making school resources available as the basis for community activity.

To a large degree these tasks are interdependent but, for our purposes, we will comment initially on the first two tasks and delay our reflection on the final two until the section on Area Focus (see page 101).

Attracting more resources from within the community

High-leverage leaders draw resources, time and energy in particular from within the local community towards the school, even from communities which at first sight appear to have very few resources to offer. They always see the potential of their parental and wider communities to contribute to the work of the school and align the expectations of teachers, families, students and neighbours.

Alignment has been helped – where schools have taken the advantage offered – by one of the most significant changes inside English schools during the term of the last government (1997–2010), the enormous increase in staff who do not have teaching qualifications (DCSF, 2009; DfE, 2010a). During this period the number of staff classified as 'teaching assistants' more than tripled (from 60,600 to 194,100), while other 'support staff' more than doubled (73,300 to 168,500). Staff not in teaching roles rose from being about a quarter of the school workforce in 1997 to 45 per cent in 2010.

While the creation of three or four jobs might not itself be a catalyst for profound change, high-leverage schools are like those reported by Craig (2005, p. 8): 'These schools have worked hard to craft gradual, accessible and reassuring pathways for their volunteers, from taster courses to local colleges, to greater responsibility within the school, to the chance of a full time job elsewhere.' High-leverage leaders purposefully recruit role models from the community around the schools and often from parents of pupils or ex-pupils. These local people are vital in the creation of linking capital. The stories they tell about the school and, in particular, about how it cares for their interests and development inevitably enhance or inhibit Alignment.

'We have parents, grandparents and other local adults working as volunteers in school. Then, workforce reform has changed the way we organise our staffing. Most of our staff can walk to work. That gives us chances to bring role models into classrooms and reflect our community. We can live our multi-cultural work day in and day out. We build social capital when local groups use our facilities and we also have good links with local churches and the mosque.'

Roy Souter, Stoke Hill Junior School

Reaching out to immediate social networks and families

High-leverage leaders do not just expect the community to contribute to the school, they are constantly looking out for opportunities to contribute to the community. This pays a double dividend: one to the school, in attendance, attitude and attainment; the other to the families and networks in, amongst other things, family learning and social cohesion. This work is not necessarily innovative or adaptive in its own right. Wilkin *et al.* (2003) concluded that there is an array of traditions of which the latest initiatives and funding schemes are only a modern manifestation. Schools, they reported, have always been a significant resource for their community although 'The enterprise, vision and energy that has gone into these developments, often in schools in difficult circumstances, has perhaps not been fully appreciated' (2003, p. 116).

High-leverage leaders do not do 'extended services' or 'big society', the buzz words of the previous and current UK governments – they are simply part of a tradition of doing what they think is necessary to educate and safeguard local children. Parenting Classes and 'Family Support Workers' are typical approaches linking parents and schools, but high-leverage leaders sponsor other positive encounters. The story told to us by the school leader who organised a bar for parents to follow Ofsted's meeting with them ahead of the school's inspection is not apocryphal, though it has to remain unattributable. The

Ofsted meeting was well attended and the 'us and them', 'don't underestimate our school' atmosphere owed something to the prospect of a party, but more to the sense of Association that had been built between school and families over several years.

Area focus

Partnership
Modelling partnership: treating partners with equal esteem and deep respect
Area focus: engaging with the wider community in a partnership role because for young people there is no 'one size fits all'

Our proposal in this section is that high-leverage leaders are adept at engaging with neighbourhood and professional communities beyond their schools so that these communities and the school become mutually supportive.

High-leverage leaders cultivate a network of associate partnerships around the school. They recognise that the school is not an island – that the surrounding world makes a difference to the school and vice versa. These associate partnerships include families, community representatives and other providers in a variety of combinations. The work of some of the partnerships is directly related to teaching and learning; others seem only marginally related to the school's core work. High-leverage leaders invest in, grow and draw on the social capital these partnerships produce.

The challenges which face high-leverage leaders and their associates in partnerships, particularly partnerships that bring together several service providers, can be summarised under seven headings (based on Close and Wainwright, 2010, pp. 443–6):

- *structural dilemmas*: schools are often metaphorically isolated by their habits and literally isolated by their campus walls;
- *ideological dilemmas*: schools are often seen by other agencies as institutions which have marginalised the issues of equity and social justice in pursuit of limited targets;
- *procedural dilemmas*: these are numerous and include apparently implacable rhythms of the timetable and academic terms;
- *inter-professional dilemmas*: views about status and hierarchy figure largely here;
- *human resource procedures*: the conditions of service vary between salaried groups, not all of whom are entitled to a long summer break;
- *political context*: different lines of accountability for different targets create different assumptions about priorities and working practices;

- *symbolic frame*: we noted in Chapter Three the importance of language as an agent for Advocacy and bonding an enterprise. This is more difficult when language varies between established groups.

Close and Wainwright describe the leadership which resolves these dilemmas as 'cultural leadership' using 'cultural conversations' in four key roles (2010, p. 447):

- leader as facilitator and coach – smoothing transitions and reducing resistance;
- leader as analyst and architect – planning partnerships and designing change;
- leader as visionary and storyteller – examining assumptions, establishing values, introducing routines;
- leader as advocate and negotiator – influencing agendas, distributing leadership, negotiating procedures.

We explained in Chapter 2 that we had developed the idea of Contextual Intelligence to describe an aspect of the leadership we encountered in our 'white working-class' research (Mongon and Chapman, 2008a). It is this, we propose, which drives what Close and Wainwright (2010) call cultural leadership. It is a recurring characteristic of high-leverage leaders, including:

- respect for the neighbourhood which is not patronising and can be critical;
- a purposeful option to work in a challenging context;
- often, but not always, a personal background shared with the pupils; and
- a commitment to equity and justice.

Their Contextual Intelligence is another contributor to Association – the inclination of high-leverage leaders to create bonds, alliances and social capital across an area. This is what makes Area Focus one of the key tools for high-leverage leaders understanding, as they do, that it has potential without ever being a panacea.

Serving a community in the north of Sheffield, the increasingly outstanding Yewlands Family of schools includes a Technology College, five primary schools and a special school.

'We had been doing bits and pieces informally together for a few years,' says Angela Armytage, the Head at Yewlands Technology College, 'when we realised we needed to make a step change in unison if we really wanted to serve this neighbourhood well. We knew that our governors, our leaders, our colleagues, even our parents and students could help one another and learn from one another, but we didn't have a framework for doing that.'

Nicola Shipman, now Executive Head of Monteney and Fox Hill Primary Schools and also a founder member of the Yewlands Family, explains: 'Everyone has a stake in everyone else's success, across and within phases as well as between the schools and the local community. If any of the schools or parts of the neighbourhood are unsuccessful, it eventually impacts on all our children. How could we serve the neighbourhood as a whole in isolation from one another?'

Nobody is ever an openly declared opponent of 'working across boundaries towards shared goals or a positive purpose'. It is another of those parenthood and apple pie 'good things' that can be so disappointing and frustrating in reality. There are always reasons to be circumspect about it. It always costs time, it usually costs money and it needs to pay a dividend. (We consider in Chapter 7 under Accountability and Governance how some of that might be explained and measured.) High-leverage collaborations establish common purpose, grow trust and manage tensions. They nudge the corporate and individual attitudes that, if mismatched, corrode the commitment of partners, inhibit practice and impair the development of shared knowledge. Attitudes towards learning, in particular, can play a critical role in deciding whether an organisation achieves collaborative advantage, or regresses into collaborative inertia (Huxham and Hibbert, 2006, p. 6). High-leverage leaders see advantage in collaboration, and Huxham and Vangen (2005, pp. 5–6) name four key advantages to suggest that they might be right:

- sharing resources if one organisation's resources do not match the task;
- sharing risk when the consequences of failure in a project are too much for one organisation to bear;
- efficiency, largely to be derived from economies of scale;
- coordination and seamlessness of different services, in particular when that is valued by the users.

Association is the approach that high-leverage leaders bring to their Area Focus. Their disposition to treat partners with respect and to build learning alliances tends, in the language of Huxham and his colleagues (2005, 2006), towards knowledge creation rather than knowledge transfer. They see learning as a prerequisite of area enterprise – which is an extension of how they regard their school enterprise. They prefer learning that is based on exchange or exploration rather than expansion or exploitation. That said, collaborations are sustained by a heady mixture of aims: explicit or implicit, selfish or altruistic, helpful or unhelpful, substantial or incidental, and so on. Sometimes the mixture can be inspirational, sometimes toxic.

Writing about collaborative and distributed leadership, Andy Coleman (2011b) highlights the synergies between, for example, distributed and relational leadership or authentic and constitutive leadership. He also draws attention to the tensions that infiltrate the best intentions – when collaboration is stifled by political management, or definitions of truth are ambiguous, or distributed leadership is designed to get others to do the dirty work. He concludes that it is not possible to entirely escape a focus on the daily practicalities that emphasise the prosaic nature of leadership. Like the leaders in Coleman's study, high-leverage leaders are disposed to enter collaborations with a disposition to Association, but they can, if circumstances absolutely demand it, be cunning and stubborn on behalf of their students and colleagues.

Focus on the community

There is good reason for high-leverage leaders to nurture a relationship with their local community.

> What sense does it make to try to reform urban schools while the communities around them stagnate or collapse? Conversely, can community-building and development efforts succeed in revitalizing inner-city neighborhoods if the public schools within them continue to fail their students? The fates of urban schools and communities are linked, yet school reformers and community builders typically act as if they are not.
>
> (Warren, 2005, p. 133)

Charting a history of disconnection between school improvement and community projects, Warren regrets that 'school leaders seldom see their school as one of a set of institutions that can anchor poor neighborhoods in partnership with other community organizations' (2005, p. 136).

High-leverage leaders avoid that disconnection by designing the relationship between their school and its community along two dimensions: the simple and practical alongside the complex and philosophical. Simply and practically, their school sits in a particular location, offers a teaching service to its young people and families, and needs to get on with it. On the other hand, they are sensitive to the complex and moral questions about what the service should be and how it should be delivered, including: 'who is the school for?', 'who owns it?' and 'what is its community?'

High-leverage leaders might well say their school is primarily for its pupils and students, then for its adult community of staff and parents, and finally for anyone whose learning and well-being can benefit from working together. That includes some younger and some older people, some in other schools, some who might benefit through their professional roles and some who do so through their domestic lives. The evidence confirms that approaches of that kind pay a dividend for schools and for communities. In the United States, community organising has created an opportunity for school-level improvement ...

> ... by building support and pressure for school restructuring, reduced overcrowding, new teaching expertise, new curriculum mandates, and additional supports for parent and community engagement.
>
> (Mediratta *et al.*, 2008, p. 6)

In turn, that has led to 'improved student outcomes in the form of higher student attendance, improved test scores, increased graduation rates, and higher college-going aspirations' (2008, p. 7).

Schools in England can also perform a key role 'in encouraging shared values and the development of social capital' through their creation of both 'bonding' and 'bridging' opportunities (Taylor, 2007). They have a direct effect on the social capital available to young people: '... both the composition of schools and the specific things that schools do can influence the development of young people's social capital' (Stevens *et al.*, 2007, p. 100).

Stevens and his colleagues concluded that 'the actions that schools took were important across all the dimensions of social capital ... [however] ... schools could achieve this in different ways' (2007, p. 101). They pointed towards 'a sense of school belonging', 'attitudes to social diversity' and 'social support' as the three key points of practice (2007, pp. 102–3). Although it is not well understood how education in turn contributes to civic engagement and social capital, education is ...

> ... a powerful generator of social capital ... more educated individuals tend to join more voluntary associations, show greater interest in politics and take part in more political activities. They are also more likely to express trust in others (social trust) and in institutions (institutional trust), and are more inclined to 'civic co-operation' – or at least to profess that they do not condone 'uncivil' behaviour.
>
> (Green *et al.*, 2003, p. 3)

If the high-leverage leaders' commitment to Area Focus is to a large degree personal and intuitive, it is also validated by the evidence above. Operationally it is visible in the last two of the four activities to which we referred on page 99:

- investing resources to create social capital and capacity;
- gifting school resources as a basis for community activity.

Investing resources to create social capital and capacity

High-leverage leaders invest school resources to help build wider social capital and cohesion. Whatever form these resources take, they still belong to the school, though they are less directly under its immediate control. This draws the school's partners together '... not as recipients of services, but as public actors and change agents, people capable of being leaders of their community' (Warren, 2005, p. 164). The activity is unlikely to pay an immediate or obviously direct dividend for the core work of the school. However, there is an expectation that the activity will have some knock-on benefit for pupils eventually and indirectly through improved well-being and cohesion across the community.

Bestowing school resources as the basis for community activity

High-leverage leaders might also bestow school resources on the community as a platform for activities that will generate community benefits, though again with little, if any, direct payback for the core work of the school. This activity draws deeply on the high-leverage school's sense of Association. It is a kind of corporate social responsibility aimed at creating the greatest possible public value from publicly funded assets. The activity might have some correlation with improvements in the school's achievement of targets, but it would be impossible to trace any causal effect. The value of the activity is expected mostly to spin out into the community and to pay, at best, a long-term dividend.

> 'Many of the adults around here don't have good memories of school and we need to persuade them onto the site and offer them good experiences when we do. We think that will begin to build some sense of ambition for themselves and of course for their children.'
>   Irene Nierzwicka, headteacher at Parkside Community Primary School, explaining the school's sessions for parent and carer training, ICT training, teaching assistant training, art lessons, dance classes, women's health sessions, weekly coffee morning for parents and carers, and re-invigorated parent–teacher association

Area Focus and Association with other schools and services

The Area Focus of high-leverage leaders extends to associating with other organisations whose work might contribute, directly or indirectly, to improved outcomes for local children and young people. In these Associations, the high-leverage leaders are well beyond the zone where their formal role is the basis for their authority. They are entering the spaces where it is more important to understand other service and sector cultures and to develop personal relationships than to depend on any formal authority from their titular position. Some of these Associations are built around groups of schools, some around a wider range of formal service and locality planning networks, and some are simply *ad hoc* arrangements with individual providers and services, including the voluntary sector. Such is the impetus in some of this work that the think tank Demos was moved to conclude:

> For many headteachers learning to extend their schools was the easy part. Already the best extended schools are learning to shrink – to build and depend upon the capacity of other organisations.
>
> (Craig, 2005, p. 10)

Our research into emerging patterns of school leadership (Chapman *et al.*, 2008, 2009; Mongon and Chapman, 2009) identified six key themes associated with success for area-based, adaptive leadership. These can be summarised as follows:

Aligned approaches

> Working together, a collaboration like this with schools and other partners, means you have to work out what you're talking about. Your view of the children, I mean the work and the language you use, is very important but it's not the only view.
>
> School leader and ECM manager

Area partnerships based on Association help schools to align individual and collective approaches around the full range of outcomes for children. Assimilated activities are not then a bolt-on to core teaching and learning work; they are integral to it.

Collaboration

> Without collaboration, our work would fall apart now. That attitude just permeates what we do, inside the school, across the Trust and with the community. It's become obvious really.
>
> School leader

There is a disposition amongst high-leverage leaders to promote collaboration within schools and across service boundaries. Collaboration with a challenging edge characterised their work with teachers, students, families and the wider communities.

Internal and external motivation

> While you have to focus on attainment, well-being and enjoyment are things which good schools should be doing without having to tick boxes. You don't need to be told what to aim for, though you might need some help doing it.
>
> Academy principal

Successful associations are not ends in themselves. They are not a reflex reaction to external agendas nor are they additional and bolt-on. They are self-generated and deep-rooted. They are part of an iterative process in which the rethinking and reconceptualising of practice promotes new structures, which in turn provide the basis for reconsidering practice. Consistent improvement in outcomes for the young people is the well-thought-out common purpose.

Internal and external effort

> I've had to learn not to deal with all the detail. I have a Head of School and a Manager for Extended Services to do that, so my role is to work on the connections and the overview.
>
> School leader

Internal effort often includes, for example, the reallocation of key responsibilities and accountability inside a school. It might also include the creation of new working practices and the redefinition of roles. External effort might include, for example, the financing of capacity – a post perhaps – to coordinate or manage a strategic partnership.

Innovation at school and system level

> I cannot imagine how we would meet the needs of our pupils and their families if we didn't work the way we are doing, if we didn't have the school federation and the community links …
>
> School leader

Theories of 'education epidemics' (Hargreaves, 2003b) or 'tipping points' (Gladwell, 2000) are important but partial explanations of the uneven and lumpy way that innovation and knowledge transfer across the system. In difficult circumstances, schools that are intrinsically motivated and are rethinking practice appear to sponsor school innovators and system innovators in their approach to local solutions.

Leadership development for the future

> She understands school systems, professional performance and student outcomes. I'd work in a school where she was headteacher.
>
> Teacher describing SLT member without a teaching qualification

> I thought I'd always be happiest teaching, but this is an unexpected revelation.
>
> School leader and extended services manager

These school leaders purposefully provide opportunities for other people to engage with the strategic leadership inside and outside school. People are supported to step beyond boundaries set by traditional expectations and qualifications.

To set up these features in associations across institutions (Mongon *et al.*, 2010, p. 32), high-leverage leaders:

- *ensure leadership sponsorship* by being a vigorous advocate, freeing staff to act, creating a no-blame culture and emphasising 'our' not 'your' children;
- *create and sustain relationships* by building a common language, nurturing trust and belief, seeking views and establishing common ground;
- *focus on outcomes* by gathering knowledge, using information, interrogating data, being clear about what makes a difference and linking purpose with practice;
- *create interdependence and watch the big picture* by having an ambitious vision, planning strategically, recognising service connections and building robust frameworks for the work;

- *facilitate others* by making space and time for them to plan, actively listening irrespective of status and creating equity in conversation;
- *show courage and commitment and build trust* by being honest, taking risks, admitting mistakes, asking for advice, demonstrating empathy and dealing with issues not personalities.

The leaders who drew up this list also highlighted the need for creative energy, the need to find adaptive solutions to persistent and quite common problems. Typically, the barriers they described included personal and institutional protectionism, separate funding streams or budget reporting, lack of supportive local or national leadership, health and safety issues and bureaucracy in general. The solutions described by the leaders were often imaginative, sympathetic and necessarily off-the-record.

> Across the 11 sites, the leadership's focus on what the adults should do in the best interest of the children allied to self-belief and determination demonstrated that any and all of those barriers can be manoeuvred aside. The levers of energy, creativity and expertise were sometimes literally in the hands of the leaders.
>
> (Mongon *et al.*, 2010, p. 18)

In these contexts, high-leverage leaders of increasingly autonomous schools in England are often stepping into the spaces created as local authority capacity evaporates. They are drawn into the brokerage roles identified as a requirement for successful networks in another of the projects to which we contributed. In broad terms (National College, 2006a) these are:

- *brokering membership* by raising awareness, generating interest, building a sense of shared purpose, articulating the compelling idea and promoting inclusivity;
- *brokering internal relationships* by focusing on the collective development work, helping to design the right activities, building trust, exploring shared values and developing a cadre of leaders across the associates;
- *brokering external connections* by supporting links with other organisations, horizon scanning for national developments and facilitating links with organisations which operate outside the locality;
- *brokering access to resources* by providing some capacity from their own resources, offering to be the fund-holder or notional contract holder for the *Association* when needed and acting as a conduit for funds from outside;
- *brokering learning and knowledge-exchange* by expanding access to knowledge and ideas, encouraging disciplined enquiry and developing the use of evidence towards the common purpose.

In the same report (2006a, p. 7) a broker is described as 'an intermediary or matchmaker engaged in the "acquisition of obligations" from different parties in a purposeful relationship'. That is not the most elegant way to describe what high-leverage leaders do, but it does capture how they apply their sense of Advocacy in Associations where they have no constitutional power.

High-leverage leaders are faced with 'adaptive challenges' that cannot be solved by direct reference to previous experience, authoritative sources or 'standard operating procedures' (Fullan, 2004). These challenges have to be solved by experiment, discovery and adjustment across their institution that permeate the systems beyond. These are explorative tactics that inevitably bring their own risks. High-leverage leaders recognise what Huxham and Vangen (2005) call 'collaborative advantage' as a way to augment resources, to share risk, to improve efficiency and to coordinate seamless services. Faced with the challenges we have described, they are drawn by both intuition and intellect towards Partnership with its constituent activities of Association, Alignment and Area Focus as the solution.

6 Organisational pathology and high-leverage leadership

Introduction

The previous chapters have set out the argument for high-leverage leadership. In Chapters 3, 4 and 5 this has involved an in-depth analysis of the core dimensions of Navigation, Management and Partnership. In Chapter 6 we move on to explore the relationship between navigation, management and partnership, improvement and school context, arguing that different emphases are required for schools at different stages of development. First we put the case for context specific improvement. This case is well rehearsed in the literature. A decade ago, Hopkins (2001, p. 59) noted:

> Authentic school improvement strategies need to pay attention to context … a wider range of improvement options should be made available to schools and more intelligence used in linking improvement strategy to need.

As long ago as fifteen years, Stoll *et al.* (1996, p. 141) argued for a more differentiated approach to school improvement involving:

> … combinations of improvement and effectiveness practices and strategies appropriate to the nature of individual schools. For a school that is ineffective and just starting the process of development, the strategies may be different from a school that has been developing for some time.

However, during the interim period, practice has tended to lag behind the research evidence of academics and the rhetoric of politicians. We draw on three contemporary examples where policy and practice has shifted to support context-specific approaches. We then move on to argue that, in schools in crisis or meltdown, the focus needs to be on Management, in particular on an analysis of the situation followed by quick and targeted action for short-term improvement. However, the managerial emphasis must not stifle Navigation and Partnership, or it becomes impossible to build the capacity for medium- and longer-term improvement, and the organisation's initial progress will stall. The managerial action must build bridges into 'Navigation'. This process is more than 're-tuning the machine', it is about confidence and capacity building, about developing a shared understanding of organisational priorities and an acceptance that current practice and relationships may be a barrier to improving outcomes.

We argue that, as capacity develops, the key task becomes balancing the focus between Navigation and Management and developing Partnership. Ultimately, for the high-capacity school to sustain improved outcomes for children, Partnership tasks must foreground both Navigation and Management activity. As 'managerial' activity decreases and 'navigational' activity increases, Partnership activity tends first to dip and then to increase again. Over the same period, the nature of the partnership activity changes from an emphasis on partnerships creating momentum for internal, institutional change to partnerships sharing capacity for attainment, well-being and community cohesion.

Understanding school pathology and capacity for change

Raising educational standards has become central to many governments' manifestos. This has led to an intensive focus on improving educational systems in diverse settings. In England, for example, we experienced wave after wave of national reform, including National Literacy and National Numeracy strategies, and National Challenge. In the United States, similar approaches have contributed to Race to the Top and No Child Left Behind, while, in Uganda, school development planning has become a focus for improvement effort. All this change has involved considerable investment of resources. In England alone, before the economic crash, government spending on national programmes and local authority support for school improvement (not including the Academies Programme) rose to £1,162 million in one year (2004–2005). This investment and its associated research and evaluation activity has created a knowledge base about what works and why in a range of educational settings. However, despite the investment and knowledge, we continue to see significant variations in student outcomes within schools and across systems. Put simply, given such investment in improving educational standards, it is somewhat disappointing that the particular school a child goes to and the specific teachers who teach them continue to play an important role in determining a child's academic outcomes and ultimate life chances.

Our response to the challenge of tackling these variations in performance and outcomes is that we must resist viewing schools as self-contained units, operating as a technical-rational machine irrespective of context. This requires policymakers to move beyond their current understandings of educational reform and school improvement. The idea that, because an intervention has 'worked well' in one context, it must be replicable in another, albeit similar, setting is flawed. For example, attempting to transplant a successful school improvement intervention from Harlem, USA, to Kent in England is likely to be difficult because of the nuance of the specific contexts in which the intervention was developed. Even if you take the international dimension out of the equation and attempt to replicate from one location to another in the same country, this is likely to be problematic, and the results patchy. One size *does not* fit all. The rhetoric for more finely tuned approaches, sensitive to specific contexts, is strong. However, for the most part, the pace of change and the desire to 'move to scale' demand simplistic blanket interventions. These tend to be interpreted, adapted, subverted or rejected in their implementation at the local level. This may sound promising – the locality deconstructing and reconstructing externally imposed change to suit its context is a form of context-specific improvement. Where it works, there is some merit for this approach. However, at best, results remain patchy, determined by leadership capacity at the local level. All too often it is the more effective schools with high-leverage leaders who have the confidence and capacity to adapt, subvert or reject, leaving others who are less sure of themselves or under more external scrutiny to implement without question, for fear of reprisals from the inspectorate or government officials.

Some recent attempts to foster 'context-specific' improvement in England have involved the development of an overarching, centrally imposed set of 'guiding principles', 'frameworks' and 'activities', supported by monitoring and critical friendship designed to provide 'space' for local innovation within a coherent framework.

The Extra Mile initiative in England was a Department for Children, Schools and Families (DCSF) project designed to raise the achievement of children from socio-economically disadvantaged areas. In the first instance, DfES advisors undertook a series of school visits to identify effective strategies for raising the achievement of this group of children. They used this information to compile a menu of areas of focus that seemed to be particularly successful in primary and secondary settings. For primaries these were:

- providing a coherent curriculum with a strong focus on speaking and listening;
- engaging pupils in their learning;
- helping pupils to articulate and manage their emotions;
- broadening pupils' horizons by providing a wide range of stimulating activities;
- providing support at transition points;
- recruiting, developing and retaining staff with empathy for the pupils and their backgrounds;
- promoting and valuing partnerships with parents/carers and the local community.

And for secondaries:

- promoting and valuing partnerships with parents/carers and the local community;
- increasing interactive and participatory learning;
- developing a listening campaign which responds to pupil and parent perceptions;
- promoting a culture of respect for local people, local culture and local values;

- broadening pupils' horizons by offering experience and opportunities they would not otherwise have;
- developing a culture of 'achievement' and 'belonging' in school;
- offering a more relevant curriculum;
- building pupils' repertoire of spoken and written language;
- developing pupils' social, emotional and behavioural skills;
- cultivating traditional values of respect, good behaviour and caring;
- tracking pupil progress and intervening promptly if they fall off the trajectory;
- developing effective rewards and incentive schemes;
- supporting pupils at important moments in their lives, especially transition points.

Schools were provided with guidance materials by the Department and a link advisor to support the design of their own approach to raising the achievement of children from socio-economically disadvantaged areas. The evaluation of this initiative is encouraging. The quantitative evidence suggests:

> There was a 20 point difference in favour of the EM group, statistically significant at the 5% level. This is equivalent statistically to compensating for one – but only one and not any combination – of the effect of FSM or 22% adverse deprivation on the IDACI scale or an 8% absence rate.
>
> (Chapman *et al.*, 2011, p. 21)

The evaluation concludes that the intervention provided a framework for improvement without being prescriptive:

> EM [Extra Mile] provided an agenda for engagement, and an overarching framework for change without being interpreted within the schools as another top-down, centrally imposed directive … the EM approach encouraged schools to reflect on their context and the action they will take to improve the situation. This 'socialised' the issues through conversation and internal (and in some cases external) collaboration. This built ownership at the school level from early on in the project.
>
> (Chapman *et al.*, 2011, p. 59)

Another example where a framework has been used to support a more context-specific approach to school improvement is the City Challenge initiative, also devised by the DfES. The initial intervention, involving a programme of intervention and support, was established in 2003 and was designed to improve outcomes in low-performing secondary schools in the London. The London Challenge has been acknowledged as a successful intervention, and 2010 school data highlight London's secondary schools continuing to outperform the rest of England on some indicators, including the number of students who achieve five good GCSEs including English and Maths. Only 1 per cent of schools in London remain below government floor targets (Ofsted, 2010b).

In 2008 the Challenge was extended to two other major conurbations, the Black Country in the West Midlands and Greater Manchester in the North-West of England. Both of these regions had similar issues to London, with pockets of excellence in some areas combined with a history of under-performance and low aspirations in others. Rather than attempting to replicate the London Challenge by 'moving up the M6 [a major highway linking London to the Midlands and the North-West]' (Woods, 2009), these initiatives took some successful practice from the London Challenge and combined them with approaches designed specifically for each region.

Strategic leaders in these two regions invested considerable time during the start-up period in understanding the context and characteristics of the London Challenge, focusing on which elements of the model would be likely to transfer directly to the new areas, which elements might work with some adaptation, and which were inappropriate. For example, The Greater Manchester Challenge invested heavily in promoting 'families of schools' as a collaborative approach to school improvement, while the Black Country initiative showed less interest in this idea. The 'Families of Schools' concept involves creating groups or 'families' of schools that share similar socio-economic characteristics. A report detailing school characteristics and results is published each year, the purpose of which is to facilitate comparison of similar types of schools and to identify schools that seem to be doing very well, often against the odds. Strategies can then be put in place to move knowledge and practice about what works in particular contexts across the family. Schools in each family are placed on a graph along the dimensions of attainment and improvement (see Figure 6.1). This highlights schools in the family that are high achieving and improving, or high achieving but not

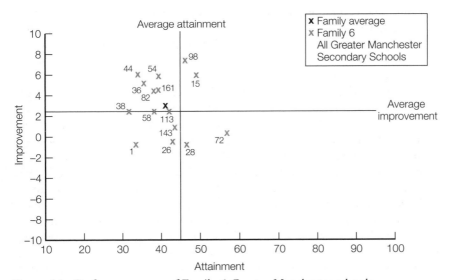

Figure 6.1   Performance map of Family 6 Greater Manchester schools

improving, as well as those that are low achieving but improving and those that are low achieving and not improving.

This analysis provides a stimulus for discussion and a starting point for celebrating success and challenging underperformance. While this approach is no panacea and can't account for the unique attributes of a school context, it offers a promising way forward. In Manchester this has led to City Challenge Advisers working with individual schools, and headteachers working together in their families to develop context-specific improvement initiatives matched to individual schools' leadership capacity and capacity for change. This approach has been a welcome development from the barrage of top-down, centrally imposed initiatives that have tended to dominate discourse over the past decade or so.

In reflecting on the failure to change schools in challenging urban areas in Chicago, Payne (2009) points to the 'ahistorical, nonsociological, and decontextualized thinking that dominates this discourse' (2009, p. 45). He argues that, if we took the time to understand the history, sociology and context, we would not continue with policies underpinned by increased accountability and by the search for better paid and high-quality teachers in a market oriented system. Payne argues that The Consortium on Chicago School Research framework offers a different way of thinking about these issues. The Consortium promotes context-specific approaches to improvement through a framework based on five principles:

1 Instructional leadership, based on principles of instructional and mutual trust;
2 Professional capacity, where continuing professional development, collective responsibility and a shared language about teaching and learning are valued as core elements of improvement;
3 Learning climate, involving positive staff–student relationships and high expectations;
4 Family and community involvement, based on effective communication and an awareness of the nature of human and social resources in the community;
5 Quality of instruction, including intellectual challenge and academic engagement.

The three approaches outlined above offer interesting and potentially fruitful ways forward if we are to move beyond standardised approaches to school improvement that fail to recognise and attend to the nuances of individual school contexts. The three approaches can be internalised by schools to generate improvement efforts matched to their particular needs and phase of development.

In previous work (Chapman, 2006) we have used a typology of school development phases based on the dimensions of teacher culture and the nature of professional relationships. In those schools (Type A schools) in the most difficult circumstances – schools in crisis with negligible capacity – teacher culture tends to be individualised within a context of autonomous professional relationships and teachers have no accountability for their work. Here survival is paramount; teachers watch their own backs and control what they can without attempting to spread their sphere of influence. There is no collective responsibility. Remarks heard in the staffroom tend to be along the lines of 'Oh, I've never had any problems with him/her/that group.' These schools are likely to be judged 'failing' at their next inspection. The leadership found in these schools is likely to be 'failed heroic' or 'laissez faire'. Common features of a Type A school include:

- lack of planning and coordination;
- high levels of teacher frustration;
- large variation in quality of practice;
- weak discipline;
- low levels of challenge to students;
- weak leadership;
- formation of cliques.

Low-capacity schools (Type B schools) are likely to be "failing schools" that have started on their road to recovery, or they may have been identified as having 'inadequate' or 'satisfactory' features. The teacher culture remains rather individualised, but the professional relationships are highly centralised. Insert Sharp accountability mechanisms pervade the discourse. Senior managers invest considerable time monitoring teaching and learning by scrutinising lesson plans and observing lessons against inspection criteria. The aim here is to eradicate unsatisfactory teaching and learning and put appropriate structures and systems in place to make the school a more effective organisation and achieve some 'quick wins'. For those Type B schools with a history of failure there is likely to be a new senior leadership team in place and there may have been significant staff turnover. Senior leaders often look to external partners for solutions in an attempt to 'jump start' improvement efforts. The school begins to become data rich, but the information tends to be held in the hands of senior managers rather than mid-level leadership or classroom teachers. The leadership in these schools is likely to tend towards the autocratic and to be perceived as rather heroic. The key features of Type B schools include:

- a top-down approach to change;
- high levels of whole-school monitoring;
- SMT and teachers' construction of 'reality' is polarised;
- a focus on the mechanistic;
- structured formalised planning;
- data-rich at a whole-school level;
- low levels of CPD;
- low levels of risk-taking.

In terms of school improvement or development phases, these are *young schools*. As confidence and capability increase and relationships develop between staff, we see the emergence of a more collaborative teacher culture. Teachers begin to develop a shared language about pedagogy and discuss students in a more positive light. This signals a significant advance in the school's development. These are features of a medium-capacity school (Type C). Professional relationships remain relatively centralised, although mid-level leaders play an important role. Departments become data-rich and mid-level leaders are increasingly responsible for capacity building within their departments and the CPD of their staff. Leadership becomes spread across the school rather than residing with a small group of senior managers. This phase of development is often very testing for the headteacher. For some of those charged with 'turning the school around', distributing authority and releasing control can be a challenge. However, heads who fail in this respect may quickly become inhibitors rather than facilitators of the capacity building process. This is an equally testing time for mid-level leaders. These leaders often feel squeezed. On the one hand they are pressurised by the new demands and expectations of senior leadership and on the other they are having to reconfigure their relationships with colleagues in their department by developing new systems and ways of working which challenge traditional notions of the role of the head of department as the individual responsible for resources and policy development. Leadership in these schools tends to be distributed in its nature. Common features of a Type C school include:

- devolution of monitoring to middle management;
- middle management makes significant contributions to the SDP/SIP;
- predominantly mechanistic view of teaching and learning;
- highly stressed middle management;
- training and development needs starting to be addressed.

In terms of school improvement and development phase, these are *adolescent schools*.

As relationships in departments and other sub-units develop, collaborative cultures intensify. There is a critical moment when the centralised professional relationships based on formal accountability mechanisms are recognised as outmoded and become viewed as a barrier to change and guardians of the status quo. This signals a shift into the fourth phase of development in which the school is becoming a high-capacity school (Type D). This is not to say that, as relationships become more autonomous, accountability becomes less important or diminishes. It changes its nature. Teachers and colleagues work for each other out of a sense of professional duty and for the collective good of the students. This leads to a more informal set of accountability mechanisms that are viewed as developmental rather than punitive in nature. So it is common to see teachers working collaboratively in lesson study groups or in educational rounds with colleagues from other departments and other schools. The school community spends more time looking to other schools and agencies for ideas and relationships that challenge the assumptions and cultural norms that have developed within the school. The school is awash with data, information being held by teachers and ultimately by students and used to inform individual learning pathways. Students play an increasingly active role in the life of the school. They feed into the refinement of the teaching and learning process, they are involved in appointments and performance management decisions. The teachers and students play an important role in the leadership of the school. In contrast to the authoritarian leadership in Type B schools at the start of the capacity building process, the leadership in Type D schools could be described as democratic. Common features of a Type D school include:

- a focus on organic growth;
- temporary membership of teams involving staff from all levels of the organisation;
- diversity of teaching practices;
- data richness at individual pupil level;
- teachers and pupils have a voice in the SDP/SIP;
- high levels of CPD;
- strong external partnerships, frequently involving sharing expertise and capacity with others and using links to challenge and generate ideas.

In terms of school improvement and development phase, these are mature schools. Figure 6.2 outlines the four phases. They can be viewed as a journey in which a school grows in maturity, moving from one phase to another, or in terms of a shift in perspectives on improvement, from one where tactical approaches dominate to a state in which strategic and ultimately sustainable approaches become the norm. Clearly, these are not mutually exclusive, and a blend of these approaches is likely to be in operation at any one time. As Hargreaves and Shirley (2009) note, short-term tactics must be combined with more strategic approaches if schools are to move forward.

Reculturing and restructuring underpin activity in each phase of improvement. The key to understanding the improvement process here is that both reculturing and restructuring are achieved through constantly redefining and reconstructing relationships in the organisation and in the wider system. Progress is impossible without understanding school improvement as a social process, concerned with building a strong and purposeful organisational culture that is underpinned by trust and mutual respect. However, the focus of improvement activity changes as the school matures. Young schools at the start of the journey tend to use tactical improvement approaches to generate quick responses to immediate challenges, and deliver visible changes to the environment. The adolescent school uses strategic improvement to build capacity to raise confidence and capability in the school. Finally, the mature school focuses on moving ideas and practice across organisational boundaries in order to sustain improvement.

In a similar vein to the requirement for context-specific approaches to improvement, tailored to each phase of development, school leaders need to draw on their professional and social intelligences to match their leadership approaches to each particular phase of development. As noted above, if their approaches are not in harmony with where the school is, the leader may become a barrier to change.

As these stratified leadership approaches evolve to reflect the needs, capacities and opportunities faced by the school, high-leverage leaders draw on Navigation, Management and Partnership at different times and in different forms to strengthen their school's capacity to manage change and sustain the trajectory of improvement.

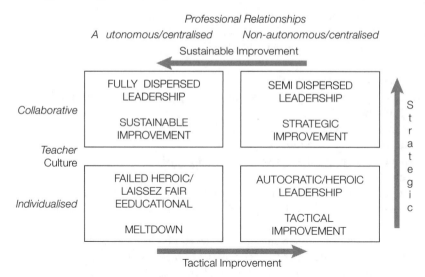

Figure 6.2 Leadership and improvement in challenging circumstances

Source: Chapman, 2004, p. 105.

Understanding the relationship between capacity for change and Navigation, Management and Partnership

The previous section highlighted the importance of understanding the improvement process and of developing improvement approaches that are matched to a school's unique context. In this section we move on to consider the relationship between context specific improvement and high-leverage leadership by focusing on Navigation, Management and Partnership. High-leverage leaders not only spread their leadership sequentially across their institutions, they adjust the focus and effort they place on Navigation, Management and Partnership as the school moves from adolescence to maturity.

Figure 6.3 shows the relative effort and focus high-leverage leaders place on Navigation, Management and Partnership as a school builds greater capacity for improvement and change management. At the left of the figure, for a *young* Type B school where capacity is low, high-leverage leaders tend to respond to the intensity of this situation by focusing their efforts on Management and Navigation activity. High-leverage leaders use Management to assess the situation through sharp analysis and a quick response, combined with action and on-going application to restructuring, putting systems in place to create the conditions for improvement. These leaders use Navigation to raise awareness and gain an acceptance that action is needed to challenge entrenched cultural norms of low aspirations and expectations. Advocacy is used to create a shared responsibility and vision about how this may be achieved. High-leverage leaders use Partnership to draw in expertise to reinforce their arguments. This often involves bringing in external consultants to support reculturing – challenging assumptions and behavioural norms and supporting restructuring and to set up and support new systems.

As a school moves into adolescence, becoming a Type C school, the relative focus and effort high-leverage leaders give to Navigation, Management and Partnership changes. For Management and Partnership, focus and effort decline. As management structures and systems become embedded and internal confidence and capability increase, management routines become more self-sustaining and require less attention. The initial burst of external partnership activity to challenge existing practice and stimulate change is no longer required. The focus of partnership activity is on developing new partnerships within school so that emerging new practice can begin to be shared across the school. The focus on Navigation is intensified. The reculturing of the organisation involves high-leverage leaders working tirelessly to raise awareness and acceptance of the vision and provide further advocacy and opportunities for colleagues.

As a school develops further capacity and exhibits the features of a mature Type D school, high-leverage leaders once again shift their focus in some areas. The focus and effort expended on Navigation continue to rise, but leadership's attention shifts away from the internal arrangements to drive school improvement and towards supporting improvement of the locality and the wider system. This is represented by a darkening of the Navigation line in Figure 6.3. High-leverage leaders in mature organisations are often searching for their next challenge. This may involve secondments, increased external consultancies with other agencies, or taking on leadership roles in other organisations. This is closely linked to partnership focus and activity. Partnership also rises as high-leverage leaders and their colleagues make new connections around the system. Partnership is not viewed as the preserve of the high-leverage leader; rather, it is an opportunity for all to share and develop their expertise and extend their professional networks. This opens up space within the organisation for others to

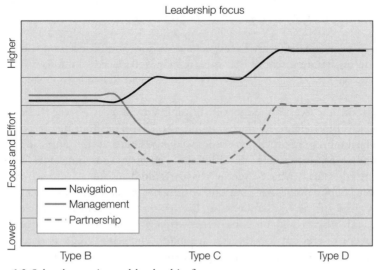

Figure 6.3 School capacity and leadership focus

take on additional leadership responsibility. The energy invested in Management continues to decline, and this decreased focus is illustrative of the progress the school has made. What was once a challenging developmental activity for a low-capacity school now goes largely unnoticed in the high-capacity school. All runs smoothly, with the exception of some low-level maintenance.

In summary, the major shift in emphasis for high-leverage leaders in mature schools is to partnership working, in which leaders scan the environment for new associations with other schools and agencies to further improve the range of experiences the school can offer its pupils and the wider community.

School capacity and *Navigation, Management* and *Partnership* in practice

In order to illustrate high-leverage leadership in action we draw on a case from our White Working-Class and New Models of Leadership projects (Mongon and Chapman, 2008a; Chapman *et al.*, 2009). By the time this research was conducted, Bartley Green School had moved from a Type A to Type D school under the leadership of one headteacher. High-leverage leaders are not fly-by-night leaders who flit from school to school after short periods of success. They tend to work in one school for a considerable period of time and often become very attached to the school and locality. At Bartley Green the headteacher had been promoted from deputy head of another school in the area to lead 13 years of continuous improvement in pupils' achievement and attainment. In 1994 only 9 per cent of students left with five good GCSEs (A*–C) compared to 77 per cent in 2007 (48 per cent including English and Maths), 79 per cent in 2008 and 90 per cent in 2009 (51 per cent including English and Maths). In 2007 Bartley Green School's CVA (contextual value added score) was 1079, the second highest in England. Bartley Green is the archetypal Type D school in challenging circumstances. As one HMI reflected:

> Anyone associated with Bartley Green School should be proud, because it is an outstanding school that is extremely well placed to improve further.
> (David Rzeznik, in Ofsted, 2008c)

Located on the western edge of Birmingham, Bartley Green School is in one of the most deprived wards within the city. The housing stock includes a significant proportion of low-rise social housing and the area suffers from significant socio-economic disadvantage, poor health indicators and low levels of education, which together have resulted in limited employment and economic opportunities. Aspirations within the community are generally low. Over a third of the 883 students at Bartley Green are entitled to free school meals, and most would be considered working-class. Boys outnumber girls – 60 per cent of students on the roll are male. The school reports that many of the pupils have never visited the countryside or an art gallery, or even been to Birmingham city centre.

Navigation, Management and Partnership in Type B settings

High-leverage leaders focus their attention on Management and Navigation in Type B settings. When the new headteacher arrived at Bartley Green (narrative from Harris *et al.*, 2002) there were considerable variations in the quality of teaching and learning, and the view of some of the staff was 'what can you do with these types of children?' This was an indication of a culture of low expectations and an acceptance that low educational standards were a likely outcome for most of the children in the school. The core belief of the headteacher was that improvement started and ended in the classroom. If conditions could be created whereby teachers could teach and students could learn, then the school would get better. The headteacher used Management to analyse the situation and diagnose what needed to be done. Action was underpinned by consistent application. For example, student behaviour was identified as an issue. This ranged from consistent low-level disruption in some classes to serious and explosive incidents in others. A system for behaviour management was developed and put in place. Discipline for Learning involved depersonalising sanctions for specific behaviours. Each student would start with 20 points and could lose a designated number of points for particular behaviours. For example, chewing gum or eating in a lesson would trigger a 2-point sanction. A 3-point sanction would trigger a letter home and a detention. When a student had lost all their points they would be placed in 'time out', where they would be set work and be removed from school at social times – they would have their break and lunch alone at different times to the rest of the school. Discipline for Learning reports for each student were printed off at the end of each week and discussed in tutorial time. Those students who did not lose points were rewarded for their good behaviour. The archiving system supported the tracking and monitoring of students and the identification of lessons and subject areas with high levels of disruption to be given additional support and intervention.

The headteacher also identified teaching and learning as an issue and instigated a system of senior team observations and reviews. This regular observation, combined with regular but unannounced 'sweeps' and 'walk-throughs', soon built up an accurate picture of the reality of classroom practice. This evidence became the starting point for managing the development of teachers or redefining their role and function. In a few cases teachers were dismissed.

In parallel, the headteacher used Navigation to develop and spell out a vision in a practical and common-sense way. She did not arrive at the school with a 'grand vision' about where the school would be in five, ten or twenty years' time. This was a day-to-day concern about what needed to be done to make the school work properly.

Whilst working on this day-to-day or 'living vision', the headteacher also set out to question the underlying assumptions and values held by some of those in the school and the wider community. She explicitly challenged the relationship between disadvantage and low educational achievement, arguing that everybody could achieve their full potential if they developed a strong work ethic and commitment to learning. Underperformance in any setting by adults or children was not tolerated. Everyone was expected to do their best and was rewarded for it. High levels of challenge and support in all areas became the norm for all. 'If we are improving on our previous best then we are succeeding' became a mantra, and could be seen on classroom walls. The school mission statement and expectations could be found in every room. During this phase of development the headteacher also invested considerable time in advocacy to build strong teams founded on communication, trust, confidence and commitment across the staff.

During this early phase of development, when the school was young in terms of improvement efforts, the focus was on Management and Navigation. However, the headteacher also used Partnership to reinforce her arguments and to challenge accepted norms of practice that did not meet her expectations. This was achieved through having visiting speakers at whole-staff in-service training (INSET), and the use of consultants, working with individuals and small groups to develop new policies and practices. For example, consultants worked with subject teams to develop new approaches to teaching literacy and numeracy.

Teachers who could not cope with proactive Management of their performance or realign their values and direction of travel to match the headteacher's Navigation tended to leave for a post elsewhere. This is a common occurrence when new leadership arrives at a Type B school.

Navigation, Management and Partnership in Type C settings

As a school moves into adolescence, the focus and activity of high-leverage leaders shifts. Management and Partnership receive less focus and attention while Navigation continues to increase in intensity. At Bartley Green the transition to a Type C school was characterised by the headteacher drawing on the increased confidence and capability of the staff to spread leadership responsibility across a wider range of people. This involved more staff taking on formal and informal leadership roles. For example, the senior leadership team was expanded to provide additional strategic leadership capacity. This also freed up some mid-level leadership roles, providing more junior staff with professional development and promotion opportunities. Whole-school initiatives, including the University of the First Age (UFA) and the Valued Youth Program (VYP), provided inexperienced members of staff with opportunities to take on informal leadership roles. During this period, department heads were offered more flexibility in their own leadership styles. Additional resources and targeted support were also made available. Mid-level leaders were made more accountable for their work. Target setting was used to reflect on and challenge mid-level leaders' and ultimately teachers' expectations and practice.

The headteacher continued to use her awareness to identify best practice within the school, but rather than continuing to have high levels of senior leadership observation of teaching she advocated a more developmental approach involving mutual support and peer observation within and across departments. This encouraged teachers to take risks and experiment with their practice and move good practice around the school. Where practice had not improved, or where staff could not respond to the challenge and support that was offered, there was an acceptance of the situation and people opted to leave or continued to be moved on. During this phase of development the local and (to a lesser extent) national reputation of the school grew. Where it had previously been difficult to attract a high-quality field of candidates for teaching positions, now people wanted to work at this improving school. However, the school continued with its policy of not filling vacant posts if otherwise suitable candidates did not hold the same values or level of talent it needed. This is a further indicator of the headteacher's astute awareness.

The relative effectiveness and efficiency of the school had grown to the extent that the systems and structures put in place during the first phase of development now ran smoothly. Management focus and activity had dipped to a point where it was subject to interim review and maintenance rather than being an important development activity in its own right. Partnership activity also declined in this phase of development. The focus on internal partnerships was designed to share expertise within the school to improve student outcomes in lower-performing areas. External partnerships were focused on extending the high-performing areas of the school. The use of Advanced Skills Teachers (ASTs) is an example of the types of networking and Partnership activity that increased as the school moved towards maturity and to becoming a Type D school.

Navigation, Management and Partnership in Type D settings

As a school undergoes the transition to a Type D school, high-leverage leaders once again shift their focus and effort. Management continues to ensure systems and structures are working efficiently and appropriate. If they are not, then there will be a spike in management activity. Navigation and Partnership increase and change in their nature.

In 2008 Bartley Green was recognised as an outstanding school in challenging circumstances, and in 2009 the headteacher was awarded an OBE in recognition of her services to education. Navigation continues to be her major focus and effort, but it has changed in nature, becoming even more outward looking. As leadership has been spread across the school, more and more staff have been involved in supporting and learning from other schools.

Bartley Green's headteacher analysed areas of strength and identified where her school might be able to offer support to others and where it needed to learn from others. For example, the pastoral deputy responsible for setting up Discipline for Learning worked with other schools across the country to support and advise them in the development of a system that would meet their needs. Subject leaders regularly work to support curriculum development in other schools. The school also receives numerous visits from other schools. The school is both a High Performing Specialist School and a Leadership Partner School, a national hub for the development of leadership and succession planning strategies. Partnerships are not restricted to adults in the school. Recently 30 students and staff from Kelly Mill School in South Carolina visited Bartley Green and worked with Year 8 students. The school has also launched its own Combined Cadet Force (CCF), traditionally the preserve of private schools. Bartley Green is the only state school with a CCF Royal Marines detachment.

The school makes a significant contribution towards the improvement of other schools and the wider system. Put simply, this is due to the high leverage Navigation and Partnership work of its headteacher.

Reflecting on school context and *high-leverage leadership*

The best high-leverage leaders draw on their intelligence to navigate, manage and work on partnerships suited to their schools' specific contexts. These leaders create a sense of urgency and demand change, but they are sensitive to the emotional and physical dimensions of school context and the natural rhythms of the school year.

In some cases, leaders manage to create an illusion of sustainable change. The structures are put in place, teams are created and standards begin to rise. On the surface all seems to be going well. The school roll grows, inspectors report on new successes and negative media attention becomes positive. For Type B schools, when the process of change has begun and praise starts to come in, there is a risk that the leader will move on to another challenge and the school will then revert to type. As previously noted, our high-leverage leaders are committed to the longer term. They have recognised when directive, authoritative leadership is necessary and they have sensed when a more distributed approach is appropriate. As Payne (2008) highlights, this sensitivity has been sadly lacking in our recent conceptualisations of leadership:

> For some time now, the official leadership model of progressives has been some variant of the facilitative, democratic, inclusive model. That model as usually presented is certainly ahistorical and decontextualized. In schools where distrust between teachers and their colleagues has built up over many years, over the short term including more people in the decision making processes gives them new weapons with which to carry out their old vendettas. There may come a point in a school's development where democratic leadership can lead to major improvements in school functioning, but that is far from saying all schools can profit from it at all points in time."
> (Payne, 2008, pp. 197–8)

It would seem that, if we are to progress by developing models which benefit from hindsight, based on our history and accounting for the subtleties and nuances of context, we need to develop high-leverage leadership, where leaders hold a detailed understanding of the power of Navigation, Management and Partnership. Most importantly perhaps, this model must include an awareness of how these elements interact with and play out in a range of school contexts.

7 Governance, accountability and impact

High-leverage leaders feel *responsible* for generating the best possible outcomes for the young people whose wellbeing and attainment are entrusted to them. They are also prepared to be *accountable* – a more systemic, less personal attribute:

> 'Responsibility' may include accountability but can also refer to the capacity for individual choice and action ('acting responsibly') exercised without reference to another persons [sic]. Accountability is always other-directed, whereas responsibility is not.
>
> (Mulgan, 2002, p. 3)

We have used concepts like 'rapport' and 'internal locus of control' to describe the characteristics on which high-leverage leaders build their individual sense of responsibility. It is those, along with their Contextual, Professional and Social Intelligence, which cause high-leverage leaders to accept accountability – the rights of others to have information about their work, to scrutinise it and to approve it. High-leverage leaders embrace that approach and recognise its advantages (Mongon and Chapman, 2008a). High-leverage leaders use governance and accountability to create powerful alliances between their schools, other services, elected government and local communities. Governance and accountability become the working connection between professional expertise and the expectations of young people, families and communities. They confer civic permissions for intervention in young people's lives and for the spending of public funds. They provide a window between different worlds, casting light on expectations that vary from one to the other. At their very best they offer scrutiny and challenge alongside partnership and association. They are anything but a bureaucratic chore.

High-leverage leaders are therefore not neutral about accountability and governance. They nurture a very active relationship with their schools' governing bodies – the Boards that are statutorily required for every school in England (see below). Their relationships with those Boards are analogous to that of a Chief Executive to the Board of Directors. High-leverage leaders are constantly nudging and influencing their governors. They also have a very active interest in designing new governance arrangements that bring individual schools, groups of schools and other providers into collaborative arrangements. These leaders are writing what Leadbeater and Mongon call a 'new story for education' (2008, p. 9), and are prepared to be judged by its outcomes. For many, this involves:

> ... the creation of a model of governance and accountability that reflects a very different conception of organising education from the tradition which locates learning within an institution to one which makes the wider community responsible for developing education.
>
> (Ranson, 2010, p. 293)

Accountability and governance in the English state school system have changed quickly and dramatically. It is so different now that the past might well be 'a foreign country', to echo L P Hartley's 1953 novel *The Go-Between*, were it not so recent and still influential. For more than a hundred years, every state-funded school in England has been required to have, in effect, a governing body. Over the past 25 years, the legal framework for that has changed from administrative simplicity to highly flexible complexity – historical practice and old habits seem to have inhibited many school leaders from appreciating just how flexible. High-leverage leaders, on the other hand, constantly exploit that flexibility, manipulating both the formal arrangements and the informal opportunities offered by the current system. They comply with national accountabilities expressed in terms of exam attainment and inspection judgements while creating parallel authorising environments (a phrase we explain later) directed towards outcomes to which they are personally committed and which they negotiate with the communities they serve.

We need to summarise how radical the changes have been and remind ourselves just how novel the interest in good institutional governance and effective leadership actually is. Until recently, leadership – by which we mean both school governance and headship – was seen by only a few politicians and researchers as a key lever in school improvement and effectiveness. So long as the headteacher and governors created no turbulence while acting as the administrative connection between autonomous teachers (who led on curriculum and pedagogy) and local government officials (who led on structure and funding), there was little expectation or possibility that they would provide high leverage. There was also, we have noted, precious little evidence on which to judge the effectiveness of schools and therefore of school leadership. The promotion of consumerism and marketisation in the education service has brought local leadership to prominence. In England, this prominence had its iconic moment in the opening of a National College for School Leadership – an institution that the BBC likened to Sandhurst, the country's prestigious military officer training academy (BBC, 1999). However, this is not just an English phenomenon: writing about Scandinavia, Per Dalin describes a recognisably similar trend:

> ... developmental characteristics that are based on a ... 'revitalisation of democracy' in which public services are brought closer to the client. Other

features of the development have all the hallmarks of deregulation and municipalisation. As a rule, this is related to demands for increased efficiency.

(Dalin, 2005, p. 7)

Dalin goes on to track similar trends in the United States, New Zealand and Netherlands (2005, chapter 1).

Though decentralisation and choice bring their own problems, they have created a previously non-existent opportunity to identify and celebrate high leverage. The following summary is a brief account of how and why school governance in England is the focus for the tensions between professional authority, government control of publicly funded institutions, ethical responsibility for the well-being of young people and the rights of families and communities in the education of their children. It illustrates the power of school autonomy and the weakness of school isolation – two of the major preoccupations for designers of education systems across the world.

Setting the context for high-leverage leadership: the recent history of school governance in England

During the second half of the twentieth century, school governance in England passed through two phases: first, national non-conformity and then local authority oversight. A third phase, institutional autonomy, emerged around the turn of the millennium. These three phases are overlapping trends. Traces of the first two – which were dominant when most of the headteachers in England today began teaching and perhaps even in their early leadership (National College, 2009b) – still persist in a system increasingly characterised by institutional autonomy.

We described the period of national non-conformity, the 'national system, locally administered', in Chapter 3. Central government prided itself on having little direct control over schools; the headteacher's authority was at best imprecise; teachers' personal preferences were the main influence on classroom activity; local authority officers often controlled admissions, appointments and budgets and the local authority determined the number of schools and school places. Most governing bodies were little more than cheerleaders for the professionals, social contributors to the life of the school and marginal fund-raisers at the Summer Fete and Christmas Bazaar. The governors' responsibility in law for the 'general direction' of the school was honoured more in the breach (Owen, 1978). Accountability for the core work in schools, teaching and learning was patchy and incoherent.

Local authority oversight lasted from about the mid-1980s until the early part of this century, mainly as a statutory response by central government to its own frustrations at being unable to influence the system strategically. Although local authorities initially assumed significant powers and responsibility for school standards, central government's mistrust of local councils was undermining this approach almost before it began. The local authorities' administrative and managerial territory became stranded between a flood of national prescription for curriculum and assessment and the rising tide of school control over local funding and other managerial functions. The local authority was being reduced to a form of supervisory oversight, intervening only in very exceptional circumstances. Headteachers, in contrast, were drawn first into an explicit administrative role, a frantic pre-leadership phase of balancing budgets, managing personnel and organising premises. Only later, arguably with a new generation emerging, did many headteachers use the budget and other functions influentially rather than bureaucratically, in effect moving from clerical administration towards Navigation and Management. Governing bodies were being drawn into a notionally more active leadership and accountability role, though that was often under the stewardship of the headteacher.

> Even when lay governors have opinions they wish to express, it seems that they face great difficulty in making their 'voice' heard, let alone in having their views taken seriously.
>
> (Whitty *et al.*, 1998, p. 100)

The third and currently prevailing phase, institutional autonomy, was trailed in the 1977 report of a central government enquiry, in part a response to the furore at William Tyndale School which we noted in Chapter 3 (HMSO, 1977). The enquiry reported that:

> ... the extent to which managing and governing bodies carried out the functions assigned to them in rules and articles was slight. In many areas they did not, in any real sense, exist at all.
>
> (1977, para. 2.11)

The government's choices, the enquiry concluded, lay between 'reforming, replacing and abolishing them' (1977, para. 3.3). The enquiry's recommendations were based on the proposition that the head should be responsible to the governing body and that:

> ... there is no area of the school's activities in respect of which the governing body should have no responsibility nor one on which the head and staff should be accountable only to themselves or to the local education authority.
>
> (1977, para. 3.15)

It was another decade before the 1988 Education Reform Act put those principles in the statute book (ERA, 1988), and even longer before they became extensively consolidated and a taken-for-granted feature of the English system. They are now consolidated in policy and law:

> With headteachers and principals free to determine how pupils are taught and how budgets are spent, the greater ... potential there has been for

all-round improvement and the greater ... opportunity too for the system to move from good to great.

(Gove, 2011)

The reality of these and similar reforms across the world is that power is not being handed to schools without constraints. In England, the defining powers and consequent accountability for school governance have been passed to a corporate body, and that, in most cases, is the lay governing body or a Trust which appoints those governors. In England, about a third of a million lay people volunteer as school governors – arguably the largest volunteer activity in the country. Over the past two decades these volunteers have become responsible in law (DfES, 2006, ch. 3, p. 3) for:

- setting aims and objectives for the school;
- adopting policies for achieving those aims and objectives;
- setting targets for achieving those aims and objectives;
- appointing, appraising and determining the pay of the headteacher.

There are, broadly speaking, three different legal frameworks for school governance in the English system. Community Schools (the present norm), Academy Schools (a fast-growing sector, funded directly by central government) and Foundation, Voluntary or Trust Schools (most commonly connected to a faith group) each have different legal bases for their curriculum, their finances, their personnel functions and their ownership of property. High-leverage leaders have to be adept at working with whichever they encounter.

We are not going to debate whether the remarkably varied context for governance across England is a good thing or not. We want to alert the reader to the range of circumstances in which high-leverage leaders operate and to consider how that affects their work. With the current national policy emphasis on Academies for many and deregulation for all, the decentralising direction of travel will persist. Schools' legal autonomy is likely to increase – offering autonomy from one another, from their local authority and from some national directives. If micro-management by central and local government reduces, the role of the school's professional executive, its leadership team, and of its Board (the governing body) will continue to expand. The key questions then become:

- how should the relationship *between* governance and executive leadership develop; and
- should legally autonomous schools choose to be isolated from or integrated with the school communities, professional communities and neighbourhood communities around them?

A framework for governance and accountability: shaping the change you want to happen

High-leverage leaders use the complexity and flexibility of the system in England to shape the governance arrangements and accountability procedures that are appropriate to the outcomes they are pursuing and the methods they want to adopt. They are compelled to do that not by external pressure but by the sense of personal responsibility and conscientiousness we described in Chapter 5. They do not treat governance as an imposition: it is a device for enhancing performance in the school and building alliances beyond it. Good governance, they know, depends more on the character of their particular governing body (over which they can have considerable influence) than on its constitutional form (over which they have no control).

We are not aware of any conclusive evidence that different legal forms of governance make a consistently significant difference to closing performance gaps or reducing variations in attainment. However, the quality of individual governing bodies, irrespective of their legal constitution, appears to make some difference (Lord *et al.*, 2009). The quality of good governance and leadership can also have a positive effect when, in a legally binding federation, they are shared between a stronger and a weaker school (Chapman *et al.*, 2009, 2011). Good governance is positively associated with higher pupil attainment, though more significantly so in the primary phase than in the secondary (James *et al.*, 2010). Governance plays a positive role when it unambiguously specifies and symbolically endorses what is expected of the school community, staff and students. That strategic role is performed with variable success in the English system and, even when it is performed well, it may be attributed to one or two governors rather than the governing body corporately (Earley 2003; Earley *et al.*, 2002). There is little empirical evidence of how governing bodies actually contribute to school improvement in practice (Earley and Creese 2003). The dynamic of cause and effect is not clear, and a self-sustaining multiplier between pupil attainment, professional leadership and governance is a possible explanation (James *et al.*, 2010). In England, this means that whether the governing body is constituted to oversee an Academy, Trust, Foundation, Voluntary or Community School seems far less important than the attitude and aptitude of governors on each governing body. This has to be a major concern for high-leverage leaders because:

> In areas of socio-economic disadvantage, for instance, schools are under enormous pressure, both because their role in overcoming disadvantage is crucial and because the challenges they face are almost overwhelming. Yet it is in precisely such areas that the model of volunteer citizens supporting and challenging the work of professionals seems most problematic. Where are these volunteers to come from, given the pressures under which people in such areas find themselves?
>
> (Dean *et al.*, 2007, p. 6)

For those reasons, high-leverage leaders are not neutral about the development of their governing bodies. James and his colleagues identify the importance of the headteacher in creating what they call 'governance capital' and we would call Association (see Chapter 5). They define 'governance capital' as:

> … the network of individuals and their capabilities, relationships and motivations that are available for the governance of any particular school"
>
> (James *et al.*, 2010, p. 83)

The school leaders in their research, like the high-leverage leaders we know, engineer this through:

> … training and development, nurturing parents who may have the potential to be good governors but initially lack the motivation, and seeking members of the local community who may have the necessary qualities.
>
> (2010, p. 84)

The evidence confirms that successful Navigation involves working with at the same time as *working on* a school's governance arrangements. High-leverage leaders therefore use the Professional and Contextual Intelligence we described earlier to recruit, advise and guide their governing bodies. It is no coincidence that school inspections in England that describe leadership as outstanding usually report the same for governance. None the less, high-leverage leaders have told us repeatedly (and we agree) that the statutory framework for governance and accountability has become inappropriate for work which is no longer confined to the technical management of pedagogy. It remains to be seen whether the most recent changes in England are more or less helpful. What we can be certain of is that high-leverage leaders will exploit the breadth and flexibility in the statutory arrangements to design governance and accountability arrangements that are commensurate with the work they do and the outcomes they are looking for.

High-leverage leaders, writing the 'new story for education', do not treat statutory demands as the complete set of matters for which they are prepared to be accountable. Their principal legal duty has for some time been 'to promote the development of pupils at the school …' (ERA, 1988, Part 1, Ch. 1(1)(2)). In reality, this was intended to mean securing the academic attainment of pupils in one school, even if competitively at the expense of pupils in other schools. Those attainments, published as national and local 'league tables', say nothing about the health and wellbeing of pupils and the communities they come from or about the benefits of Partnership. During the first decade of this millennium, some of those other outcomes were recognised, though often obscured in the jargon of New Labour – the political party then in national government. The jargon included 'extended services', 'Education Action Zones' and 'Every Child Matters' – all aimed at using the capacity of schools to improve academic attainment and other kinds of outcomes for young people (Chapman and Gunter, 2009). High-leverage leaders are concerned about the wider set of outcomes, and they rode that New Labour wave for all it could offer. They may now 'drop', as surfers say, into the following wave, 'The Big Society'. 'Big Society' is a much criticised phrase repeatedly relaunched by the coalition government which came into power in 2010 to describe its intention to give:

> ... citizens, communities and local government the power and information they need to come together, solve the problems they face and build the Britain they want.
>
> (Cabinet Office, 2010)

For high-leverage leaders, the operational work with children and communities that lies behind this jargon-fuelled political arm wrestling is an enduring concern. That kind of work, we explained particularly in Chapter 5 when we wrote about Association and Area Focus, requires new service configurations at the point of delivery and improved collaboration to create them. The 1988 Act reflected a fashion in England for what Heifetz and Linsky (2002) and later Fullan (2005) might characterise as technical solutions – the application of a limited range of school effectiveness techniques to local attainment and therefore to governance. In contrast, the work of high-leverage leaders is highly demanding of what the same authors call adaptive approaches – dealing with what Tim Brighouse and David Woods (2008) call 'the messy business' of school leadership (2008, Ch. 2). Despite legislative tinkering with the 1988 framework, it is now 'increasingly out of kilter with the organisational models and culture of the age, which are increasingly networked, collaborative and open' (Leadbeater, 2008, p. 17). It is certainly out of kilter with the ambitions of many high-leverage leaders.

What, then, might an appropriate governance framework for supporting high-leverage leadership look like? We have explored with Charles Leadbeater the idea of a tripartite model that might encourage innovation in public services and the creation of Public Value (Mongon and Leadbeater, 2011). The same model provides a useful device for reflecting on high-leverage leadership that requires:

- *an authorising environment* (though not permissive);
- *new capacity* (though not necessarily increased);
- *appropriate measures of value* (though not just numerics).

Our previous chapters have focused on the ways in which high-leverage leaders create the second of those, new capacity, to meet need in the organisations and localities where they operate. We have described the Navigation of their organisations, the Management of effective action and the Partnership activity through which they improve the lives of young people and their families. We have written about their need to nuance their work against the health and strength of their organisation at different times. New capacity, adaptive innovation alongside technical application in support of a living vision, cannot survive in a vacuum. It requires supportive and transparent governance with agreed objectives. Communities, parents, staff, students and taxpayers are entitled to know and to have some say in what those purposes are and how well they are being pursued. It is those two aspects, the authorising environment and appropriate measures of value for high-leverage leadership, that we now want to consider in some detail.

The authorising environment

To whom are high-leverage leaders answerable for their stewardship of public funds and their care of young people? To whom *should they be* answerable? Where does their authority come from? These questions boil down to asking who owns the school and its purposes and in what sense are they owned? For high-leverage leaders these are not technical questions; they are pressing moral matters that require adaptive solutions based on authentic relationships – what we have called Association.

Defining 'ownership' is less important to high-leverage leaders than making themselves accountable in different ways to different stakeholders, including government, governors, pupils, families, staff, other schools and services and the neighbourhood. Across all those groups, there are some clear strands in the way these leaders approach accountability, whatever the formal, statutory arrangements.

- They have high standards for everyone around them and they expect those around them, in turn, to have high standards for their leadership – a mutually reciprocal formula.
- They prefer strong governance arrangements. The clarity of purpose and expectation which good governance endows also creates enough space for disciplined innovation and provides no room for complacency.
- When their work does move beyond the core of teaching and learning, high-leverage leaders, in England at least, are becoming involved in the local design of governance arrangements which are fit for that more complex purpose.

These three strands echo the findings in a study of English schools adapting to the first wave of the new legislative framework for governance in the 1990s. The authors reported distinctions between those schools which used the new freedoms to create 'community oriented public management' rather than a 'neo-liberal market orientation' (Martin *et al.*, 2000, p. 122). The researchers concluded that the schools most likely to survive and to succeed in adverse circumstances were those that saw their new governance freedoms as an opportunity:

- to engage with community regeneration;
- to draw the local community into the governance arrangements;
- to treat learning as both an entitlement and a shared responsibility for everyone involved.

Our proposal is that high-leverage leaders appear to operate in five interlinked 'authorising environments', each with overlapping though distinctive sources of capacity and measures of value. The five authorising environments are:

- Personal
- Associate
- Institutional
- Contextual
- National.

Personal authorisation

- *Personal authorisation* is based to a large degree in the leaders' own dispositions – the permissions they give and demands they make on themselves.
- The *capacity* associated with personal authorisation is provided by the leaders' energy and activity.
- The *appropriate measures of value* are intrinsically personal and often moral or ethical.

In Chapter 5, Management, we described three of the key characteristics shown by the high-leverage leaders in our research. We wrote that they had a strong sense of self-confidence, personal responsibility and conscientiousness. The first two, self-confidence and personal responsibility are central to understanding each leader's personal 'authorising environment'.

Self-confidence 'authorises' high-leverage leaders to persist not only when first efforts are unsuccessful but also when outside agencies are diffident or even hostile. It is an attribute with the potential to create its own virtuous circle. It should not be confused with arrogance, even when their outward features sometimes look similar. Arrogance will eventually and always undermine leverage by being incompatible with Advocacy and Association. In contrast, many – probably most – of the high-leverage leaders in our projects tended to worry about the fragility of their success – though their colleagues might be surprised to learn this.

Personal responsibility 'authorises' high-leverage leaders to examine the outcomes of their work critically and to test whether they are personally satisfied with the results. They determinedly influence the variables at their disposal and are prepared to be personally accountable for those.

Associate authorisation

- *Associate authorisation* is drawn from the bonds which high-leverage leaders create between themselves, the adults and the children who are working together daily.
- The *capacity* associated with associate authorisation is derived from the synergy of a community working more in harmony than in friction.
- The *appropriate measures of value* are partly personal and partly communal. For adults and students they invoke the sense of a 'job well done', of professional pride and personal esteem.

The reciprocated permission and approval which high-leverage leaders seek from young and old alike draw their school communities into what we called Association (Chapter 5). Because they know and understand that a community with a shared sense of endeavour will be a stronger community, they work hard to explain their actions to its principal recipients, to canvass their opinions and to gain their communal authorisation.

High-leverage leaders also understand the value of Navigation and Partnership – in particular of Advocacy and Association. Associate authorisation is one of the processes that takes some schools beyond distributed leadership (see Chapter 5). High-leverage leaders encourage their associates to become self-regulating, personally responsible individuals by nurturing a self-regulating, collectively responsible community in which to display those skills. Our descriptions of Advocacy and Association showed how these leaders purposefully encourage staff and students to take personal responsibility for their own achievement and shared responsibility for the communal outcomes, rather than superficially subscribing to rules which they then persistently undermine. High-leverage leaders factor iconic symbolism into the fabric of school life – student commissions of enquiry, staff working parties and community groups – demonstrating that accountability operates up and down, across and round the school community.

'Relationships with senior management are what defines the school …'
Middle Leader, Cardinal Hume School

'There is a cultural feel to the school as soon as you walk through the door … There are different levels of leadership that we all feed off … There is every single form of leadership and the vision filters through them all.'
Teacher, Guildford Grove Primary

'Why is this a good school? It's respect that we hold in the teachers and the teachers give back to us.'
Pupil, Robert Clack Secondary School

Institutional authorisation

- *Institutional authorisation* is provided to high-leverage leaders by the governance arrangements to which they owe their primary legal account-ability. These are mainly school governing bodies, though other arrangements are emerging in the English system.
- The *capacity* associated with institutional authorisation is derived in part from the contribution which individuals on the governing body make to the work of the school and in part from the space and impetus it creates as a body by approving and supporting the school leadership.
- The *appropriate measures of value* will include those required by law, notably student attainment. They may also include other measures which

may or may not be required by law but are agreed by the governing body, for example school ethos, student wellbeing, self esteem, contributions to community cohesion and wider contributions to community development and regeneration.

We noted earlier in this chapter that it is not clear what the balance of contribution to school improvement and effectiveness is between high-leverage leaders and governors. About a fifth of headteachers have described their governing body as very effective, and a similar proportion described it as ineffective (PWC, 2007). The national inspectorate, Ofsted, has reported that, in 90 per cent of schools where leadership and management was excellent or very good, governing bodies were also judged to be at least good at fulfilling their responsibilities.

Schools at Garforth near Leeds in the north of England have created a Trust with an alliance of trustees including the secondary school, four primary schools, the local further education college, the primary care trust and the Learning and Skills Council. Each of the school governing bodies can focus on teaching and learning while the Trust provides a vehicle for shared activity across children's services. It also provides the hub to share planning, facilities and provision to guarantee the core extended services offer to families across the locality. The Trust can also sponsor local enterprise, including its own retail sites, to improve the personalised curriculum offer to young people.

(Mongon *et al.*, 2010)

High-leverage leaders' contracts reflect the range of corporate approaches which can be adopted by governing bodies in England, including:

- executive headship where one leader is responsible for more than one school;
- shared headship where two leaders share the headship of a single school;
- reciprocal appointments where a school shares its site, and perhaps its premises, with another provider, typically a pre-school Children's Centre, and where governance and/or leadership might also be shared;
- trust arrangements in which a group of trustees operating as a corporate, not-for-profit charitable organisation appoint some of the governors at several schools;
- collaborations in which some, but not all, of the functions of two or more governing bodies are legally combined;
- federations in which a single governing body oversees two or more schools which might or might not share a single headteacher.

The authority to adopt any of these arrangements rests with the governing body of a school that would almost certainly take into account, but not necessarily accept, the advice of the headteacher, their school's *de facto* chief executive. For high-leverage leaders there are three important implications:

1   To all intents and purposes, the law in England allows governing bodies to organise themselves and to design their relationships with other schools and services in almost any imaginable format. High-leverage leaders are careful that the format should reflect the priorities in their work.
2   The relationship between the school leader and the governing body is now more than ever the one they create – whether they do so by choice or negligence. High-leverage leaders are not negligent. The balance of power between the leader and the governors, in particular the Chair of Governors, will depend as much on personalities and personal relationships as on formal authority.
3   Values and priorities which might previously have been invested in the day-to-day core activity can now be expressed in the long-term structural, constitutional arrangements to which the governors commit the school. The high-leverage leader's advice and the governing body's decisions on the constitutional framework for the school become one of the iconic symbols to which we referred in Chapter 2. They are a public demonstration of the kind of place we want to be and how we will do things – not least how we will work with others around us.

These important features of institutional authorisation reinforce the recurring theme in the present chapter. High-leverage leaders are not, and cannot afford to be, neutral about governance.

Contextual authorisation

- *Contextual authorisation* is created when school leaders expand their sphere of influence into the neighbourhood and professional communities around their school. In the absence of legally determined formulae for the governance of collaborative activity, high-leverage leaders create *ad hoc*, fit-for-purpose arrangements.
- The *capacity* associated with contextual authorisation comes from 'collaborative advantage', the reduction in duplication and increases in efficiency, about which we wrote in Chapter 5.
- The *appropriate measures of value* are in part the institutional measures imposed by national policy and institutional authorisation on each of the partners. Other measures of value do emerge. They often involve a social or emotional dimension that would be difficult to track even in a single organisation, more so in a collaboration.

We want to explore contextual authorisation by drawing an analogy with a business model. So long as an enterprise's outputs or outcomes remain limited to a core range – anything, for example, from tins of beans to pupil attainment

– authorisation and accountability can be relatively clear and simple. If the range is extended, becoming more risky and innovative, authorisation and accountability are likely to become more opaque and complex.

Companies that extend themselves beyond a relatively tightly defined scope for their service or product may perhaps do so because they want to ensure their raw material supplies or maybe influence the placement of their products in the market. They might therefore take control of their suppliers and/or outlets. They can create a chain of command along the line of supply, production and sales.

Similarly, schools might want to extend the scope of their provision so that learning can be improved (perhaps across all ages), and so that adult life chances can be enhanced across the local community. They might also want to influence closely associated but arguably tangential factors such as health and wellbeing. Expansion of that kind might involve linkage in several directions. Although recent legislation in England has encouraged the creation of 'chains' of schools, these are more analogous to a commercial cartel of similar suppliers than to a commercial chain connecting supply, production and sales. Schools still do not usually have the option of taking over other services or of creating a centrally managed chain of command across a sequence of potential contributors – though there are now a very small number that do this. High-leverage leaders therefore imitate those options by developing voluntary connections characterised by equity and empowerment. They create collaborations and alliances with varying patterns of authority, power and influence across the institutions, organisations and communities on which their children and young people depend.

At George Green's Secondary School in London's East End, Stella Bailey, the school's Director of Extended Services, is a trustee of the Isle of Dogs Community Foundation – a voluntary, charitable foundation responding to local needs and sponsoring community activities. The school created the Island Sports Trust (IST) as a charitable, not-for-profit organisation to facilitate and manage the community's use of the school's sports facilities. IST has eight trustees, is now an employer of local residents, and shows a small annual trading surplus. The school adopted a more informal arrangement in the Docklands Youth Service (DYS) – a network of 20 youth service providers – as the consortium backing its contract to provide the local youth service. The substantive contract is with the school, while the DYS is one of the key guiding influences on the youth work.

The further the roles adopted by school leaders move from the core of teaching and learning on a single school site, the more adaptive both the leadership and governance arrangements need to be. Contextual authorisation in informal and *ad hoc* relationships requires an Association of authoritative figures, some of whom derive their authority from a formal, corporate position and some from very informal circumstances – for example, as community representatives.

Lesley Farmer, Principal at Hailsham Community College, and four of her primary colleagues created an informal but substantive and effective partnership Board. With no statutory constitution or powers, the Board provided oversight, coordination and governance for more than three dozen agencies across the town. Four of the schools have since become a Cooperative Trust.

Institutional authorisation often plays an important role in contextual authorisation, either by supporting or by dampening the impetus of partnerships. Institutional authorisation can provide impetus to wider partnerships or strangle them. 'In the absence of formal governance arrangements, responsibility for supporting the governance of partnerships falls to partners' own corporate governance mechanisms' (Audit Commission, 2005, p. 62). The high-leverage school leader therefore manages her relationship with the governing body to ensure that its members understand, support and then scrutinise the executive decisions she needs to make in contextual associations.

National authorisation

- *National authorisation* is produced by the occasionally contrary combination of legal framework, statutory targets and policy rhetoric which central government wraps around school leaders.
- The *capacity* associated with national authorisation is partly derived from the resources, in particular funding, which central government arranges for schools and in part from the encouragement it offers school leaders to work, even more so to innovate, in areas within their competence.
- The *appropriate measures of value* are often standardised, numeric and easy-to-measure performance indicators across a limited number of outcomes for young people.

In England, all three main political parties are committed to the rhetoric of localism, devolving more and more discretion directly to councils, communities and service users, encouraging them to pool budgets and to commission services rather than providing them directly. However, in the education service, deference to localism is almost always accompanied by a tightening of national accountability towards a limited range of student outcomes.

Under the headline 'Every Child Matters', the last Labour government promoted policies to integrate services for children and to focus as intently on health and wellbeing as on academic attainment. The coalition government formed in May 2010 is in turn exploring similar themes through quite different tactics, in education through its commitment to school autonomy and more widely through the 'Big Society' policy to which we referred earlier (Cabinet Office, 2010). Schools are being refocused on their core activity of teaching and learning, although increased local autonomy, the government claims, will allow schools greater opportunities for collaboration with other public and private organisations (DfE, 2010b).

If the differences between political parties continue to play out mainly in structural and funding arguments, the national authorising environment for high-leverage leaders may not be very different. Their approaches may become more mainstream as politicians across the spectrum promote more collaborative, community based initiatives designed to change consumer behaviour and to build capacity in communities as well as delivering services to them. Much will depend on how local autonomy is defined for schools by central government and the extent to which a techno-managerial approach to teaching and learning, focused tightly on exam attainment, comes to dominate the culture of school leadership. High-leverage leaders will still domesticate national policies to the needs of the school, retain the focus on high-quality teaching and learning and deliver high student attainment outcomes; and they will still allow staff and students to work on locally agreed priorities.

Appropriate measures of value

The raison d'être of the governance and accountability we have been describing in public services – schools in this case – is their focus on appropriate measures of value. A public service that cannot explain its value cannot have a secure moral basis or a justifiable claim on the public purse. For both those reasons, high-leverage leaders are keen to demonstrate the value of their work and to use the evidence of its value to motivate themselves, the adults they work with and the young people they are working for. They are occasionally frustrated by the reluctance of others to accept measures outside the framework of national performance indicators. They are also occasionally frustrated by their own inability to be precisely articulate about the measures appropriate to their work.

> 'Families tell us that we are making a difference to their lives in many ways but we have little hard evidence at the present time to prove this. We know, for instance, that crime has reduced in the area ... We know that the emotional and mental health of some of our more vulnerable young people is improving ... We believe that the health of the community will be improving ... but we are a long way from proving it all.'
>
> Headteacher, Garforth Community College

The appropriate measures of value by which the work of high-leverage leaders can be judged may need to be different in the five different authorising environments – personal, associate, institutional, contextual and national. There is therefore a portfolio of measures on which high-leverage leaders can draw in different circumstances and from time to time. All high-leverage leaders accept that attainment tests for children at given ages are important for their school, internally and externally. Many believe that these are necessary but not sufficient measures, an incomplete account of what they are trying to achieve. The need to complement these with additional measures of engagement, commitment, wellbeing and other non-academic achievement requires new and sometimes *ad hoc* measures of value. This presents high-leverage leaders with four challenges:

1 *Measuring inputs.* It is relatively easy to measure school budgets, teacher-to-pupil ratios and the number of days a school is open. It is more difficult to measure the marginal or opportunity costs of activities at the margins of the school day or curriculum. It is very difficult to measure the input value of staff enthusiasm, parental commitment, peer influence and community culture.

2 *Evaluating processes.* In schools, the teaching process has a direct effect on learning outcomes. Lesson observation and inspection contribute to our understanding of that process. Other processes inside or outside the school, when focused on personal and community development, become more diffuse and less easy to observe and describe.

3 *Measuring outputs.* The units of measurement for the core of the school's work are pupils and exams. It is relatively easy to publish test results, especially if there is a national requirement to do so and the figures are provided by central government. It is far less easy to establish the unit of measurement for outcomes when relationships, networks, social and emotional wellbeing or community cohesion are the focus of an activity.

4 *Managing timescales.* High-leverage leaders initially trade the pay-offs between quick-fix improvement programmes and sustainable improvement (see Chapter 6). When successful, the quick fixes provide temporary relief from external pressures and the space to innovate for the longer term. It follows that some high-leverage activity will incur short-term costs and only pays a dividend in the longer term. This is an uncomfortable juxtaposition for the leaders and those they are working with or accountable to.

All four of these challenges, like governance arrangements, become more complex and intangible as the focus of high-leverage activity moves outside and further from the classroom. Along the same inward–outward spectrum it becomes increasingly difficult to track from input to impact or from costs to pupil outcomes. 'Partnerships are sometimes compared to a black box. Inputs and outputs are visible but the mechanisms enabling the transformation from input to output are not' (Giguere, 2001, p. 18).

'How do you count the number of young people that you've "saved" as a result of local knowledge and close partnership with social services? How do you count the number of young people who haven't been out in the streets stabbing each other because you've provided other things for them to do?'

Stella Bailey, Director for Extended Services, George Green's Secondary School

---

Public service accountability, Giguere concludes, is insular and constrained by inconsistent national policy demands. Local, individual services, including schools, are rarely required to integrate the policy objectives assigned to the partners with whom they are expected, or need, to associate. Despite the evidence that schools which are outwardly engaged in effective networks are more likely to have specific goals and partners who feel included and empowered (Hill, 2006, p. 7), high-leverage leaders are faced with the difficult question, 'How do we know that the full breadth of our work is effective, efficient and worthwhile?'.

Without good evidence, high-leverage leaders are stuck with nothing more than an opinion, and that is not sufficient to fuel ambitious enquiry, to aid accountability or to fulfil any of the other purposes to which they want to put the evidence. They need evidence of the need for change and a clear view about what evidence would demonstrate success after change. Some of their more innovative work in school and in association with the surrounding communities is what David Hargreaves calls 'disciplined innovation' (Hargreaves, 2003a), driven by dissatisfaction with the *status quo* and an informed belief that more can be achieved. Hargreaves (2003b) writes that every school has to pose the questions: what is the most important and urgent problem area and where do we think we could innovate successfully? The answers, he writes (2003b, p. 38), come from exploring three questions:

- What do we need to know to be better equipped in this problem area?
- What do we currently know about this problem area?
- What do we need to do to close the gap?

Hargreaves's 'discipline in innovation' is recognisably akin to the high-leverage leaders' use of Analysis (Chapter 4) combined with Awareness and driven by Advocacy (Chapter 3). Some of this 'disciplined innovation' begins in competition with long-standing approaches to the work and to traditional measures of success. High-leverage leaders therefore accept the discipline that change and innovation require evidence of necessity and then can only be sustained if they are successful and can be seen to be successful.

In their approach to outcomes, evidence and accountability, many high-leverage leaders are more or less intuitively following the framework of Mark Friedman's 'Outcomes based Accountability' (Friedman, 2005). They are constantly alert to Friedman's central question, 'what would we do differently if outcomes really mattered?' (2005, p. 6). They connect, as Friedman suggests they should, the performance of their organisation to wider population outcomes by recognising that, although they can be a significant contributor, in the case of educational attainment the most significant service contributor, they can never be the only one. Many follow lines of questioning similar to those Friedman (2005, p. 12) proposes:

- Who are our customers?
- How can we measure if our customers are better off?

	Quantity	Quality
Effort	How much did we do?	How well did we do it?
Effect	Is anyone better off?	

Figure 7.1 Framework for discussing impact

Source: Based on Portsmouth, 2006, p. 14.

- How can we measure if we are delivering services well?
- How are we doing on the most important measures?
- Who are the partners who have a role to play in doing better?
- What works to do better, including low-cost and no-cost ideas?
- What do we propose to do?

Faced with key questions such as the three in Figure 7.1, high-leverage leaders are keen to avoid the temptation to which many public services appear to succumb, which is to concentrate on answering the most easily measured, 'how much did we do?'.

This temptation relies on the delusion that, 'because our intentions are virtuous, then, provided we *do* more, our results will look after themselves'. It is a delusion which draws service providers into 'box-ticking the completion of endless activities listed in action plans' (as one leader described it to us) in the belief that evidence of effort is itself an end rather than a means to the ends.

High-leverage leaders are interested in the answers to all three questions in Figure 7.1, but above all in knowing 'is anyone better off?' They have to combine rigorous Analysis and Application (Chapter 4) with the care for language and symbolism that we described as Advocacy (Chapter 3). The criteria chosen to judge success need to be resolutely monitored and at the same time they need to speak to the school community and its partners about core values. This in turn requires high-leverage leaders to balance four key aspects of accountability:

1 Accountability to externally derived standards, of which national targets for exam success and inspection judgements are the most obvious examples.
2 Accountability to locally derived standards, of which a school's ambitions to improve student wellbeing or contribute to community cohesions would be examples.
3 Accountability by progress in service development, which is an important tool when there is pressure for evidence of sustainable impact over implausibly short timescales and evidence of good foundation-building has to suffice.
4 Accountability by impact on outcomes, which is the end to which other forms of accountability are the means, demonstrating that the work is changing the achievement and life chances of young people.

	Progress evidence	Outcomes evidence
National standards	Ofsted reports	Pupil attainment
Local standards	Narrative accounts from providers, associates and service users	Indicators agreed with associates

Figure 7.2 Sources of evidence

Figure 7.2 illustrates how these four features interact and where high-leverage leaders are turning for the evidence in each case.

In the following paragraphs we consider the national and local indicators separately.

National indicators

One of the recurring themes in this book has been the acceptance by high-leverage leaders of central government's apparatus for high external accountability. They accept the importance of success measured by the quality of teaching, learning and attainment. That is, as we described in Chapter 4, not an external imposition, the academic success of young people is their core compact with their local community.

> 'School improvement has to be your driver. Education provides the keys to the kingdom and every child deserves a set.'
>
> Headteacher, Garforth Community School

High-leverage leaders understand the status of exam passes in individual lives and in the national psyche. When we wrote about their sense of Application, we noted their determination to deliver and then to build on consistently good pupil attainment. One school leader summarised that for us: 'The numbers do not lie: those end of term percentages show either what you've achieved or what you still have left to do.'

High-leverage leaders also know that they are vulnerable to trial by national inspection, especially in some of the most challenging contexts. In England this means inspectoral visits commissioned by the national inspectorate, Ofsted – about every four years but more regularly if there are concerns about performance.

In England, about one in 40 primary schools and one in 25 secondary schools is judged inadequate (Ofsted, 2009, p. 56) and 'Schools serving deprived communities are more likely to be in a category of concern' (2009, para. 143).

> 'I can't organise our work around what the inspectors might ask me one day. So when they do arrive, I organise the inspectors' work around what we want to tell them.'
>
> Primary School Leader

This is a risk that high-leverage leaders cannot leave to chance. They manage the inspection process primarily by ensuring that their pupil attainment is good or better because teaching and learning are good or better – the implacable focus on teaching and learning that we called Application (Chapter 4). They also, in their own often-repeated phrase, 'manage the inspection teams'. A significant part of that anticipation and management is in the preparation of evidence for the inspectors. The high-leverage leader quoted above, like most, is familiar with the Inspection Framework, the publicly available guide to how the inspectors work and make judgements. He organises the school's day-to-day work around its own priorities but evidence of the impact of each activity can be organised around the headings in the inspection framework. This leader's approach to Analysis, Action and Application means he can show how much, how well, and with what impact each activity has been done.

Local indicators

Local indicators add a powerful dimension to the work of high-leverage leaders. They deploy their Professional and Contextual Intelligence, using Advocacy, Analysis and Association, to agree priority outcomes within the school and across the locality. Rarely, if ever, using the phrase 'Outcomes Based Accountability', they nevertheless use a mindset similar to Friedman's (2005) framework (see page 144). They use that approach both to drive the work: 'what exactly are we trying to achieve and how would we do that?'; and account for it: 'what exactly is better for our children and families and how can we be certain?'

High-leverage leaders tell us that it is important to choose the indicators that are critical to success and to choose them in advance. Because some things are amenable to numeric assessment and analysis while some are best done by narrative accounts, the choice of reporting style is also important. We wrote in Chapter 4 that high-leverage leaders use information analysis rather than data analysis. Their Professional Intelligence leads them to combine numeric and narrative sources because they know that neither is capable of providing a rounded account of the real world they inhabit. In the local context, some of the numeric data collated by partners and associates and from social care, health, youth justice and other children's services can be presented alongside traditional education data to demonstrate the school's association with, if not its direct impact on, other outcomes for young people. To that, they add the narrative accounts provided by their staff, students and associated partners.

Clifton Green Primary School in York has used narrative in the reports for its Healthy Minds Projects. Annually and over the years, the accounts are a powerful history of the work. Two paragraphs from the Project's 2008–9 report summarise how a programme for new pupils whose first language is not English benefitted children and adults.

"All the children respond extremely well in small group situations and feel secure that they are receiving good support to help them learn. Small-group work also enables behaviour issues to be tackled more effectively which has resulted in minimal disruption to other children.

The success of this work has created a confidence from the teaching assistants. Four have gained Senior Teaching Assistant status, six gained Higher Lever status, and four teaching assistants are now qualified Learning Mentors. Four are Team Leaders in the Performance Management of other teaching assistants. A group of these teaching assistants was invited to give a presentation about their work at an annual Teaching Assistants' Conference."

Clifton Green 2009

High-leverage schools might, for example, share targets with their local partners to reduce antisocial behaviour inside the school and in the surrounding streets. This involves shared work and shared accountability. Friendship surveys and tracking incidents inside the school can be combined with citizen surveys and data provided by the local authority and police services to show the levels of improvement. The stories that children tell about the school and that adults tell about the neighbourhood can be added to this mix. High-leverage leaders know this is not absolute evidence of cause and effect but that, if it recurs often enough, it is reasonable to hypothesise cause and effect.

George Green's Secondary School in London's East End and The Westwood Secondary School in Coventry can each associate their community relationships with improved student behaviour in school. They also both use local crime statistics to show how their neighbourhoods are improving compared with others in the same police areas.

High-leverage schools also point to the local reduction in the numbers of young people who are not in employment, education or training (NEETs in the education service vernacular) and to the number of young people gaining nationally recognised qualifications in youth service provision, further education and higher education. Many believe that their Partnership work creates scaffolding across the neighbourhood and service communities and sustains young people who have good school-leaving qualifications but not the social or emotional infrastructure to see them safely into the early stages of adulthood.

Parental involvement and support are key indicators of progress for many high-leverage leaders and are often associated with a wider commitment to community regeneration in poor areas. They are pursued in the belief that they will contribute to increased aspiration and attainment for their children.

Measures we have come across include parental attendance at 'partnership meetings' – which deal with community issues and not directly with schooling or educational subjects. This is an approach taken by many schools, as we noted in Chapter 5, to build 'social capital'. Recording parental visits to the site before school starts in the morning is another measure.

> 'Keep hold of the wider picture and perspective. View learning in the widest sense and view it as long-term. Too many schools have structures in place that lead to goals that we don't really believe in, hurdles that we have to jump through. Don't lose sight of what learning really is about.'
>
> Headteacher, Delaware Primary School

The corollary, pupil engagement with the community outside school, is also a much-used indicator. Schools use a variety of monitoring exercises and surveys to track their students' involvement in and impact on community activities.

In conclusion, high-leverage leaders are astute in their use of outcomes, accountability and governance. They use nationally determined indicators and governance arrangements to establish their primary authority and the core purpose of their organisations. National determination is, however, prey to what Strike (2007, ch. 7) identifies as three vices:

- *goal displacement*: when providers either narrow their field of concern or reduce their ambitions to match precisely the minimum of the given indicators;
- *motivational displacement*: when providers lose personal, intrinsic motivation and care only about higher scores for external accountability;
- *gaming*: when providers find ways to meet performance indicators other than by providing better services, often in unethical if not harmful ways.

High-leverage leaders therefore use their Advocacy and Association to create a local-level approach which matches their interests and those of their colleagues and associate partners, which reinforces the personal, internal motivation of the key actors, and which draws deeply on a shared, ethical commitment to the agreed outcomes. These leaders understand that the evidence they produce serves two essential purposes. The production of evidence is never an end in itself. In its different forms, it first provides an account to other agencies and also to other people, families and children, of the quality of the work completed. It also simultaneously provides adults with the information they need to make informed judgments about how to improve the service they offer.

8 Reflections on high-leverage leadership in education

We have fulfilled two of the three aims we set ourselves in the introduction to this book.

- We have celebrated the work of the great school leaders and leadership teams we have been close to over the past decade or so.
- We have assembled our description and analysis of that work in a way which allows others to understand it and to reflect on their own practice through it.

In this chapter, we turn to our third aim: to explore the lessons that should be learned from the work of high-leverage leaders. We will:

- describe the importance of taking the principles of high-leverage leadership to scale from institutional through area to national levels, in particular the importance of fractal features in Navigation, Management and Partnership across levels;
- propose the necessity to move beyond a narrow use of 'system leadership' as a generic, vogue phrase;
- emphasise the importance of national education systems learning the lessons of their own experiments;
- explore how the framework of Navigation, Management and Partnership could be used to critique and improve not just institutional but also system leadership.

These are the four critical and distinct lessons to be learned from our analysis.

Taking the principles of high-leverage leadership to scale

Our thinking about the three levels in the education system was helped by Allenby and Sarewitz's (2011) Level 1, 2 and 3 descriptions of the complexity of human interdependence with new technology and its consequences for Enlightment Rationality. In an era of incomprehensible technological complexity and change, they argue, we have to escape the constraints of current assumptions about rational certainty but hold firm to our values if we are to have any prospect of directing our destinies. We think there is an analogy to be drawn between their high-level analysis and our communal grasp of the education system at three levels – institutional, area and national.

Institutional Level. At this level, high-leverage leadership might be described as a techno-social function, an approach designed to apply particular 'technical' skills in a social milieu to achieve a defined purpose. We have described that techno-social function; we have located it in the school improvement and effectiveness literature; we have created a particular framework to explain it. The techno-social function of high-leverage leadership is visible, applied and can be replicated. This function is not easy to provide; its delivery requires a complex and continuous struggle with existing practices. At this level, in the education service, the function is confined to the purposeful achievement of improved outcomes, especially academic attainment, usually in one and rarely more than two schools. We call this first level Institutional. The techno-function of high-leverage leadership at Institutional Level is generally amenable to rational analysis. So why, if we can describe it and analyse it, do we all struggle to explain why high-leverage leadership does not permeate across more schools at the Institutional Level and occur in every school that might benefit from it. This is something to do with the second and third levels.

Area Level. At this level high-leverage leaders engage with and are influenced by a more complex network. They bring their techno-social function to engage with a series of interconnected local activities and actors. The school leaders and their approaches become connected to and have an effect on families, neighbourhood groups, other local providers, local employment and local democracy. This bilateral, sometimes multilateral, reciprocity between inside and outside the school cannot be avoided and happens even when school leadership excludes wider concerns as best it can and confines itself to managing the core activity of teaching and learning. The effect might be greater or less, benign or malign, but it is always there. High-leverage leadership, which initially creates impressive outcomes for young people, will also have a longer-term influence on wider wellbeing and 'sense of place'. In broad terms, these leaders are modelling and then contributing to the resilience that the OECD (2011) has correlated with higher outcomes for young people from disadvantaged homes. Because an Area Level network is inevitably more complex than one at Institutional Level, the impact of the high-leverage leader is more difficult to track the further he or she moves away from managing attainment and other immediate outcomes for pupils. It is more difficult to apply rational analysis to understand how high-leverage leadership engages, influences or is influenced by the complex network at Area Level, still more so to prove what impact that engagement has on attainment or any other outcomes for students or anyone else.

National Level. This level is an apparently rational but actually chaotic network consisting mainly of subsidiary intricate networks including area networks. Despite the efforts of political leaders to create an illusion of coherence and control, at the National Level fragmentation and complexity are inevitable and pervasive. The visible parts of the national system, government policy and legislation, are the equivalent of that part of a swan that can be seen above water. The important action is happening out of sight. The activity and outcomes of high-leverage school leadership are churning away though none of us can properly grasp how they are influencing or are influenced by the 'national system'. In part, this can be described directly in terms of the relationship between national policies and school leaders; how these intentionally attempt to change one another. The unintended consequences are often more important: the way national policymakers take partial aspects of high-leverage leadership, promulgate them systemically and expect them to be embedded ubiquitously; the way that high-leverage leaders domesticate and cannibalise national policies to create local benefits. To these unforeseen consequences we can add the social and economic positioning in adult life of young people who have benefitted from high-leverage school leadership (not least the small but important number who return to work in the school). It also includes the relationship of neighbour-hoods and communities to national economic or social policies (and vice versa). Simply, the National Level begs the question of where high-leverage leadership fits in with the country's massive tectonic forces – social, political and economic.

We tend to become absorbed with the Institutional and Area Levels because they exist at a recognisable scale and are tolerably systemic (the cause and effect in their connecting parts makes some kind of sense). We think we can pretty much understand them and spot the levers that operate them. In contrast, our attempts to bring order to the National Level are riddled with unintended consequences. We usually attribute these to shortcomings at Institutional and Area Levels rather than to the endemic national incoherence. In England, that is typified by the national prescriptions for curriculum, pedagogy, assessment and leadership: in broad terms these are the National Curriculum, the National Strategies, league tables of attainment for 11- and 16-year-olds and the National College for School Leadership. All these produced some benefits alongside unintended, widespread and generally unwelcome consequences.

In Allenby and Sarewitz's (2011) analysis the relevance of enlightment thinking, rational analysis, the attribution of cause and the prediction of conse-quence, appear to diminish as systems become more complex. So, as we move from the relative certainties and coherence of the Institutional Level through Area Level and towards the uncertainties and even contradictions of the National Level, our capacity to grasp the system conceptually, still less managerially, is eroded. In the context of that shift, what does our framework of Navigation, Management and Partnership have to offer? These three and their subsets are the necessary features of high-leverage leadership. In Chapter 3, we wrote about the importance of the fractal nature of high-leverage institutions and the importance of behaviours, patterns, structures and processes being similar at small-group, department, faculty, and whole institutional levels. Our proposal here is that this is as important at Area Levels and National Levels as at the Institutional Level. High-leverage leadership at school level will only flourish if the National and Area Levels share the same triple helix DNA of Navigation, Management and Partnership that some schools already have available at Institutional Level.

Our observation is that the key elements of Navigation and Partnership, namely Advocacy and Association, are difficult, though not impossible, to maintain at Area Level and diminish towards disappearance at National Level. Consequently Management, in particular Action and Application, increases in direct proportion to fill the gaps and at National Level does so with increasingly dysfunctional results. This conceals what needs to be made explicit: that Advocacy and Association become more important as rational analysis, the attribution of cause and the prediction of consequences become less secure. Values and ethics become even more important foundations for behaviour when administration and managerialism have even less control over it. Values and ethics need to become the impetus for continuous learning and adaptive activity, or ignorance – because we cannot fathom the national system – will overwhelm us. If our tripartite framework is the template for high leverage at Institutional Level, then Area Levels and, even more so, National Levels need to become more obviously fractal in their replication of its principles.

In the following section, we will reflect on our second lesson, the extent to which the particular national interpretation of the phrases 'System Leader' and 'System Leadership' in England undermine the national capacity for Association.

Moving beyond a narrow use of system leadership

Without digging too deeply into definitions of what constitutes a system, we need to be clear about our use of the phrase high-leverage system leadership. In England at least, the phrase system leadership has a prevalent orthodoxy. It is widely used to describe the circumstances in which headteachers take on the responsibility of leading more than one school, leading partnerships and federations, leading on the delivery of other provision for children and in some cases even leading on the redefinition of relationships between schools and communities. Hopkins and Higham (2007) identified a five-point taxonomy to define the range of activity which, they propose, constitutes 'system leadership':

1 developing and leading a successful school improvement partnership between several schools;
2 choosing to lead and improve a school in extremely challenging circumstances;
3 partnering another school facing difficulties and improving it;
4 acting as a community leader to broker and shape partnerships and networks of wider relationships across local communities to support children's welfare and potential;
5 working as a change agent or expert leader.

The National College for School Leadership in England has similarly defined elements of system leadership to include headteachers providing executive leadership of more than one school, the leadership of networks of schools, the leadership of schools extending their provision for children beyond teaching and the leadership of communities in community development (National College,

2007). By this definition, the College estimates that almost two-thirds of school leaders (63 per cent) are system leaders, '... a term used to describe the various ways in which leaders support other leaders to improve outcomes for children and young people beyond their own schools' (National College, 2011a). The College's annual awards include one for 'outstanding contribution to system leadership'.

The OECD has reported on Flanders (Belgium), England, Finland, Victoria (Australia) and Austria as 'jurisdictions' promoting system leadership by school leaders. Reportedly, in part this is being pursued by leadership development across those systems and in part by '... creating possibilities for co-operation that promote going beyond leaders' own schools to promote improvement' (Pont *et al.*, 2008, p. 10). Pont and her colleagues repeatedly make the point that, in order to be 'system leaders' by this definition, those involved need to have been successful school leaders.

We share the enthusiasm of all these authors and many others for the approach they are describing and recognise the benefits brought by this dispersion of expertise across schools when excellent school leaders are involved (see Chapter 6). However, we regret that the originally helpful phrase 'system leadership' is becoming synonymous with a partial concept. Taking the phrase to describe something close to the leadership of a parallel set or series of schools, often quite locally, leaves a conceptual gap for thinking about the leadership for Area and National Levels of education services. It also leaves individual schools as the primary unit of analysis. This is because we are easily seduced by Institutional Level simplicity and choose to ignore the complexity, uncertainty and sometimes downright incomprehensibility of Area Level and National Level effects. That is not because those effects are unimportant but because they are difficult to grapple with. In England, some school leaders are being badged by the National College as 'National Leaders of Education' and others as 'Local Leaders of Education', '... so creating a critical mass of system leaders' (National College, 2011b). The figures we quoted in Chapter 6 and earlier in this chapter combine to send messages that the National College is creating the critical mass, when already two-thirds of leaders are involved in this activity, and that only a minority are competent to be accredited by the College in that role. This corralling of leadership to a minority in formal leadership roles runs directly counter to the high-leverage requirement for moving even beyond distributed leadership and cultural leadership and into Association.

That might be a welcome development for those whose inclination is to believe that leadership is more about control than impetus and who would also want to diminish the significance of Area and National Levels in order to make the former irrelevant and the latter untouchable. System leadership should, we think, be used to describe the activity of design and oversight at National or Area Level. Otherwise, the work from those levels becomes caricatured as legal rather than cultural, managerial rather than visionary, technical rather than developmental, bureaucratic rather than innovative. Above all, work at those levels is rarely described as leadership of the system. System leadership becomes the preserve of school leaders and we are invited to believe that no other system leadership is required – in effect, there is no need for a system beyond individual schools or a marginal inter-school level.

We think that this is a loss to the complex understanding of national or area systems. Given the growing body of evidence for higher tiers, '… both to support and drive and, in other cases, to hinder and obstruct improvement in schools and learning' (Barber *et al.*, 2010, p. 23), it is important that we have a language which acknowledges those tiers and their systemic overview. So, when we use the term 'system leadership', we will mean the leadership of the national and regional or district systems.

To describe relatively local and mainly cross-institutional leadership we will use the phrase 'catenate leadership' with the adjective deriving from a verb often used in chemistry and meaning arranged in chains or rings. Our experience and the wider research is that these catenate leaders operate broadly in four spheres:

1   as leaders of a particular brand when several schools are operated, as the English Academy system allows, at public expense by non-profit-making private providers;
2   as leaders of a network of schools, often but not always within a geographically defined area, which share one or more common interests in the improvement of outcomes for young people;
3   as leaders in a small grouping of two or more schools for which they hold executive responsibility;
4   as leaders alongside others by providing coaching, mentoring and other development opportunities to their colleagues in nearby schools.

We agree with Pont and her colleagues (2008) that '… to maximise the value of system leadership one needs to view it within the context of a learning organisation' (2008, p. 255). Technical and administrative problems will always be demanding, and their solutions will always make vital but uncelebrated contributions to success, but '… system leaders will need to work adaptively to lead people and organisations beyond restrictive boundaries, perceived wisdoms and entrenched cultures where they exist as barriers to improvement' (2008, p. 255). Findings like these, alongside our own observation of 'catenate leadership', confirm that to be effective this area of leadership draws on the repertoire of good institutional leadership skills which are encompassed by our framework of Navigation, Management and especially Partnership. That is not surprising if the best catenate leaders are recruited from amongst the best institutional leaders.

The importance of national education systems learning the lessons of their own experiments: learning nothing and forgetting nothing

In a phrase attributed to Talleyrand, the Bourbon kings, returning to rule France in the early nineteenth century after the French Revolution, '*n'ont rien appris, ni rien oublié*: having learned nothing and forgotten nothing, they were doomed to repeat their historic errors again … and again. We are concerned that many national systems appear trapped in a similar cycle. In England, for example, the system appears to be gripped by a volatile, endemic and ceaseless exploration incapable of arriving anywhere or knowing anything with confidence. This centrally flooded white-water ride runs contrary to what we have written about Advocacy and Analysis in particular. The absence of a living vision, the weak platform for enquiry as initiative and the incoherence of professional development combine to undermine the system's high-leverage capacity.

On the following pages we will criticise the accelerating helter-skelter of experiment to which school leadership in England has been exposed over the past 20 years or so. Our view is that the turmoil those experiments have created is now impeding the system's pursuit of excellence and equity. Neither excellence nor equity can benefit more than marginally from the disjointed and sometimes contradictory policies that have been rushed into the English education system from all political sides. We have argued earlier that high-leverage leaders are successful at defending their schools from systemic confusion and skilled in using the torrent of initiatives to their school's advantage – much like a wrestler using an opponent's impetus to add strength to their own movement. We conclude that the approaches embedded in our Framework can be used not only by local leaders within and across organisations but also by policymakers, executives and administrators in other parts of the system. High-leverage activity works across and should work through the system

The public education service is a continuous and massive social experiment. It has been like that in England since its origins in the late nineteenth century. It is bad enough that there are none of the agreed points of reference to which the physical sciences can turn as the basis of the next enquiry. Matters are made worse when the switching of variables becomes increasingly frequent and turbulent, as it has been over the past two decades. This has confused the nature of the experiment as well as preventing any useful analysis from being completed, still less understood or spread. In England, the major systemic and curricular changes – other than periodic rises in the school leaving age – appeared to work through most of the 20th century on a cycle of around two decades. The pace changed with the 1988 Education Reform Act, which presaged the introduction of a national curriculum, a national assessment framework, publication of student performance school by school, funding based largely on pupil numbers, more open student enrolment and the opportunity for schools to opt away from local authority supervision to a quasi-independent status. That Act was promptly followed by the 1992 Education (Schools) Act that established the new national inspectorate, Ofsted, to employ private contractors to inspect every school and to publish the consequent reports. Three more Education Acts followed in that decade, in 1993, 1996 and 1997, to consolidate the preceding versions.

In 1998, and then in 2002, the then Labour government passed significant Education Acts introducing selection by aptitude, earned autonomy (high-attaining schools being released from aspects of the National Curriculum) and greater diversity in secondary education (increasing numbers of specialist schools and academies with strong private-sector connections). These Acts additionally gave the Secretary of State subsidiary powers to experiment with aspects of the system, in effect to legislate for change, without further parliamentary authority.

This led to a series of policy initiatives, some of which had legislative authority and some of which were carried forward by the weight of political *force majeur*. They included a number of 'National Strategies', an unprecedented intervention in classroom practice by central government in England, promoting particular pedagogic and curricular approaches to raise standards in 'core subjects'. Policy was promoted through major publications in successive years. In 2004, the 'Five Year Strategy for Children and Learners', was described as 'the death knell of the comprehensive system' for its promotion of increased specialisation and school autonomy (the *Guardian*, 2004). In 2005, 'Higher Standards, Better Schools for All' was the title of the policy documents which preceded yet another major Act – the Education and Inspection Act 2006. Among its many detailed provisions, the 2006 Act allowed all schools to become 'Trust Schools' by forming links with external partners who would be able to appoint the majority of the governors, own their own assets, employ their own staff, set their admission arrangements and apply for additional flexibilities. Local authorities would be corralled into a role promoting choice, diversity, high standards and the fulfilment of potential for every child while responding to parental concerns about the quality of local schools. The final three years of the Labour Government saw three more Education Acts: the 2008 Education and Skills Act, the 2009 Apprenticeships, Skills, Children and Learning Act, and the 2010 Children, Schools and Families Act. The 2009 Act is notable for the 153 new powers it gave to central government ministers, and the 2010 Act for its truncation by the dissolution of Parliament and the government's defeat in the consequent general election.

Experiment has not ended there, and at the time of writing the coalition government formed in 2010 already has several initiatives, a major cut-back on new school building and one Education Act under its belt (the Academies Act 2010). The Academies Act aims to increase the number of state-funded independent Academies and to facilitate the creation of 'Free Schools' funded by the state and run by local groups of parents. The government, in its pursuit of more freedoms and autonomy for schools, is also reducing in number, size and influence the organisations established by previous governments to manage the system.

Experiment – what David Hargreaves (2003) might call 'disciplined innovation' – is not a bad thing: it is an essential feature of vibrant and improving organisations or systems. We are not opposed to experiment or innovation, but we are not describing 'disciplined innovation'. We are describing a series of national experiments in which

- *hypotheses* have been distorted by ideology;
- *methods* have been manipulated by political expediency; and

- *conclusions* have been obscured by the recurring loss of communal memory.

The international literature confirms that England is not the only democracy with this frenetic experience. The frantic introduction of one wilful and incomplete experiment after another magnifies tensions that are inherent in any national system. We will note what those tensions are and explain why we believe our framework could contribute to a form of system leadership that resolves them.

Reflecting on Navigation, Management and Partnership

There are also a number of tensions relating to navigation. First, there is a lack of clarity relating to awareness. There is no consensus about what the key issues and agenda are because there is no agreed sense of purpose. Second, the system is characterised by 'buck-passing'. No-one takes responsibility, national governments are set against local governments, schools against districts, the centre against the local. This creates a system underpinned by mistrust where acceptance is viewed as weakness and failure. Therefore, relational trust, a feature associated with improving academic achievement in primary schools in the United States, tends to be low (Bryk and Schneider, 2002). Third, constant change is bewildering for providers. The language of improvement changes as political regimes change. These symbolic changes are important and limit advocacy.

The tensions relating to management are threefold. First, in terms of analysis the system is data-rich but not information-wise. Educationists and the public are confused about what is valid information and about what weight to give to differing narratives. For example, Ofsted claims to appraise the quality and standards of education and works on the assumption that it is providing an independent and objective assessment of individual schools:

> An appraisal of the quality of and standards of education in the school ... The function of the report is to evaluate, not prescribe or speculate; reports must be as objective as possible.
>
> (Ofsted, 1993, p. 7)

However, the picture Ofsted constructs is biased towards decontextualised quantitative information that tends to be given more weight and credibility compared to qualitative insights and explanations. Furthermore, as networks, chains, federations and other collaborative arrangements emerge, more pupils and staff are moving between schools. This blurring of institutional boundaries means the 'school' is an outmoded unit of analysis. This further distorts any picture painted by a flawed accountability system.

Second, in terms of action, political interference ensures a rapid pace of change. This means the focus of effort keeps shifting, and support is often late, marginalised or never appears. This is problematic because schools are constantly having to readjust their focus and priorities to reflect the latest policy direction, and associated accountability measures have to be put in place to ensure compliance. Therefore, considerable energy is invested for minimal reward. Reflecting on reforms in Canada, Andy Hargreaves highlights a similar set of issues:

> Despite the Ontario government's access to world-class advice on change implementation, almost everything which is known about successful change management was absent in the speed with which the government rushed through its reform agenda, the scope of issues the reforms addressed, and the quality and levels of support that were provided to (or withheld from) teachers responsible for implementing them.
>
> (Hargreaves, 2003, pp. 79–80)

Third, in practical terms the monitoring of performance is externalised and the imbalance between internal and external accountability limits the potential of high-leverage activity so that tenacity is undermined. Put simply, what is valued is not always seen as important because of account-ability mechanisms. This is contrary to high-leverage systems. For example, in Finnish schools, self-evaluation has been linked to improved classroom practices (Webb *et al.*, 1998).

For Partnership, there are a number of important tensions within systems. First, for Association, there is a lack of emotional intelligence, empathy or linking capital in the system. Put simply, the explosive mix of policies blending competition and collaboration does not create the conditions that bring people together in a meaningful way. Second, there is no alignment within the system; instead, there are competing agendas at every level. Even parents are treated as consumers rather than partners. Third, in terms of area focus, the system has encouraged competition rather than partnership. Recent shifts have supported new cross-school partnerships at the expense of broader relationships with other services. The tensions we have described are inherent in large systems. They cannot be resolved, nor will they evaporate. However, our observation is that they can be magnified or alleviated, emphasised or diminished by the ways in which actors choose to play their parts.

Over the past 20 years Management has been underplayed and Navigation overemphasised. This has led to a situation where some school leaders have become so wrapped up in the rhetoric and spin of leadership that they fail to pay attention to the detail and complexity of operational management. In some settings this has resulted in leadership and management roles becoming separated within a senior team. The role of the principal or headteacher is reduced to that of a figurehead, a public face, while other senior leaders are concerned with the management of the school. The emergence of the title of 'operational principal' is evidence of this shift. More recently, during the past five years, Partnership has emerged as an important dimension of leadership. However, structures rather than relationships have dominated the discourse and there has been an emphasis on transaction and exchange that serves to maintain the *status quo*, rather than on values or purpose which would be more likely to stimulate development.

Navigation, Management and system leadership

Several education systems around the world have generated leaders who are adept at change management in challenging settings. This cadre of leaders is particularly evident in England. They belong to a government-recognised club of National Leaders of Education (NLEs); they have a track record of success evidenced through Ofsted inspections; they demonstrate great skill and tenacity at turning around failing schools, and they work as system leaders to support the improvement of schools with a prolonged history of underperformance. In the autumn of 2006 the New Labour government identified 68 NLEs, and their schools became designated 'National Support Schools'. By 2008 their numbers had risen to 180 (Higham, Hopkins and Matthews, 2009). The current government has pledged its support to the policy and is investing up to £7.3 million to swell the number of NLEs from 393 in 2010 to 1000 by 2014. A DfE press release claimed primary schools receiving NLE support in 2007–8 saw a ten-point increase in pupils achieving their expected levels, and in secondary schools that received support, pupils' achievement at GCSE improved at twice the national average (DfE, 2010c).

The best of these 'system leaders' pay particular attention to building alliances which resonate with specific school contexts, have high expectations of the outcomes of partnerships and perhaps most importantly use partnerships to strengthen capacity for change.

There are three key issues in the identification of future system leaders. First, in their preparation future leaders must understand the importance of vision and advocacy within leadership. Until now this has been an under-valued and underdeveloped area. Second, future leaders must also be aware that, as a system becomes more fragmented and autonomy increases, leaders' management skills become more important. Finally, leaders' ability to build external alliances will become increasingly important as system fragmentation and increased autonomy become the norm. Again, these are both important areas which to date have been undervalued and underdeveloped.

In future systems, system leaders at the national and district level need to be clear about what is expected of schools and, in particular, what levels of variation in practice and performance are tolerable. System leaders also need to be clearer about the expected outcomes and manage them assiduously. And finally, the space needs to be created for partnership working. The purpose of partnerships needs to be clear and they must be built on strong relationships rather than benign structures. These partnerships must be rewarded and respected. Put simply, the system needs to be responsible for the deployment, development and sustainability of system leadership.

The purposes of education systems are not usually self-evident, easily discernible or agreed – they are more often obscure and contested. The tensions we described earlier tend to push school leaders to one or another of two extremes, creating an hourglass-shaped disposition across their profession. Where each of them settles will depend in part on how the glass is shaken and in part on the granularity of their own context and personality. It will not be easy to settle in the middle ground. At one end of the hourglass the leaders will tend to be technocrats, leaders who see themselves primarily as the technical managers of pedagogy. Their focus will be on the oversight of teaching and learning leading to success measured by academic attainment in national tests. That focus will define their appeal to some parents in a market-style school economy.

Leaders at the other end of the hourglass are sociocrats, by which we mean leaders who see education and schooling as predominantly social activities founded on strong relationships within and across institutions, services and communities. Their focus is on the creation of a wider range of social relationships – of which high-quality pedagogy is one – which deliver high attainment alongside other outcomes for children and young people.

High-leverage leaders will tend to be sociocrats. They recognise that sustainable improvement is built on enduring relationships within a school, between a school and its community and, eventually, across the community. The challenge facing national educational systems is whether their authorising environments and the professional development of their potential leaders are capable of delivering school leaders of that type in sufficient numbers and in the right places to achieve the step changes in outcomes which the 21st century seems to require. Authorising environments and professional cultures which look to an idealised past and in which the 3Rs and Mr Chips (Hilton, 1934) are the zeitgeist will be a poor legacy for future generations. They will not produce the living vision, the curriculum framework, the strategic service design or the relationships that today's pupils will need to survive communally as tomorrow's citizens. There are enough examples of high-leverage leaders and their impact inside the education systems we have worked in or read about for the systems to learn from them and to benefit from their qualities. That cannot be achieved by centralist direction or free market operations. The medium is indeed part of the message. Whether national governments can realise, as high-leverage leaders do, that education is not a matter either of command and control or of individual inclination but of association built by trust and shared commitment, remains to be seen.

References

Ainscow, M. and West, M. (2006) *Improving Urban Schools: Leadership and Collaboration*, Maidenhead: Open University Press.

Allenby, B.R. and Sarewitz, D. (2011) *The Techno-Human Condition*, London: MIT.

Audit Commission (2005) *Governing Partnerships: bridging the accountability gap*, London: Audit Commission.

Auld, R. (1976) *William Tyndale Junior and Infant Schools Public Inquiry. A Report to the Inner London Education Authority*, London: ILEA.

Ball, S.J. (2003) *The more things change ... educational research, social class and "interlocking" inequalities*, London: Institute of Education.

Barber, M., Whelan, F. and Clark, M. (2010) *Capturing the leadership premium: How the world's top school systems are building leadership capacity for the future*, available online at http://www.mckinsey.com/clientservice/Social_Sector/our_practices/Education/Knowledge_Highlights/Capturing%20the%20leadership%20premium.aspx/ (accessed 9 August 2011).

BBC Education (1999) *'Sandhurst for schools'*, available online at http://news.bbc.co.uk/1/hi/education/481243.stm/ (accessed 9 August 2011).

BBC News (2011) 'UK pupils "among least likely to overcome tough start"', Report on OECD PISA project, 17 June 2011, available online at http://www.bbc.co.uk/news/education-13794591 (accessed 24 June 2011).

Beckett F (2004) 'Business class', *Guardian* 9 July, available online at http://www.guardian.co.uk/politics/2004/jul/09/publicservices.schools (accessed 12 August 2011).

Bell, L., Bolam, R. and Cubillo, L. (2003) *A systematic review of the impact of school leadership and management on student outcomes*, London: EPPI-Centre, Social Science Research Unit, Institute of Education, University of London. Available online at: eppi.ioe.ac.uk/cms/LinkClick.aspx?fileticket=G74GsI2AJ3Q%3d&tabid=317&mid=1220&language=en-US/ (accessed 9 August 2011).

Biddle, B.J. (2001) *Social Class, Poverty and Education: Policy and practice*, London: Routledge Falmer.

Boreham, N. and Reeves, J. (2004) *Strategies for School Improvement: Transferring the Concept of Organizational Learning from an Oil Refinery to a Local Authority Education Department*. Paper presented at the Annual Conference of the British Educational Research Association, UMIST, Manchester, Thursday 16 September 2004. Available online at https://dspace.stir.ac.uk/bitstream/1893/1154/3/BERA-2004-(WL)-Strategies-for-School-Improvement.pdf/ (accessed 9 August 2011).

Brighouse, T. and Woods, D. (2006) *Inspirations: A collection of commentaries to promote school improvement*, London: Continuum.

Brighouse, T. and Woods, D. (2008) *What makes a good school now?* London: Continuum.

Brooke-Smith, R. (2003) *Leading Learners, Leading School*, London: Routledge Falmer.

Brophy, J.E. and Good, T.L. (1970) 'Teachers' communication of differential expectations for children's classroom performance: Some behavioral data', *Journal of Educational Psychology*, 61: 365–74.

Bryk, A.S. and Schneider, B. (2002) *Trust in schools – A core resource for improvement*, New York: Russell Sage Foundation.

Bush, T. (2003) *Theories of Educational Leadership and Management*, London: Paul Chapman.

Bush, T. and Glover D. (2002) *School Leadership: Concepts and evidence*, Nottingham: National College.

Cabinet Office (2010) *Building the Big Society*, London: Cabinet Office. Available online at http://www.cabinetoffice.gov.uk/sites/default/files/resources/building-big-society_0.pdf/ (accessed 9 August 2011).

Caldwell, B. (2008) 'Reconceptualizing the Self-managing School', *Educational Management Administration Leadership*, 36: 235–49.

Chapman, C. (2004) 'Leadership in Schools Facing Challenging Circumstances', *London Review of Education*, 2(2): 95–108.

Chapman, C. (2006) *Improving Schools Through External Intervention*, London: Continuum.

Chapman, C., Ainscow, M., Bragg, J., Hull, J., Mongon, D., Muijs, D. and West, M. (2008) *Emerging Patterns of School Leadership: Current trends and future directions*. Nottingham: National College.

Chapman, C., Ainscow, M., Mongon, D., Muijs, D. and West, M. (2009) *Emerging Patterns of School Leadership: A deeper understanding*, Nottingham: National College.

Chapman, C. and Gunter, H. (eds) (2009) *Radical reforms: perspectives on an era of educational change*, Abingdon: Routledge.

Chapman C. and Harris, A. (2004) 'Strategies for School Improvement in Schools Facing Challenging Circumstances', *Educational Research*, 46(3): 219–28.

Chapman, C., Lindsay, G., Harris, A., Muijs, D., Arweck and Goodall, G. (2006) *The role of school-to-school collaboration as a strategy for raising education standards in urban contexts: The Federations Policy*. Paper presented to American Education research Association Annual Meeting, San Fransisco, 7–11 April.

Chapman, C., Muijs, D., Collins, A. and Sammons, P. (2009) *The Impact of Federations on Student Outcomes*, Nottingham: National College.

Chapman, C., Muijs, D. and Macallister, J. (2011) *The Impact of Federations on Student Outcomes*, a follow-up study, Nottingham: National College.

Chatwin, B. (1986) *Songlines*, Philadelphia: Franklin Press.

Clarke, P. (ed.) (2005) *Improving Schools in Difficulty*, London: Continuum.

Clifton Green School (2009) *Emotional and Social Intervention Programmes: Report on fifth year – September 2008–July 2009*. Unpublished. York: Clifton Green Primary School.

Close, P. and Wainwright, J. (2010) 'Who's in charge? Leadership and culture in extended service contexts', *School Leadership and Management*, 30(5): 435–50.

Coleman, A. (2011a) 'The significance of trust in school based collaborative leadership', *International Journal of Leadership in Education* [forthcoming].

Coleman, A. (2011b) 'Towards a Blended Model of Leadership for School-based Collaborations', *Educational Management Administration & Leadership*, 39(3): 296–316.

Collins, J. (2001) *Good to Great: why some companies make the leap and others don't.* London: Random House.

Connolly, P. (2006) 'The effects of social class and ethnicity on gender differences in GCSE attainment: a secondary analysis of the Youth Cohort Study of England and Wales 1997–2001', *British Educational Research Journal*, 32(1): 3–21.

Copland, M.A. (2003) 'Leadership of Inquiry: Building and Sustaining Capacity for School Improvement', *Educational Evaluation and Policy Analysis*, 25(4): 375–95.

Corbett, A. (1972) 'The school governors we want', *Where, The Education Magazine for Parents*, 69 (May/June).

Cordingley P., Bell M., Rundell B. and Evans D. (2003) 'The impact of collaborative CPD on classroom teaching and learning'. In: *Research Evidence in Education Library*. London: EPPI-Centre, Social Science Research Unit, Institute of Education, University of London.

Cordingley, P., Bell, M., Thomason S. and Firth, A. (2005) 'The impact of collaborative continuing professional development (CPD) on classroom teaching and learning.' London: EPPI-Centre, Social Science Research Unit, Institute of Education, University of London. Available online at http://eppi.ioe.ac.uk/cms/LinkClick.aspx?fileticket=TFVw%2bEl3y08%3d&tabid=136&mid=959&language=en-US (accessed 12 August 2011).

Craig, J. (2005) *Taking the wide view: report of six ContinYou/NCSL conferences,* London: DEMOS.

CUREE (2009a) *How can we identify the most vulnerable pupils?* Available online at www.tlrp.org/pa/index.php?option=com_content&task=view&id=189&Itemid=40/ (accessed 22 December 2009).

CUREE (2009b) *Gathering evidence through observing others.* Available online at http://www.nationalcollege.org.uk/docinfo?id=33195&filename=gathering-evidence-through-observing-others.pdf/ (accessed 22 December 2009).

Cuthbert, C.D. and Hatch, R. (2008) *Educational Aspiration and Attainment amongst young people in deprived communities.* Available online at http://www.crfr.ac.uk/spa2009/Cuthbert%20C,%20Hatch%20R%20-%20Educational%20aspiration%20and%20attainment%20amongst%20young%20people%20in%20deprived%20communities.pdf/ (accessed 15 June 2011).

Dalin, P. (2005) *School Development: theories and strategies,* London: Continuum.

Davies, B. (ed.) (2009) *The Essentials of School Leadership* 2nd edition, London: Sage Publications.

Davies B. and Davies B.J. (2009) 'Strategic Leadership', in Davies, B. (ed.), *The Essentials of School Leadership*, 2nd edn, London: Sage Publications.

Davies, B and West-Burnham, J. (eds) (2003) *Handbook of Educational Leadership and Management,* London: Pearson/Longman.

Davis, J. (2002) 'The Inner London Education Authority and the William Tyndale Junior School Affair, 1974–1976', *Oxford Review of Education*, 28(2): 275–98.

Day, C., Harris, A., Hadfield, M., Tolley, H. and Beresford, J. (2000) *Leading Schools in Times of Change,* Buckingham: Open University Press.

Day, C., Sammons, P., Hopkins, D., Harris, A., Leithwood, K., Gu, Q., Brown, E., Ahtaridou, E. and Kington, A., (2007) *The impact of school leadership on pupil outcomes: interim report.* Nottingham: DCSF. (Research report DCSF-RR018.) Available online at: http://www.education.gov.uk/publications//eOrdering Download/DCSF-RR108.pdf/ (accessed 9 August 2011).

Day, C., Sammons, P., Hopkins, D., Harris, A., Leithwood, K., Gu, Q. and Brown, E. (2010) *10 Strong Claims about Successful School Leadership.* Nottingham: National College.

Day, C., Sammons, P., Hopkins, D., Leithwood, K. and Kington, A. (2008) 'Research into the impact of school leadership on pupil outcomes: policy and research contexts', *School Leadership and Management*, 28(1): 5–25.

Day, C., Sammons, P., Leithwood, K., Hopkins, D., Gu, Q., Brown, E. and Ahtaridou, E. (2011) *Successful School Leadership.* Buckingham: Open University Press.

DCSF (2008a) *The extra mile: how schools succeed in raising the aspirations in deprived communities*, Nottingham: Department for Children, Schools and Families. Available online at: publications.teachernet.gov.uk/eOrderingDownload/3882_ The%20Extra%20Mile_web.pdf/ (accessed 9 August 2011).

DCSF (2008b) Table 4.3.1 in *Youth Cohort Study and Longitudinal Study of Young People in England: the Activities and Experiences of 16 year olds: England 2007.* (Statistical bulletin.) London: Department for Children, Schools and Families. Available online at http://www.dcsf.gov.uk/rsgateway/DB/SBU/b000795/ index.shtml/ (accessed 9 August 2011).

DCSF (2009) *School Workforce in England (including pupil:teacher ratios and pupil:adult ratios)*, January 2009 (Provisional) SFR 09/2009. Available online at http://www.dcsf.gov.uk/rsgateway/DB/SFR/s000844/SFR09_2009PDFv2. pdf (accessed 16 September 2011).

Dean, C., Dyson, A., Gallannaugh, F., Howes, A. and Raffo, C. (2007) *Schools, governors and disadvantage*, York: Joseph Rowntree Foundation.

Dennis, N. (1980) 'Sociology, Education and Equality in the Sociology of Education: a review of Halsey, Heath & Ridge's Origins and Destinations', *Oxford Review of Education*, 6(2): 111–31.

Desforges, C. and Abouchaar, A. (2003) *The impact of parental involvement, parental support and family education on pupil achievement and adjustment: a literature review*, Research Report No 433, London: DfES.

DfE (2010a) *School Workforce in England (including pupil:teacher ratios and pupil:adult ratios)*, January 2010 (Provisional) SFR11/2010. Available online at http://www.dcsf.gov.uk/rsgateway/DB/SFR/s000927/index.shtml (accessed 16 September 2010).

DfE (2010b). Available online at http://www.education.gov.uk/inthenews/ inthenews/a0061085/gove-teachers-not-politicians-know-how-best-to-run-schools (accessed 15 August 2011).

DfE (2010c) News and press notices available at http://www.education.gov.uk/ inthenews/inthenews/a0067809/new-leadership-for-children-in-need (accessed 10 May 2011).

DfE (Department for Education) (2011a) *A Guide to becoming an academy*, London, Department for Education. http://www.education.gov.uk/schools/leadership/ typesofschools/academies/becominganacademy/b0061257/how-to-become-an-academy (accessed on 17 May 2011).

DfE (Department for Education) (2011b) Research and Statistics Gateway. Available at http://www.education.gov.uk/rsgateway/index.shtml (accessed 13 June 2011).

DfE (Department for Education) (2011c) *School Spending Data*. Available at http://www.education.gov.uk/schools/adminandfinance/financialmanagement/b0072409/background (accessed 24 January 2011).

DfEE (1999) *The Department for Education and Employment, Learning Elements of the Single Regeneration Budget* http://www.lifelonglearning.co.uk/srb/content.htm (accessed 27 October 2010).

DfES (2005) *Extended schools: Access to opportunities and services for all – A prospectus,* Nottingham: DfES.

DfES (2006) *A guide to the Law for School Governors* London: HMSO.

DfES (2007) *Making great progress – schools with outstanding rates of progression in Key Stage 2*, Nottingham: Department for Education and Skills available at http://www.education.gov.uk/publications/standard/publicationdetail/Page1/DFES-00443-2007#downloadableparts (accessed 24 January 2011).

Dimmock, C. (1999) 'Principals and school restructuring: conceptualising challenges as dilemmas', *Journal of Educational Administration*, 22(5): 131–40.

Dimmock, C. and Walker, A. (2005) *Educational Leadership: Culture and Diversity,* London: Sage Publications.

Donnachie, I. (2000) *Robert Owen. Owen of New Lanark and New Harmony*, East Linton: Tuckwell Press.

Drucker, P.F. (2007) *The Essential Drucker*, Oxford: Butterworth-Heinemann.

Earley, P. (2003) 'Leaders or followers? Governing bodies and their role in school leadership', *Educational Management and Administration*, 31(4): 353–67.

Earley, P. and Creese, M. (2003) 'Governors and school improvement', *Research Matters No. 20*. London: Institute of Education.

Earley, P., Evans, J., Gold, A., Collarbone, P. and Halpin, D. (2002) *Establishing the Current State of School Leadership in England.* London: DfES.

Edmonds, R.R. (1979) 'Effective schools for the urban poor', *Educational Leadership*, 37(1): 20–4.

Elmore, R.F. (2004) *School reform from the inside out: Policy, practice, and performance*, Cambridge, MA: Harvard University Press.

Engels, N., Hotton, G., Devos, G., Bouckenooghe, D. and Aelterman, A. (2008) 'Principals in schools with a positive school culture', *Educational Studies*, 34(3): 157–72.

Englefield, S. (2002) *Leading to success: judging success in primary schools in challenging contexts*. (Practitioner enquiry report.) Nottingham: National College.

ERA (1988) *Education Reform Act 1988*. London: National Archives. Available online at http://www.legislation.gov.uk/ukpga/1988/40/contents/ (accessed 9 August 2011).

Evans, R. (2007) 'The Human Side of School Change', in *The Jossey-Bass Reader on Educational Leadership*, 2nd Edn, San Francisco: Jossey Bass.

Feinstein, L., Duckworth, K. and Sabates, R. (2004) *A model of inter-generational transmission of educational success*. (Wider benefits of learning research reports No. 10.) London: Centre for Research on the Wider Benefits of Learning, Institute of Education, University of London. Available online at http://www.learningbenefits.net/Publications/ResReps/ResRep10.pdf/ (accessed 11 August 2011).

Feinstein, L., Sabates, R., Anderson, T.M., Sorhaindo, A. and Hammond, C. (2006) *What are the effects of education on health?* OECD Copenhagen Symposium on

Measuring the Effects of Education on Health and Civic Engagement. Available online at http://www.oecd.org/dataoecd/15/18/37425753.pdf (accessed 11 August 2011).

FFT (2011) Fischer Family Trust Data Analysis Project. Available online at http://www.fischertrust.org/dap_overview.aspx/ (accessed 11 August 2011).

Fink, D. (2005) 'Developing Leaders for their future not our past', in Coles, M.J. and Southworth, G., *Developing Leadership: creating the schools of tomorrow*, Maidenhead: Open University Press.

Flint, N. (2010) *Schools, Communities and Social Capital*, unpublished research associate report produced by the headteacher of Aspinal Primary School, Manchester, for the National College.

Foucault, M. (1977) *Discipline and Punish: The birth of the prison*, London: Penguin.

Foucault, M. (1980) *Power/Knowledge: Selected Interviews and Other Writings 1972–1977*, edited by Colin Gordon, London: Harvester.

Friedman, M. (2005) *Trying Hard is Not Good Enough*, Victoria, Canada: Trafford Publishing.

Fullan, M. (2001) *Leading in a Culture of Change*, San Francisco: Jossey-Bass.

Fullan, M. (2003a) *The moral imperative of school leadership*, Thousand Oaks: Corwin Press.

Fullan, M. (2003b) *Change forces with a vengeance*, London: Routledge.

Fullan, M. (2004) *Systems Thinkers in Action: Moving beyond the Standards Plateau*, London/Nottingham: DfES Innovation Unit/NCSL.

Fullan, M. (2005) *Leadership and Sustainability: System Thinkers in Action*. Thousand Oaks: Corwin.

Fullan, M. (2006) *Turnaround Leadership*, San Francisco: Wiley and Son.

Fullan, M. (2008) *The Six Secrets of Change*, San Francisco, John Wiley. Quote available on the National College website at http://www1.nationalcollege.org.uk/index/leadershiplibrary/ldr-magazine/back-ldr-issues/ldr-january-2010/ldr-jan-10-practical-steps-how-to-tackle-variation.htm (accessed 11 June 2010).

Gardner, H. (1983) *Frames of mind: The theory of multiple intelligences*. New York: Basic.

Gazeley, L. and Dunne, M. (2005) *Addressing working class underachievement*. (Research commissioned by Multiverse.) Falmer: University of Sussex.

Giguere, S. (2001) *Local partnerships for better governance*, Paris: OECD.

Gillborn, D. (2008) *Racism and Education: Coincidence or conspiracy*. London: Routledge.

Gladwell, M. (2000) *The Tipping Point: How little things can make a big difference*, London: Little, Brown.

Gleeson, D. and Husbands, C. (eds) (2001) *The Performing School*, London: RoutledgeFalmer.

Goldthorpe, J.H. and McKnight, A. (2004) *The economic basis of social class.* (CASE paper 80.) London: Centre for Analysis of Social Exclusion, London School of Economics and Political Science. Available online at http://sticerd.lse.ac.uk/dps/case/cp/CASEpaper80.pdf (accessed 11 August 2011).

Gove, M. (2011) Speech made at the Education World Forum, London, 11 January 2011. Available online at http://www.education.gov.uk/inthenews/speeches/a0072274/michael-gove-to-the-education-world-forum (accessed 18 May 2011).

Grace, G. (1995) *School Leadership. Beyond educational management: an essay in policy scholarship*, London: Routledge.

Gray, J., Hopkins, D., Reynolds, D., Wilcox, B., Farrell, S. and Jesson, D. (1999) *Improving Schools: Performance and Potential*, Buckingham: Open University Press.

Green, A., Preston, J. and Sabates, R. (2003) *Education, Equity and Social Cohesion: A Distributional Model*, London: The Centre for Research on the Wider Benefits of Learning, Institute of Education.

Greenleaf, R.K. (2003) *The Servant Leader Within: A Transformative Path*, New Jersey: Paulist Press.

Grint, K., (2001) *The Arts of Leadership*. Oxford: Oxford University Press.

Gronn, P. (1996) 'From Transactions to Transformations: A New World Order in the Study of Leadership?' *Educational Management & Administration*, 24(1): 7–30.

Gronn, P. (2000) 'Distributed Properties: A New Architecture for Leadership', *Educational Management Administration & Leadership*, 28: 317–38.

Gronn, P. (2003) 'Without leadership?', in Davies, B and West-Burnham, J. (eds) *Handbook of Educational Leadership and Management*, London: Pearson/ Longman; pp. 60–6.

GTCE (2005) *Consulting pupils about teaching and learning*, General Teaching Council for England. Available online at http://www.gtce.org.uk/pdf/tla/rft/ pup_learn0605 (accessed 11 August 2011).

GTCE (2009) *Accountability in Teaching – Key messages from two research studies*, General Teaching Council for England. Available online at http://www.gtce.org. uk/documents/publicationpdfs/accountability_findings0909.pdf (accessed 10 February 2010).

Hallinger, P. and Heck, R.H. (1996) 'The principal's role in school effectiveness: An assessment of methodological progress, 1980–1995', in Leithwood, K. and Hallinger, P. (eds) *International Handbook of Educational Leadership and administration*, Dordrecht: Kluwer.

Hallinger, P. and Heck, R.H. (2010) 'Collaborative leadership and school improvement: Understanding the impact on school capacity and student learning', *School Leadership and Management*, 30(2): 95–110.

Hansard (1981) *House of Commons Debate 29 January 1981*, vol. 997 c489W.

Hargreaves, A. (2001) 'Emotional geographies of teaching', *Teachers' College Record*, 103(6): 1056–80.

Hargreaves, A. (2003) *Teaching in the knowledge society: education in the age of insecurity*. Buckingham: Open University Press.

Hargreaves, A. (2004) 'Distinction and disgust: the emotional politics of school failure', *International Journal of Leadership in Education*, 7(1): 27–41.

Hargreaves, A. and Shirley, D. (2009) *The Fourth Way*, London: Sage.

Hargreaves, D. (2003a) *Working laterally: how innovation networks make an education epidemic*, Nottingham: DfES.

Hargreaves, D. (2003b) *Education Epidemic: Transforming Secondary Schools through innovation networks*, London: Demos.

Hargreaves, D. (2010) *Creating a self-improving school system*, Nottingham, National College. Available online at http://www.nationalcollege.org.uk/docinfo?id=133 672&filename=creating-a-self-improving-school-system.pdf (accessed on 16 May 2011).

Hargreaves, A. and Hopkins, D. (1996) *The Empowered School*, London: Cassell.

Harris, A. and Chapman, C. (2002) *Effective leadership in schools facing challenging circumstances*. Nottingham: National College of School Leadership. Available online at: http://www.canterbury.ac.uk/education/protected/spss/docs/ effective-leadership.pdf (accessed 7 June 2011).

Harris, A., Chapman, C., Muijs, D., Russ, J. and Stoll, L. (2006) 'Improving schools in challenging contexts: exploring the possible', *School Effectiveness and School Improvement*, 17(4): 409–24.

Harris, A., Day, C., Hadfield, M., Hopkins, D., Hargreaves, A. and Chapman, C. (2002) *Effective Leadership for School Improvement*, London: Routledge.

Harris, A., Gunraj, J., Clarke, P. and James, S. (2006a) *Improving schools in exceptionally challenging circumstances: tales from the frontline*. (Improving Schools series.) London: Continuum.

Harris, A., Jamieson, I. and Russ, J. (1995) 'A Study of "Effective" Departments in Secondary Schools', *School Organisation*, 15(3): 283–99.

Harris, A. and Muijs, D. (2004) *Improving Schools Through Teacher Leadership*, London: Open University Press.

Harris, A., Muijs, D. and Chapman, C. (2003) *Raising attainment in schools in former coalfield areas*. (Research report 423.) Nottingham: DfES. Available online at https://www.education.gov.uk/publications/eOrderingDownload/RR423.pdf (accessed 7 June 2011).

Harris, A. and Spillane, J. (2008) *Distributed School Leadership: Developing Tomorrow's Leaders*, London: Routledge.

Heifetz, R. and Linsky, M. (2002) *Leadership on the line*. Boston: Harvard Business School Press.

Henchey, N. (2001) *Schools that make a difference: Final report. Twelve Canadian Secondary Schools in Low Income Settings*. Kelowna, BC: Society for the Advancement of Excellence in Education.

Higham, R., Hopkins, D. and Ahtaridou, E. (2007) *Improving school leadership: Country background report for England*, Paris: OECD.

Higham, R., Hopkins, D. and Matthews, P. (2009) *System Leadership In Practice*, Buckingham: Open University Press.

Hill, K. (ed.) (2006) *The impact of networks on pupils, practitioners, organisations and the communities they serve*, Nottingham: National College of School Leadership.

Hills, J. and Stewart, K. (eds) (2005) *A more equal society?: New Labour, poverty, inequality and exclusion*. Bristol: Policy Press.

Hilton, J. (1934) *Goodbye Mr. Chips*, London: Hodder and Stoughton.

HMSO (1977) *A New Partnership for Our Schools: Report of the Committee of Enquiry (The Taylor Report)* London: HMSO. HMRC statement of aims. Available at www.hmrc.gov.uk/ (accessed 24 June 2011).

Hopkins, D. (2001) *Meeting the Challenge: An Improvement Guide for Schools Facing Challenging Circumstances*, London: DfES.

Hopkins, D. and Higham, R. (2007) 'System Leadership: Mapping the Landscape', *School Leadership and Management*, 27(2) April: 147–66.

Hopkins, D., Reynolds D. and Gray, J. (2005) *School Improvement – Lessons from Research*, Nottingham: DfES/Innovation Unit.

Horner, L., Lekhi, R. and Blaug, R. (2006) *Public Value: Deliberative Democracy and the Role of Public Managers*, London: The Work Foundation.

House of Commons Work and Pensions Committee (2008) *The best start in life?: alleviating deprivation, improving social mobility, and eradicating child poverty: second report of session 2007–8. Vol. 1: Report, together with formal minutes* (HC 42-I), London: The Stationery Office. Available online at http://www.

publications.parliament.uk/pa/cm200708/cmselect/cmworpen/42/42.pdf (accessed 11 August 2011).

Huxham, C. and Hibbert, P. (2006) *Give and Take: Understanding attitudes to learning in the collaborative process*, London: Advanced Institute of Management Research, London Graduate School of Business.

Huxham, C. and Vangen, S. (2005) *Managing to collaborate. The theory and practice of collaborative advantage*, London: Routledge.

Innovation Unit (2009) *The Bridge Change Leadership Framework*, London: Innovation Unit. Accessed on 21/10/2001 at http://www.innovationunit.org/knowledge/free-resources/toolkits/bridge-change-leadership-framework

IRS (2011) *The Agency, its Mission and Statutory Authority*, Washington, DC: Internal Revenue Service. Available online at: http://www.irs.gov/irs/article/0,,id=98141,00.html (accessed 7 June 2011).

Jackson, C. (2006) *Lads and ladettes in school: gender and a fear of failure*, Maidenhead: Open University Press.

Jackson, M. and Gretton, J. (1976) *William Tyndale: Collapse of a school – or a system?*, London: Allen and Unwin.

James, C. Brammer, S., Connolly, M., Fertig, M., James, J. and Jones, J. (2010) *The 'hidden givers': a study of school governing bodies in England*, Reading: CfBT.

James, C.R., Connolly, M., Dunning, G. and Elliott, T. (2006) 'Lessons from successful schools in disadvantaged settings: it's both what you do and the way that you do it, that's what gets results!', *Management in Education*, 20(4): 14–17.

John Lewis Partnership (2011) *Our Commitments*. Available online at http://www.johnlewispartnership.co.uk/Display.aspx?MasterId=bb9e575f-01e3-4228-8da5-7f782f182dd4&NavigationId=555 (accessed 7 June 2011).

Johnson, D.W. and Johnson, R.T. (1989) *Leading the Cooperative School*. Edina, MN: Interaction Book Co.

Jussim, L. and Harber, K.D. (2005) 'Teacher Expectations and Self-Fulfilling Prophecies: Knowns and Unknowns, Resolved and Unresolved Controversies', *Personality and Social Psychology Review*, 9(2): 131–55.

Kegan, R. and Laskow Lahey, L. (2003) *How the Way We Talk Can Change the Way We Work*, New York: Jossey Bass.

Kirsch, I., de Jong, J., Lafontaine, D., McQueen, J., Mendelovits, J. and Monseur, C. (2002) *Reading for change: performance and engagement across countries: results from Pisa 2000*, Paris: OECD.

Knapp, M.S. (2001) 'Policy, poverty and capable teaching: assumptions and issues in policy design', in Biddle, B.J. (ed.) *Social class, poverty, and education: policy and practice.* (Missouri symposia on research and education.) New York: RoutledgeFalmer; pp. 175–212.

Lakomski, G. (2005) *Managing without Leadership: Towards a Theory of Organizational Functioning*, Oxford: Elsevier.

Lambert, L. (2009) 'Constructivist Leadership', in Davies, B. (ed.) *The Essentials of School Leadership*, 2nd edn, London: Sage Publications.

Leadbeater, C. (2008) *What Next? 21 Ideas for 21st Century Learning*, London: The Innovation Unit.

Leadbeater, C. and Mongon, D. (2008) *Leadership for Public Value: Achieving valuable outcomes for children, families and communities*, Nottingham: National College.

Leigh, A. (2007) *Estimating teacher effectiveness from two-year changes in students' test scores.* Canberra: Research School of Social Sciences, Australian National University. Available online at http://econrsss.anu.edu.au/~aleigh/pdf/TQPanel. pdf (accessed 11 August 2011).

Leithwood, K. and Jantzi, D. (2009) 'Transformational Leadership', in Davies, B. (ed.) *The Essentials of School Leadership*, 2nd edn, London: Sage Publications.

Leithwood K., Day C., Sammons P., Harris A. and Hopkins D. (2006) *Seven Strong Claims about Successful School Leadership*, London: DfES.

Lord, P., Hart, R., Martin, K. and Atkinson, M. (2009) *Narrowing the Gap in Outcomes: Governance.* (LGA Research Report.) Slough: NFER.

Louis, K.S., Leithwood, K., Wahlstrom, K.L. and Anderson, S.E. (2010) *Investigating the Links to Improved Student Learning*, Final report of Research Findings, Minneapolis: University of Minnesota.

MacBeath, J. (2008) 'Distributed Leadership: Paradigms, Policy, and Paradox', in Leithwood, K. Mascall, B. and Strauss, T., *Distributed Leadership According to the Evidence*, London: Routledge.

MacBeath, J. and Dempster, N. (2009) *Connecting leadership and learning: principles for practice*, London: Routledge.

Malen, B. (2005) 'Educational Leaders as Policy Analysts', in English, F.W. (ed.) *The Sage Handbook of Educational Leadership*, London: Sage Publications.

Marcos, J. and Macaulay, S. (2008) *Organisational Resilience: The Key to Anticipation, Adaptation and Recovery*, Cranfield: Cranfield School of Management. Available online at http://www.som.cranfield.ac.uk/som/dinamic-content/cced/documents/ org.pdf (accessed 17 May 2011).

Marks & Spencer plc (2010) *Corporate Governance Statement.* Available online at http:// corporate.marksandspencer.com/documents/specific/investors/governance/ governance_statement.pdf (accessed 7 June 2011).

Martin, J., McKeown, P., Nixon, J. and Ranson, S. (2000) 'Community active management and governance of schools in England', in Arnott, M.A. and Raab, C.D. *The Governance of Schooling: comparative studies of devolved management*, London: Routledge.

Mediratta, K., Shah, S., McAlister, S., Fruchter, N., Mokhtar, C. and Lockwood, D. (2008) *Organized Communities, Stronger Schools: A Preview of Research Findings*, New York: Annenberg Institute for School Reform, Brown University.

Midwinter, E. (1972) *Priority Education. An account of the Liverpool Project*, Harmondsworth: Penguin.

Midwinter, E. (1973) *Patterns of Community Education*, London: Ward Lock.

Ministry of Education (1944) *The Principles of Government in Maintained Secondary Schools*, Cmd. 6523 (1944) followed by Administrative Memorandum, No. 25, January (1945) quoted in Owen, J. (1978) 'A New Partnership for Our Schools: The Taylor Report', *Oxford Review of Education*, 4(1): 4.

Ministry of Education (1951) *Education 1900–1950*, Cmd. 8244, London: HMSO.

Mongon, D. (2010) *The 2009 Inspection Framework: well-being and community cohesion*, Nottingham: National College. Available online at http://www.nation-alcollege.org.uk/docinfo?id=132924&filename=inspection-framework-2009.pdf (accessed 10 September 2010).

Mongon, D., Allen, T., Farmer, L. and Atherton C. (2010) *Emerging patterns of leadership: co-location, continuity and community*, Nottingham: National College of School Leadership. Available online at http://www.nationalcollege.org.uk/

docinfo?id=132913&filename=emerging-patterns-of-leadership.pdf (accessed 22 September 2010).

Mongon, D. and Chapman, C. (2008a) *Successful leadership for promoting the achievement of white working class pupils*, Nottingham: National College of School Leadership.

Mongon, D. and Chapman, C. (2008b) *Successful leadership for promoting the achievement of white working class pupils. Vignettes: Twelve accounts of school life*, Nottingham: National College of School Leadership.

Mongon, D. and Chapman C. (2009) *Emerging patterns of school leadership: ECM perspectives*, Nottingham: National College.

Mongon, D. and Leadbeater, C. (2010) *Understanding valuable outcomes for children, families and young people*, Nottingham: National College of School Leadership.

Mongon, D. and Leadbeater, C. (2012) *School Leadership for Public Value: schools creating valued outcomes for children, families and communities*, London: Institute for Education.

Moon, N. and Ivins, C. (2004) 'Survey of Parental Involvement 2003/04, DfES RR589', *Oxford Review of Economic Policy*, 21(3): 357–72.

Morris, H. (1925) *The Village College. Being a Memorandum on the Provision of Educations and Social Facilities for the Countryside, with Special Reference to Cambridgeshire* (Section XIV). Available online at http://www.infed.org/thinkers/et-morr.htm (accessed 3 June 2011).

Muijs, D., Ainscow, M., Dyson, A., Raffo C., Goldrick, S., Kerr, K., Lennie, C. and Miles, S. (2007) *Every Child Matters: leading under pressure: leadership for social inclusion*, Nottingham: National College of School Leadership. Available online at http://www.nationalcollege.org.uk/index/docinfo.htm?id=17163 (accessed 12 August 2011).

Muijs, D., Ainscow, M., Dyson, A., Raffo, C., Goldrick, S., Kerr, K., Lennie C. and Miles, S. (2010) 'Leading under pressure: leadership for social inclusion', *School Leadership and Management*, 30(2) April: 143–57.

Muijs, D., Harris, A., Chapman, C., Stoll, L. and Russet, J. (2004) 'Improving schools in socioeconomically disadvantaged areas – a review of research evidence', *School Effectiveness and School Improvement*, 15(2): 149–75.

Muijs, D., Harris, A., Chapman, C., Stoll, L. and Russet, J. (2005) 'Improving Schools in Socio-Economically Disadvantaged Areas: A Review of Research Evidence', in Clarke, P. (ed.) *Improving Schools in Difficulty*, London: Continuum.

Muijs, D. and Reynolds, D. (2005) *Effective Teaching*, London: Paul Chapman.

Mulford, B. (2010) 'Recent Developments in the Field of Educational Leadership: the challenge of complexity', in Hargreaves, A., Lieberman, A., Fullan, M. and Hopkins, D. (eds) *Second International Handbook of Educational Change*, Dordrecht: Springer; pp. 187–208.

Mulgan, R. (2002) *Accountability Issues in the New Model of Governance, Discussion Paper No.91, April 2002*. Available online at https://digitalcollections.anu.edu.au/bitstream/1885/41701/3/No91Mulgan.pdf (accessed 10 June 2011).

National Audit Office (2006) *Improving poorly performing schools in England*, Report by the Comptroller and Auditor General, HC 679, session 2005–2006. London: The Stationery Office.

National College (2006a) LEA involvement in school networks, Nottingham: National College.

National College (2006b) *Narrowing the gap. Reducing within-school variation in pupil outcomes*, Nottingham: National College. Available online at http://www. nationalcollege.org.uk/index/docinfo.htm?id=17307 (accessed 13 June 2011).

National College (2007) *System Leadership: Lessons from the Literature*, Nottingham: National College.

National College (2009a) *Building Effective Integrated Leadership*, Nottingham: The National College for Leadership of Schools and Children's Services.

National College (2009b) *School Leadership Today*, Nottingham: The National College for Leadership of Schools and Children's Services. Available online at http://www1.nationalcollege.org.uk/download?id=21843 (accessed 10 June 2011).

National College (2010a) *What are new models and partnerships?* Nottingham: The National College for Leadership of Schools and Children's Services. Available online at http://www.nationalcollege.org.uk/index/leadershiplibrary/leadingschools/ modelsandpartnerships/what-are-new-models-of-leadership.htm (accessed on 16 May 2011).

National College (2010b) Quote on the National College website at http://www1. nationalcollege.org.uk/index/leadershiplibrary/ldr-magazine/back-ldr-issues/ ldr-january-2010/ldr-jan-10-practical-steps-how-to-tackle-variation.htm (accessed 11 June 2010).

National College (2010c) *Leadership for Narrowing the Gap*, Nottingham: The National College for Leadership of Schools and Children's Services. Available online at http://www.nationalcollege.org.uk/index/leadershiplibrary/leadingschools/ leading-change/key-initiatives/narrowing-the-gap/leadership-for-narrowing-the-gap-project-resources (accessed 13 June 2011).

National College (2010d) *Leadership for parental engagement*, Nottingham: The National College for Leadership of Schools and Children's Services. Available online at http://www.nationalcollege.org.uk/docinfo?id=134336&filename=lead ership-for-parental-engagement.pdf (accessed 17 September 2010).

National College (2011a) *System Ready*, Nottingham: The National College for Leadership of Schools and Children's Services. Available online at http://www. nationalcollege.org.uk/index/leadershiplibrary/ldr-magazine/back-ldr-issues/ ldr-june-2010/ldr-jun-10-need-to-know.htm (accessed 21 February 2011).

National College (2011b) *National Leaders of Education and National Support Schools*, Nottingham: National College. Available online at http://scms.ncsl.org. uk/index/professional-development/national-leaders-of-education.htm (accessed 28 May 2011).

OECD (2001) *Knowledge and skills for life: first results from the OECD Programme for International Student Assessment (PISA) 2000*, Paris: OECD.

Ofsted (1993) *Framework for the inspection of schools*, London: Ofsted.

Ofsted (2002a) *Achievement of Black Caribbean pupils: three successful primary schools*, London: Ofsted. Available online at http://www.ofsted.gov.uk/resources/ achievement-of-black-caribbean-pupils-three-successful-primary-schools (accessed 11 August 2011).

Ofsted (2002b) *Achievement of Black Caribbean pupils: good practice in secondary schools*, London: Ofsted. Available at http://www.ofsted.gov.uk/resources/ achievement-of-black-caribbean-pupils (accessed 1 August 2011).

Ofsted (2007) *The Annual Report of Her Majesty's Chief Inspector of Education and Children's Services and Skills 2006/2007*, London: Stationery Office. Available online at http://www.education.gov.uk/b0056633/

research-on-the-role-of-school-governors/4-effectiveness (accessed 14 October 2010).

Ofsted (2008a) *White boys from low-income backgrounds: good practice in schools*, London: Ofsted. Available online at http://www.ofsted.gov.uk/resources/ white-boys-low-income-backgrounds-good-practice-schools (accessed 11 August 2011).

Ofsted (2008b) *Using data, improving schools*, London. Ofsted. Available online at http://www.ofsted.gov.uk/Ofsted-home/Publications-and-research/Browse-all-by/Documents-by-type/Thematic-reports/Using-data-improving-schools (accessed 13 June 2011).

Ofsted (2008c) Bartley Green School, A Specialist Technology and Sports College: Inspection report (David Rzeznik HMI), London: Ofsted. Available online at http://www.ofsted.gov.uk/filedownloading/?id=879149&type=1&refer=0 (accessed 15 August 2011).

Ofsted (2009) *The Annual Report of Her Majesty's Chief Inspector of Education and Children's Services and Skills 2008/2009*, London: Stationery Office.

Ofsted (2010a) *The Annual Report of Her Majesty's Chief Inspector of Education, Children's Services and Skills 2009/10*, London: Stationery Office.

Ofsted (2010b) *London Challenge*, London, Ofsted. Available online at http://www. ofsted.gov.uk/resources/london-challenge (accessed 11 August 2011).

Oplatka, I. and Addi-Raccah, A. (2009) 'Is "educational leadership" a national-contextual field of study? Some insights from an analysis of the field's major journals', in Wiseman, A.W. (ed.), *Educational Leadership: Global Contexts and International Comparisons* (International Perspectives on Education and Society, Vol. 11), Bingley: Emerald; pp. 399–418.

Owen, J. (1978) 'A New Partnership for Our Schools: The Taylor Report', *Oxford Review of Education*, 4(1): 37–49.

Payne, C.M (2008) *So much reform so little change: The persistence of failure in urban schools*, Cambridge, MA: Harvard Education Press.

Pelage, A. and Evetts, J. (1998) Structural and Cultural Dimensions of Secondary Headteacher Careers in France: similarities and differences with British patterns, European Journal of Education, Vol 33, No 4, pp. 458–468.

Plowden (1967) *Children and their primary schools: a report of the Central Advisory Council for Education (England), vol. 1, The Report*, London: HMSO.

Pont, B., Nusche, D. and Hopkins D. (2008) *Improving School Leadership Volume Two: Case Studies in System Leadership*, Paris: OECD.

Portsmouth (2006) *Portsmouth Children's Trust Development Team, Turning The Curve Toolkit*. Available at http://tna.europarchive.org/20081106120944/http://www. everychildmatters.gov.uk/resources-and-practice/EP00201/ (accessed 11 August 2011).

PWC (2007) *Independent Study into School Leadership*. DCSF Research Report RR818A, DCSF-RW005. London: PricewaterhouseCoopers.

RAISE (2011) RAISEonline, Ofsted/DfES. Available online at https://www. raiseonline.org/About.aspx (accessed 13 June 2011).

Raffo, C., Dyson, A., Gunter, H., Hall, D., Jones, L. and Kalambouka, A. (2007) *Education and poverty: a critical review of theory, policy and practice*, York: Joseph Rowntree Foundation. Available online at http://www.jrf.org.uk/bookshop/ eBooks/2028-education-poverty-theory.pdf (accessed 15 June 2011).

Ranson, S. (2010) 'From Partnership to Community Governance', *FORUM*,

52(3). Available online at http://www.wwwords.co.uk/rss/abstract. asp?j=forum&aid=4177 (accessed 24 June 2011).

Reynolds, D. (2007) *Schools Learning From Their Best (the within-school variation project)*, Nottingham: National College.

Riehl, C.J. (2000) 'The principal's role in creating inclusive schools for diverse students: a review of normative, empirical and critical literature on the practice of educational administration', *Review of Educational Research*, 70(1): 55–81.

Riley, K.A. (2008) 'Reconfiguring urban leadership: taking a perspective on community', *Management in Education*, 22(2): 31–9.

Rivkin, G.S., Hanusehk, E.A. and Kain, J.F. (2005) 'Teachers, schools, and academic achievement', *Econometrica*, 73(2) March: 417–58. Available online at http://www.epi.org/page/-/old/books/teacher_quality_exec_summary.pdf (accessed 6 October 2010).

Robinson, V., Hohepa, M. and Lloyd, C. (2009) *School Leadership and Student Outcomes: Identifying What Works and Why Best Evidence Synthesis Iteration*, Wellington: New Zealand Ministry of Education.

Rockoff, J.E. (2003) *The Impact of Individual Teachers on Student Achievement: Evidence from Panel Data*, Cambridge, MA: Harvard University. Available online at http://129.3.20.41/eps/pe/papers/0304/0304002.pdf (accessed 13 June 2011).

Rosenthal, R. and Jacobson, L. (1968) *Pygmalion in the classroom: teacher expectation and pupils' intellectual development*, New York: Holt, Rinehart & Winston.

Rubie-Davies, C.M. (2007) 'Classroom interactions: exploring the practices of high- and low-expectation teachers', *British Journal of Educational Psychology*, 77: 289–306.

Rubie-Davies, C.M. (2010) 'Teacher expectations and perceptions of student attributes: Is there a relationship?', *British Journal of Educational Psychology*, 80: 121–35.

Rubin, B.C. and Silva, E.M. (2003) *Critical voices in school reform: students living through change*, London: RoutledgeFalmer.

Rutter, M., Maughan, P., Moretimore, P. and Ousten, J. (1979) *Fifteen Thousand Hours: Secondary Schools and Their Effects on Children*, Cambridge, MA: Harvard Education Press.

Ryan, W. (2008) *Leadership with a moral purpose*, Carmarthen: Crown House Publishing.

Sammons, P. (2007) *School effectiveness and equity: making connections: a review of school effectiveness and improvement research – its implications for practitioners and policy makers*, Reading: CfBT Education Trust. Available online at www.cfbt.com/evidenceforeducation/pdf/Full%20Literature%20Review.pdf (accessed 18 December 2009).

Sammons P., Hillman, J. and Mortimore P. (1995) *Key characteristics of effective schools: a review of school effectiveness research*, London: Ofsted.

Sammons, P., Sylva, C., Melhuish, E., Siraj-Blatchford, I., Taggart, B., Barreau, S. and Grabbe, Y. (2008) *The Influence of School and Teaching Quality on Children's Progress in Primary School. Research Report No DCSF-RR028*, London: Institute of Education, University of London.

Sammons, P., Taggart, B., Siraj-Blatchford, I., Sylva, C., Melhuish, E., Barreau, S. and Manni, L. (2006) *Effective Pre-school and Primary Education 3–11 Project*

(EPPE 3–11). Summary Report: Variations in Teacher and Pupil Behaviours in Year 5 Classes, London: Institute of Education.

Sammons, P., Thomas, S. and Mortimore, P. (1997) *Forging links: Effective schools and effective departments*, London: Sage.

Sanders, W.L. and Rivers, J.C. (1996) *Cumulative and Residual Effects of Teachers on Future Student Academic Achievement*, Tennessee: University of Tennessee Value-Added Research and Assessment Center. Available online at http://www.mccsc. edu/~curriculum/cumulative%20and%20residual%20effects%20of%20teachers.pdf (accessed 7 October 2010).

Senge, P. (1990) *The fifth discipline: the art and practice of the learning organization*, New York: Doubleday/Currency.

Sergiovanni, T.J. (2001) *Leadership: What's in it for schools?*, London: RoutledgeFalmer.

Smith, G., Smith, T. and Smith T. (2007) 'Whatever Happened to EPAs? Part 2: Educational Priority Areas – 40 years on', *FORUM*, 49(1 & 2): 141–56.

Smith, W.O.L. (1957) *Education: an introductory survey*, Harmondsworth: Penguin.

Southworth, G. (2004) *Primary School Leadership in Context: leading small, medium and large sized schools*, London: RoutledgeFalmer.

Stevens, P., Lupton, R., Mujtaba, T. and Feinstein, L. (2007) *The development and impact of young people's social capital in secondary schools*, London: Centre for Research on the Wider Benefits of Learning, Institute of Education.

Stoll, L., Reynolds, D., Creemers, B.P.M. and Hopkins, D. (1996) 'Merging school effectiveness and school improvement: Practical examples', in Reynolds, D., Creemers, B.P.M., Hopkins, D., Stoll, L. and Bollen, R. (eds) *Making Good Schools*, London: Routledge.

Strike, K.A., (2007) *Ethical Leadership in Schools: Creating Community in an Environment of Accountability*, Thousand Oaks: Corwin Press.

Stringfield, S., Reynolds, D. and Schaffer. E. (2008) *Improving secondary students' academic achievement through a focus on reform reliability. Four- and nine-year findings from the High Reliability Schools project*, Reading: CfBt.

Sutton, L. Smith, N., Dearden, C. and Middleton, S. (2007) *A child's-eye view of social difference*, York: Joseph Rowntree Foundation. Available online at http://www.jrf.org.uk/bookshop/eBooks/2007-children-inequality-opinion.pdf (accessed 15 June 2011).

Szreter, S. (2004) 'The state of social capital: Bringing back in power, politics, and history', *Theory and Society*, 31(5): 573–621.

Tauber, R. (1998) 'Good or bad, what teachers expect from students they generally get!' ERIC Digest. Washington, DC: ERIC Clearinghouse on Teaching and Teacher Education, ED426985. Available at http://www.edpsycinteractive.org/ files/teacherexpect.html (accessed 27 July 2010).

Taylor, M. (2007) *Neighbourhood Management and Social Capital, Research Report 35*, London: Department for Communities and Local Government.

TDA (2009) *Reducing in-school variation. Making effective practice standard practice*, Nottingham: National College. Available online at http://www.tda.gov.uk/~/ media/resources/isv/isv_guide.pdf (accessed 13 June 2011).

Tikly, L., Haynes, J., Caballero, C., Hill, J. and Gillborn, D. (2006) 'Evaluation of Aiming High: African Caribbean Achievement Project.' (Research report 801.) Nottingham: DfES.. Available online at https://www.education.gov.uk/publications/eOrderingDownload/RB801.pdf (accessed 7 June 2011).

Timperley, H.S. (2005) 'Distributed leadership: developing theory from practice', *Journal of Curriculum Studies*, 37(4): 395–420.

Timperley, H.S. (2006) 'Learning Challenges Involved in Developing Leading for Learning', *Educational Management Administration & Leadership*, 34(4): 546–63.

Timperley, H.S. (2008) *Teacher professional learning and development*. Educational Practice Series – 18. International Academy of Education & International Bureau of Education, Paris: UNESCO. Available online at http://www.ibe.unesco.org/fileadmin/user_upload/Publications/Educational_Practices/EdPractices_18.pdf (accessed 7 June 2011).

Togneri, W. and Anderson, S. (2003) 'How High Poverty Districts improve', *Educational Leadership*, 33(1): 12-16.

Total Place (2010) *Total Place: better for less*. Available online at http://www.local-leadership.gov.uk/totalplace/ (accessed 1 February 2011).

Walker, A. (2004) *Priorities, strategies and challenges: proactive leadership in multi-ethnic schools*, Nottingham: National College. Available online at http://www.ncsl.org.uk/media-893-09-priorities-strategies-and-challenges.pdf (accessed 8 October 2008).

Warren, M.R. (2005) 'Communities and Schools: a new view of urban education reform', *Harvard Education Review*, 75(2): 133–73.

Watkins, C., Carnell, E. and Lodge, C. (2007) *Effective learning in classrooms*, London: Paul Chapman.

Webb, R., Vulliamy, G., Hakkinen, K. and Hamalaianen, S. (1998) 'External inspection or school self evaluation? A comparative analysis of primary schools in England and Finland', *British Educational Research Journal*, 24(5): 539–57.

West, M., Ainscow, M. and Stanford, J. (2005) 'Sustaining improvement in schools in challenging circumstances: a study of successful practice', *School Leadership & Management*, 25(1): 77–93.

West-Burnham, J. and Otero, G. (2006) *Leading together to build social capital*, Nottingham: National College of School Leadership.

Whitty, G., Power, S. and Halpin, D. (1998) *Devolution and Choice in Education: The School, the State and the Market*, Buckingham: Open University Press.

Wiliam, D. (2009) 'Designing teacher learning that benefits students: the role of school and college leaders', Annual Conference of the Association of School and College Leaders, Birmingham, March. Available online at http://www.ascl.org.uk/mainwebsite/resources/document/designing%20teacher%20learning%20that%20benefits%20students%20-%20dylan%20wiliam.pdf (accessed 17 May 2011).

Wilkin A., Kinder K., White R., Atkinson M. and Doherty P. (2003) *Towards the development of 'extended' schools*. (DfES Research Report 408.) London: NFER.

Woods (2009) 'Moving up the M6', keynote presentation at BERA Educational Effectiveness and Improvement SIG, Manchester, November.

Wright, C.Y. and Weekes, D. (2003) 'Race and gender in the contestation and resistance of teacher authority and school sanctions: the case of African Caribbean pupils in England', *Comparative Education Review*, 47(1): 3–20.

Wrigley, T. (2003) *Schools of Hope*, Stoke-on Trent: Trentham.

Index

14–19 Pathfinders 31
Academies Act 157
Academy Leadership 9
Academy Schools 28, 32, 131, 155, 157
achievement *see* attainment
Accelerated School Network 25
Acceptance 23, 25, 35, 46–8, 87
accountability 70–1, 118, 127–8, 133, 135, 144–56 *see also* governance
Action 23, 61–2, 72–5,
adaptive approaches 134
Advanced Skills Teachers (ASTs) 125
Advocacy 23, 25–6, 35–6, 51–3, 87–8
Alignment 23, 84–5, 96–101
ambiguity management models 9
Amstrad 1
Analysis 23, 27, 61–72, 147
Apple 1
Application 23, 27, 61–2, 75–82
Apprenticeship, Skills, Children and Learning Act 2009 157
area-based initiatives (ABIs) 31
area-based leadership 106–8
Area focus 23, 84–5, 101–6, 159
Area Level 151, 153–4
associate authorisation 136–7 *see also* authorising environments
associate partnerships 33, 101–2
Association 23, 84–95, 106–7
asymmetric partnerships 33
Atkinson, Sir William 2
attainment *see also* league tables *and* Extra Mile *and* outcomes *under* pupil *and* outcomes *under* student
  academic 28, 41, 85, 133, 146
  data 62–72, 77, 81
  educational 76–7
  and ethnicity 97
  and professional behaviour 47

pupil 47, 76–7, 79–81, 89, 122, 132–3, 142
  school 115–16
audits 70
authorising environments 21, 134–42
autonomy 28, 40, 129–30, 141
Awareness 23, 25, 35–46

Bartley Green School 122–6
BASRC (Bay Area School Reform Collaborative) 67
Beacon schools 31
'behaviour trails' 70
behavioural trust 87
Big Society, The 32, 100, 133–4, 141
Black Country Challenge 115
Blair, Tony 2
Boyson, Rhodes, Minister of Education 30
British (Non-conformist Church) Schools 29
budget management 40, 63–4

Callaghan, Prime Minister Jim 39
Cambridge Village Colleges 30
capillary transmission 26, 57
'catenate leadership' 155
Centre for Economics of Education 64
Chatwin, Bruce 58
Children, Schools and Families Act 2010 157
Children's Trusts in England 15
City Challenge 114–15
Clifton Green Primary School 147
Collaboration 10, 30, 103–4, 107
collegial management models 8
Collins flywheel effect 19

Combined Cadet Force (CCF) 126
common purpose 88–9, 103, 107
community
 contribution to 100–3
 of followers 60
 local 104–6
 neighbourhood 22, 29–30, 85–7,
  90–1, 148
 resources 99–100
 school 86–91, 118
'community oriented public
 management' 135
Community Schools 30, 131
conscientiousness 18–9, 22, 82–3
Consortium on Chicago School
 Research 116
constructivist leadership 60
contextual authorisation 139–41 *see also*
 authorising environments
Contextual Intelligence 19, 21–2
contingent leadership models 9
conversations 58–9, 70, 73
cooperative leadership 25
Copland, M. A. 67–8
cultural conversations 102
cultural distribution 92–3
cultural leadership 102
cultural management models 9
curiosity 65
Cycle of Enquiry 67

data 27, 147–8
 analysis 27, 61–73, 147
 attainment 62–72, 77, 81
 financial 63–4
 presentation 66–7
 qualitative 68–70
Department of Education 40
Department of the Environment,
 Transport and the Regions 31
Department for Children, Schools and
 Families (DCSF) 113
deprivation 98 *see also* socio-economic
 disadvantage
disadvantage *see* socio-economic
 disadvantage
Discipline for Learning 123, 125
'disciplined innovation' 144, 157
distributed leadership 66–8, 91–5,
 103–4
Docklands Youth Service 140

Edmonds, Ronald 4
Education Act 1870 29

Education Action Zones (EAZs) 31,
 133
Education Acts, history of 156–8
Education and Inspection Act 157
Education and Skills Act 2008 157
Education Priority Areas 30
Education Reform Act 1988 37, 130,
 156
Education (Schools) Act 1992
 156
education system 28, 156
 history 29–32, 156–8
 levels 150–3
Else, Jean 2
equality of opportunity 43–4, 96
'ethical leadership' 41–3
ethics 42–3, 153 *see also* morality *and*
 values
Every Child Matters 133, 141
Excellence in Cities (EIC) 31
extended services 100, 133
Extra Mile (EM) 113–14

Families of Schools 115
Family Support Workers 100
Federation Leadership 9
Fischer Family Trust data analyses 63 *see
 also* analysis *under* data
Five Year Strategy for Children and
 Learners 157
formal management models 8–9
Foundation Schools 131
fractal system 57–8
free school meals (FSM) 63, 79, 122
Free Schools 28, 157
French schools 40
Friedman, Mark 144–5
Fullan, Michael 41, 54

George Green's Secondary School 140,
 143, 148
Goodwin, Sir Fred 1
Google 51
Google Scholar 3
governance 10–1, 36–7, 39–40,
 127–41 *see also* governors *under*
 school
governance capital 133
government
 and autonomy 28
 funding 6, 31, 63, 141–2, 156
 and governing bodies 129–30
 investment 3, 112, 160
 jargon 133–4

policies 31–2, 40, 99–100, 141,
    156–8
reforms 32, 112
research 6
Greater Manchester Challenge 115–16
Gronn, Peter 3, 93–5

Hailsham Community College 141
Hargreaves, David 144, 157
Headteachers 4–5 *see also* leadership
    authority 49, 63, 106, 129, 139
    and colleagues 116, 118
    and governing bodies 37, 131–3,
        139
    moral purpose 42
    roles 9–11 37–41, 80, 130, 159
    and system leadership 9, 153
    values 4, 41–2
    vision 4, 123
Healthy Minds Projects 147
Her Majesty's Revenue and Customs
    (HMRC) 51–2
high-capacity schools 118
high-leverage leadership, definition of 2
Higher Standards, Better Schools for
    All 157
holographic system *see* fractal system
human intellectual competence *see*
    intelligences

ideological trust 87
Industrial Schools 29
information analysis 69, 147
Innovation Unit 53
Insert Sharp 117
INSET (in-service training) 124
Inspection Framework 147
inspections 6–7, 15, 38, 64, 100, 146–7
    see also Ofsted
institutional authorisation 137–9, 141
    see also authorising environments
institutional autonomy 129–30 *see also*
    governance
Institutional Level 151–4
instructional leadership models 9
'intelligences' 18–19, 22
Internal Revenue Service (USA) 51
interpersonal management models 8
interpersonal skills 21
Island Sports Trust (IST) 140
Isle of Dogs Community Foundation
    140
ISV (in-school variations) 68, 71, 74,
    81

Jobs, Steve 1
John Lewis 51

Kegan, Robert 59
Kelly Mill School 126

Lahey, Lisa Laskow 59
Lakomski, Gabriele 93–5
language 53, 58–9, 70
language shifts 59
Leading Edge Partnership Programme,
    the 31
leadership *see also* headteachers *and*
        distributed leadership
    behaviour 21, 37, 54, 83
    characteristics 4, 16, 102, 136 *see also*
        personality traits *under* leadership
    development 108–9
    framework 5, 10–13, 22–3
    history 3–4
    importance 3–7
    investment 3
    issues 6, 12–3, 28, 160
    and management 7–8, 10, 26, 125,
        158–9
    models of 8–9, 22–4, 91–5, 126,
        134
    morality 37, 41–3
    personality traits 18–19, 82–3 *see also*
        characteristics *under* leadership
    practices 6, 10–13, 17, 44, 54–5, 80
        see also models
    research 6
    responsibilities 10, 21, 18, 40, 85,
        106, 127, 153 *see also* system *under*
        leadership
    and sense of purpose 41–4, 88–9
    skills 11, 19, 21
    strategies 16–17
    and student outcomes 4–9, 12, 20,
        44, 66, 151
    styles 18
    system 9–10, 153–5, 160
    theories 7–9, 66, 93–5
    types 117–19
    values 4, 15
Leadership Incentive Grants 31
league tables 133, 152
Learning and Skills Council 138
learning orientation 55–6
'learning zone' 32, 94
Leicestershire community colleges 30
Leverage, concept of 14
'living vision' 24–6, 35–6, 51–3

local authorities 15, 38–9, 109, 129–30, 157
local authority oversight 129–30 *see also* goverance
local autonomy 141–2
local indicators 147–8
Local Leaders of Education 154
London Challenge 114–15
low-capacity schools 117

maintenance-development dilemma 11
management 26, 61–2
   behaviour 27, 123
   budget 40, 63–4
   leadership and 7–8, 159
   models 8–9
   resource 40
   school 38, 118, 121
   skills 11
   tensions 158–60
management of commitment 42
MacBeath, John 92–3
McDonald's 51
managerial leadership models 8, 93
Marks & Spencer 51
mission statements 25, 51–2
model communities 29
models of educational management 8–9
models of leadership 8–10, 23, 91, 93
moral leadership models 9, 37
moral purpose 41–2, 44
morality 37, 42 *see also* ethics *and* values
monitoring 17, 81, 117, 159 *see also* data
Morris, Henry 30

National (Anglican Church) Schools 29
national authorization 141–2 *see also* authorising environments
National Challenge 112
National College for Leadership of Schools and Children's Services in England (National College) viii, 31–2, 59, 99, 128, 152, 153–4 *see also* National College for School Leadership
National College for School Leadership viii, 3, 153 *see also* National College for Leadership of Schools and Children's Services
National Curriculum, 152
national indicators 146–7, 149
National Leaders of Education (NLEs) 154, 160

National Leaders of Education in England 9
National Level 151–4
National Literacy 112
national non-conformity 129 *see also* goverance
National Numeracy 112
national policy 30, 131, 139 *see also* policies *under* government
National Strategies 152, 157
National Support Schools 160
NEETs (not in employment, education or training) 148
'neo-liberal market orientation' 135
Networked Learning Communities 31, 87
No Child Left Behind 112

OECD 56, 81, 151, 154
Ofsted (Office for Standards in Education, Children's Services and Skills) 44, 146–7, 156, 158 *see also* inspections
operation principal 159
Outcomes Based Accountability 144–5, 147
Owen, Robert 29

panoptic leadership 7
Panoptican 6
parental involvement 69, 97–8, 148–9
Parenting Classes 100
participative leadership models 8
partnership working 12, 122
perceptual trust 87
performance measuring *see* attainment *under* data
performance orientation 55–6
personal authorisation 136 *see also* authorising environments
personal modelling 54
personal responsibility 18, 22, 136
personality traits 18–19, 22
phases of leadership 4–5 *see also* leadership
Phoenix School 2
Plato 36
political issues 45–6
political management models 8
post-modern leadership models 9
practice, key aspects of 82
Professional Intelligence 19, 27, 61
pupils *see also* students
   achievement 113–14, 122

attainment 76–7, 79–81, 89, 132–3,
    142 *see also* attainment *under* data
    and ISV
behaviour 18, 57–8, 79, 123, 148
outcomes 15, 44, 77, 133
respect 88, 90
socio-economic disadvantage 47,
    113–14

Question Time 2

Race to the Top 112
Ragged Schools 29
RAISEonline (Reporting and Analysis
    for Improvement through School
    Self-Evaluation) 63 *see also* analysis
    under data
Raising Achievement for Teaching and
    Learning (RATL) Programme 15
Ratner, Gerald 1
recruitment 20, 28, 79–80
relational trust 87
research objectivity 6
resources 40, 99–100, 105–6, 109
Risinghill School 3
Rowntree, Seebohm 29
Ruskin College, Oxford 39

School Boards 37, 39, 127
school
    autonomy 28–9, 40–1, 130–1,
        156–7
    development phases 116–17
    explicit features 48, 50–1
    governors *see* governance
    improvement 6, 112–20
    implicit features 48–50
    management 38
    partnerships 28–9, 31–2
    stages of enquiry 67–8
    types 116–19, 120–6
    volunteers 100, 131
servant leaders 42
shadow system 57–8
Single Regeneration Projects 31
social capital 92–3, 100–1, 105
Social Intelligence 20–1, 27, 86
socio-economic disadvantage 15, 43–4,
    78–81, 113–14, 122, 132
sociocrats 161
Specialists schools 31
staff *see also* teachers *and* teaching
    assistants *and* support staff
    confidence 54, 117, 124

development 11, 17, 54–7, 80, 91,
    124–5
expectations of 48, 91
performance 28, 76
quality 20, 79–80
recruitment 20, 28, 79–80
relationships 14, 20, 65, 91, 118
resilience 50
responsibilities 11, 116, 124
standard operating procedures (SOPs)
    81–2
students *see also* pupils
    ambitions 37, 97–8
    attainment 47, 76–9, 89, 122 *see also*
        attainment *under* data *and* ISV
    background 15, 44, 78–9, 96–7 *see*
        also socio-economic disadvantage
    behaviour 123
    and ethnicity 97
    outcomes 47–8, 76–7, 89–90,
        97–9, 105, 112 *see also* London
        Challenge
    tests 142–3
subjective management models 9
Sugar, Lord 1
support staff 99–100 *see also* staff
system leadership 9–10, 153–5, 160

Talleyrand 155
teachers *see also* staff
    behaviour 48–9, 78–9
    culture 116–18
    development 54–8, 79–80, 123–4
    expectations 48–9, 97
    quality 18–20, 27–8, 73, 75–80,
        88–9
    recruitment 20, 28, 79–80
teaching assistants 55, 99–100, 148 *see*
    also staff
technical solutions 134
Timperley, Helen 56–7, 66
Tottenham Hotspur Football Club 1
Training and Development Agency for
    Schools (TDA) 68–9
transactional leadership models 8
transformational leadership models 8,
    93
Trust Schools 131, 157

Union Schools 29
University of the First Age (UFA) 124

value, appropriate measures of 142–9
Valued Youth Program (VYP) 124